Ask For The Ancient Paths

by

Jessica Jones

Dedication

This book is dedicated to Linda who taught me that this "sight" I have is actually a gift and blessing from God. I knew that in my mind, but it had never made its way to my heart. She helped me overcome the years of mockery and abuse I suffered at the hands of others, within and without the church, because of this unusual gift I had received before birth. I consider Linda one of two friends that I have put in the rank of sister, confidant and true friend, who accepts me regardless of what I tell her, someone who I can be totally vulnerable with and who tells me the objective truth about questions of my heart. Thank you, Linda, for your diligent lectures, encouragements and acceptance.

Acknowledgments

S pecial thanks to Susan Fryer who labored through two raw manuscripts, without whose help this work would not have become the polished book it is. Special thanks to Esther Warner and Ivan Roman who gave me the encouragement to finish this book. Special thanks to Mike Kerry who gave me encouragement and valuable editorial comments.

Book Proceeds

Half of all proceeds from this book will be donated to Be Free Ministry, a ministry dedicated to the healing of both hearts and bodies of all who would come. I pray these proceeds multiply and benefit all those who the Lord wishes to reach.

Jeremiah 6:16

Thus says the LORD:
"Stand in the ways and see, and ask for the old paths,
where the good way is, and walk in it;
then you will find rest for your souls."

Foreword

Five years ago, I began to have a great number of visions that left me speechless and in a state of continual awe. In many cases, these visions were so outside the realm of those things I had been taught that I researched every facet of the things I saw with scripture and science. The visions and the research took me to new levels of understanding I never imagined possible.

This is the compilation of those visions given to me over a four-year period. After receiving the whole vision and placing the events into chronological order, which took me about one year, they began again, this time filling in details throughout.

Because of the unusual position where I stood during these visions, often to the right side of the throne of God, or in the middle of events and conversations, I asked the Lord, "How could this be?"

He answered, "You are not a prophet but a reporter and it is your job to report all that you see and hear." This is what I have done in as much detail as I possibly could.

As the vision progressed and I began to put it into its proper chronology, I realized that I had been seeing parts of this whole vision most of my life. I am still seeing parts of the whole vision in greater detail.

As a very small child, my first recollection of God, was asking Him where He came from. Finally, in the fall of 2004 I received the answer to this question. This is the beginning of the vision. He has stirred in my heart the desire to know the details of creation and in particular to understand the spiritual things I have witnessed.

I cannot write all that I have seen for it would be too much. But I have written what the Lord has directed me to.

Table Of Contents

PROLOG

A Little About Myself

The enemy decided before I was even born to take me out, but the Lord intervened to thwart his plans at every turn.

Before birth, it was suggested that my mother have an abortion, but she refused. Because of a time miscalculation, the doctors then removed me from her womb two months early through cesarean birth and sent me home to die. Born with skin cancer and insufficient blood volume in my two-pound body, I was sickly and barely clung to life. The Lord saved me from blindness often caused by the incubator lights, as well as physical and brain damage from uncontrolled oxygen levels by sending me home to His care. Premature babies had a very low survival rate in the early fifties, and those that did survive usually suffered irreversible physical and emotional damage.

Once home, I was placed in an isolation tent for two years. I was placed on the kitchen table with a constant pot of steaming water beneath the blanketed shelf I lay on. The only contact with humans was when my mother force fed me or changed my bedding. I lived in isolation suffering from chronic bronchial pneumonia. To cure this, our family physician ordered a daily regimen of whiskey, which slowly destroyed my stomach. It was a miracle I survived the ill-timed birth and isolation of those first two years.

By the age of three, I slept in a dresser drawer because of my small stature. Finally over the bronchial pneumonia, the skin cancer

xix

flared up and had to be treated with radiation therapy. Once that was cured, juvenile diabetes set in, along with a number of other ailments. Throughout my years the attacks did not stop as a bizarre number of physical injuries, abuses and ailments plagued my life.

It wasn't until fifty-three years later that I discovered the depth of the Lord's love and the extent of His intervention in my life. It was not until then I realized, through a download of revelation, the reality of my life and its purpose.

Over the past six years, the Lord has been undoing and restoring, through healing and deliverance, everything the enemy had stolen. It was not until recently, I have had restored to me the visions I experienced in those first four years of age and realized God's unencumbered mercy towards me. My first remembered vision was when I was two days old.

I learned that during the first four years of my life, I spent my entire time in heaven in continual vision.

I remember playing in the luscious green fields with several angels twirling me around, being sung to sleep by a chorus of melody, and being held tightly in the Father's arms as I sat on His lap. I asked all sorts of questions, and He laughed and freely answered every question. Outside His Throne Room, there were massive lawns filled with vivid colors that stretched hundreds of miles and the air was filled with the fragrance of a multitude of flowers. There was only sunlight and I do not remember ever getting tired. Angels held me and played with me...there did not seem to be any notion of time in those days. They told me stories upon endless stories of life in the heavens, and I slept in their arms, held close to their bosom, listening to the comfort of their heartbeat.

When these visions came flooding back to me, the veil that covered them rent, I wept because I suddenly realized that I had never been abandoned by the Lord as I once thought. He went to extraordinary lengths to save me from every attack the enemy threw at me.

My angelic friends were numerous and my life in heaven was filled with joy and laughter. But these precious angels, who are still with me to this day, were not only in my visions...they guarded me here on the earth as well.

When I was four or five, while my sister was looking after me, she pushed me over the top of our four-foot tall headboard and dropped me behind it to the floor. It was her payback for my being born. I remember screaming and crying because I could not climb over, under or around the bed. I was trapped and my parents were not home. To her dismay, an angel lifted me up and placed me gently on the bed.

When I was four years old, finally physically capable of interacting with the natural world around me, I remember sitting on the Father's lap. He held me tight in His large arms and hugged me. Then He said, tears in His eyes, "You have to go away for a little while."

The next moment I was back in my bed, crying. Within a matter of days I was besieged by a world of fallen angels who terrorized my every waking and sleeping moment. This would continue through many years.

I did not know at that time that the Lord had given me a peculiar vision in which I saw the natural and spiritual world equally well. I did not know at that time that what I saw no one else did, especially not a family who was barely Christian. I did not understand that I had, because of my four years in heaven, a spiritual sight that was more stimulated than my natural sight that had been damaged by incubator lights.

Out of the protective hands of the Father, the fallen spirits took me to such depths of visual depravity at four years old that my mind was branded and distorted for five decades. They pulled me into the pits of their agonizing hell and world of evil, tutoring me in all their ways, laws and rituals.

Changed completely by the age of seven, I gave myself over totally to the world of fallen angels, forgetting completely the visions of heaven where I had once lived.

It was not until fourteen years later that I began the long and difficult road back to the Lord. But I was trapped between two worlds—the fallen world of sin and the call on my life. Neither world gave me any understanding of the things that I saw. It would be another two decades before I would get the answers explaining what this ability really was.

The hardest thing for me was to comprehend that the things I saw and heard were not seen or heard by others. The reaction of people towards me was to steer clear of me, and as I look back, I can totally appreciate their response. It took me years of continued isolation, as friends and associates kept me at a distance, to learn to stop talking about the things I saw. But by then, the damage had been done. I was alone in a world of people I did not comprehend or relate to because I had spent most of my life in the spiritual world.

What I had was not so much a vision, as we have come to understand them, as a peculiar way of seeing things. I see what is in the heart of a person as well as their physical appearance. Often I will see them as an object, a word or an essence, and that is how I recognize them from that moment on.

An example of this is the lady who I always see as standing behind a barely open front door. She is a wonderful, gentle person, but the *fear* on her shadowed face as she peered through the open crack is her nature. True to her nature, she is a woman who, although a wonderful hostess to people she knows, is terrified of the world outside.

Another example is the woman I see whose arms are always wrapped around the feet of Jesus. It is her nature, desperation and passion to always be in intimate relationship with Jesus, positioning herself at His feet. Although I will always remember her name, I will invariably identify her by her nature, which is total submission, in this case identified by *feet*.

Others I have seen as *rage, a castle turret, an angry bear, ego, a plethora of spirits, a stallion,* etc. One man I saw as a whirling vortex of consuming emptiness. In vision, Jesus personally introduced one woman to me as His wife. He took me around each room of His house and showed me the touch she had in each room.

These pictures may change as the person changes, but with every person I have ever met, I have seen their nature plainly visible upon them. There have been no exceptions.

This may be an odd way of thinking of people, but when I am shown visions of someone, or the Lord wants to point them out to me, He shows them to me by their nature, not their name. Although

He knows everyone's name, that is how we communicate—by pictures of people's natures.

It has, at times, been difficult not to react to what I am watching while talking or listening to someone. In my teen years, after once again reaccepting the Lord as my Savior, I was attending an unaffiliated church. One evening one of the three pastors spoke, a man in his late thirties. In vision, as he was speaking, as if it was shown on a big screen T.V., I watched as he raped a young girl. I spoke to the elders of the assembly and told them what I had seen and that he was going to molest a member of the congregation if he had not already done so. Two men picked me up, each taking one arm, and carried me up the stairs and deposited me at the end of the driveway. It was only one month later that the man was arrested in Ontario, Canada for raping a fourteen-year-old parishioner.

This *sight* I lived with has ostracized me in every situation. It separated me from my family who thought I was insane, from the church that thought I was of the devil, and from the world that thought I was a freak. This revelation had kept me on a tortured path of complete loneliness and isolation from the day I was born...a path it has taken me over half a century to overcome.

Then one day, when I was forty-eight, I discovered what it was to be a seer. It was the beginning of the healing process and being freed from the influence of fallen angels. I still saw things the same way, but I began to differentiate between what I was seeing in the natural, in the spiritual, and what things actually meant.

One morning, I attended a deliverance meeting in Georgia. A young woman sat in front of me. I ducked and stretched trying to see around her three heads, all of which were staring at the speaker. Finally, I got up and moved. Later, the staff, seeing my odd behavior, asked me what the problem was. Upon hearing what I saw, they confirmed it by explaining to me that the woman suffered from multiple personalities.

This was a turning point of acceptance for me, and the day another level of healing began.

I have seen angels, devils and the natures of people. I have seen the hearts of people and watched as their hearts did not match their words. It has been a difficult and fascinating time. These spirits and angels are all around us; hundreds of thousands of them can be seen at any time. The people of God have guardians sent to protect and minister to them, as many as two-dozen ministering and soldier angels. Just as busy around people are the fallen angels of Lucifer who are on assignment to cause harm and division.

While driving down the highway, I have seen fallen spirits dart in and out of cars and trucks, while other vehicles had an angel at each corner standing guard...and they take their post very seriously.

My fifty-third year has been a year of monumental and very deep healing. Visions have been restored. Health has been restored. And I was instructed to write the four-year vision the Lord gave me a few years ago. For me, God was asking me to do something that would again place me in a level of great vulnerability...a place that has never served me well before.

It is only in obedience that I write the things God has shown me, which will most likely draw a lot of criticism from both church and world. However, when God speaks, it is better to listen and obey.

CHAPTER ONE

Eternity Before Creation

I was transported to the center of an endless expanse of black space. There was no sensation of cold or hunger or even time. There was a very pale light within the core of the expanse that was visible while being invisible at the same time. There was nothing around in any direction except what I perceived as complete emptiness. Although I was in space, there were no stars or solar systems or substance of any recognizable kind. One could say, there was nothing...except this soft light. Off in the distance, in every direction, I could see the line of the horizon in the pale, almost invisible light.

While I was still trying to orient myself, I heard a voice speak in a very deep, resonant, and incredibly authoritative tone, "Look and observe." I could not discern where it came from, as I was the only one around.

At this point, the veil over my eyes was removed and I found that I could look into the very essence of this space. My vision was given the unlimited ability to be magnified to the nth degree so that I could see the absolute minutest particles at the greatest magnification. As large as the expanse was, the particles were infinitely small. I saw that this essence was filled with particles and every particle was individually emanating a slight pulse of light.

As I focused deeper and deeper into the essence of this expanse, I began to see that the space I had previously thought was empty was actually filled to overflowing with an element so infinitesimally small I was amazed at the minuteness. Each element was like a cell, part of the whole. There was googolplex (10^{100}—largest number known by man) upon googolplex of cells, each joined to the other by a unity of purpose.

As the essence became magnified in my sight, I could run my fingers through it. It ran over my hands like a very pale, translucent golden liquid that was not really a liquid at all. It rolled over my fingers like tiny cells...like little, tiny beads of golden honey.

I spoke out loud, asking the Lord what this element was, but He answered, "Go. Explore to the ends of the horizon." At this point, my vision returned to normal, I looked up at what I thought was the horizon, and as soon as it appeared in my thought, I was there in less time than a millisecond, looking at a new horizon and traveling to that point. I traveled this way for what seemed like years, but was in fact only a matter of seconds as I was speeding faster than the speed of light or thought. First I went to the east, then to the west. I went to the north and south. I traveled to the top and bottom, and even explored every angle. No matter how far or where I traveled, there was always another horizon before me just as far away.

This was a colossal expanse without end.

Suddenly, I found myself in the exact center of this space. How I knew I was at the center, I am not certain. It was simply a knowing. I looked around, and before my eyes, there arose one man, whose hair and beard were white. He was clothed in the most brilliant, purest white light. His face shone and He was wrapped in light as if He were wearing clothes. At His presence, the entire expanse became a brilliant visual light. Beside Him, on His right side, arose another man who was also clothed in light and whose face shone of light. Beneath them rose a ziggurat, step pyramid, with one throne upon it. The man with the beard sat down upon the throne while the other stood at His side, and around them rose a mist, which encircled and engulfed them.

I realized in a moment that this mist and the elements of the expanse was the Holy Spirit and that I had actually been traveling inside the Holy Spirit. The Father, Son and Holy Spirit were one in union, purpose, heart and character. And I also realized that they always were, for in Them is everything. I bowed down before Them and began to worship, the fear of the Lord engulfing me.

The Lord said to me, "Arise and look upon my face and tell me what you see." I arose and gazed into the face of the Father who sat upon the throne. I saw at once His countenance as well as His heart and spirit. There was a smile upon His face and a tremendous joy in His heart, which seemed to reach out towards me and swallow me up whole. I saw upon His face what I could only describe as *endless possibility*. There was the knowing of this by His expression, the words written on my heart at the same time as they were spoken in my ear. There was no possibility of mistake.

I knew in my heart that before Him was the possibility to create anything He chose. He could be whatever He wanted to be. In that instant, I saw that He could have been a God of great cruelty, taking delight in creating an endless number of creatures to torture and maim if He so chose. After the unfathomable period of time in the isolation of being before creation, He could have been anything He chose. But He chose to follow His nature.

Above His head appeared words, which circled the heads of the Father, Son and Holy Spirit, slowly spiraling downward. The words appeared at the same time they called their name. They constantly cried out what they were as they circled and finally settled upon the very being of the Godhead, covering and clothing Them. The voices of the words shouted so loud they echoed throughout the expanse, literally reaching even the most unending distant corner. As they appeared, they were written in what I can only describe as *Angelese*, not actually knowing what the first language of the Godhead is called. As they appeared, they spoke out their names and the spirit within me translated them into English so that I might understand their meaning. "I Am," "The Self-Existent One," "Most High," "Everlasting God," "God All Sufficient," "The Lord of Hosts," "God Of The Covenant," "Mighty God," "The Lord Will Provide," "The Lord Who Heals," "The Lord Who Sanctifies," "Lord God," "The Lord Is There," "Holy One," "Savior," "Righteous," and hundreds more. It seemed there was no end to the names of Their nature.

I then looked into the Father's face again and my breath left me. His face had the features of a man, but in His face was everything that would ever be created: universes, galaxies, people, angels, animals, stars, planets…everything. The deeper I looked into His face, the more I could see of what would be created. Everything was already there, planned and already existing in the *endless possibility* that was His being.

I realized at that moment, that the Holy Spirit would draw out of His being, the God realm, what was already there to bring it into the spiritual realm, just as we are to draw out of the spiritual realm what is already there to bring it into the natural realm. Absolutely everything that has been or will ever be created was first in the Father.

I felt as if I was dead; I couldn't move, but my eyes were transfixed on His face. I could not tear them away from searching out everything I saw in His face. In natural time, I actually searched His face for close to two hours. I was transfixed and could have spent eternity just looking into the depths of His beautiful face. I knew that there would never be enough time to know everything that was there, but that I would gladly spend an eternity gazing into His face if I was permitted that honor.

But He reached out a hand towards me, breaking my transfixed concentration. The Lord said unto me, "Watch."

My life came back into me and I slowly stood up; I stood off to one side, a little before and to the right of the throne where the Father sat, and simply watched everything that went on. The Son stood because the Son had a tremendous amount of work before Him.

I looked around and noted that there was nothing that could be seen except the expanse of space I had previously explored and the throne standing majestically upon a platform. There were a great number of steps leading to the platform that stood on the top step. The Father sat upon the throne, and standing to His side and moving about was the Son.

Creation of Lucifer

I saw the Father speak to the Son, and the Son opened His mouth and spoke words. The Holy Spirit went out from about the throne, yet never really leaving the throne, and circled in an area in the middle of the space just before the throne. When the Holy Spirit left the area, I saw a most beautiful angel.

He stood perched, as it were, in nothingness before the steps and throne. He was at eye level with the Father who sat upon the throne, and he stood straight, arms by his side. His hair was red and curled. His eyes were fresh pools of a most captivating blue; his face was finely featured and of perfect complexion. He wore a short white tunic that glistened with every color of a rainbow, all below a halo of pale golden hue. Upon his brow was a thin crown adorned with a single row of the deepest hued jewels, absolutely flawless and perfect.

As I watched, his fingers twitched and his eyelids fluttered, and he opened his eyes slowly. The very first thing he saw was the Father's face. There was, from the Father's eyes, such a great profundity of love it was hard to keep one's life under the weight of their stare. When he beheld the Father's gaze, he fell on his face in one fluid movement and worshipped the Lord—partly from fear and partly instinctual. The love was so intense that it drove Lucifer to his knees. I could barely remain where I was in the presence of His look, but obedience kept me in place. Then I saw the Son step down the stairs. He put His hand upon the angel's shoulder, and said, "Arise Lucifer, my friend."

The angel rose, trembling. I heard the Father say, "You are the first. You will bear witness to all that I will do. You will give testimony to the nations. You will teach those that follow the things that I have done. For in you will be the sum of all wisdom."

Again, Lucifer fell upon his face and worshipped the Godhead, staying there for a very long time. This time, though, it was not from fear.

I was released to join him, the sheer impact and weight of the Father's love driving me to my face.

CHAPTER TWO

Creation Of The Universes

The next three things the Lord created were two universes and the Lake of Fire within the expanse. Today, science calls the great expanse of the Holy Spirit the Ekpyrotic Universe, and the two universes the Light and Dark Branes—two flat universes within a large shell universe. The Lake of Fire was created next, placed in the absolute furthest corner of the expanse, a place no man will ever be able to explore. Although I have seen it from a very far distance, I have not as yet been permitted to search it out. I do know that to even go near it is to be consumed by the very heat emanated from the Lake itself.

These two universes were one within the other, one dark, the Second Heavens, and the other light, the First Heavens. The one held all dark matter, only visible through scientific methods of measuring and scanning, and the other held all light matter, everything visible to the naked eye. They moved within each other, one seen and the other in secret, moving back and forth as the laws governing them so ordered.

The dark matter had a heavier gravitational pull that would not permit any *body* from the light universe trapped within its boundaries to remain intact, for the heavier gravitational forces within it would pull asunder anything of light matter substance. The dark matter produced a searing, scorching heat even though they did not produce sufficient visible light to be seen—the energy going into heat instead of light. This is the place found in the book of Luke and the temporary place reserved for those who choose not to follow their Creator.

Luke 16:22-31 ...The rich man also died and was buried. And being in torments in Hades, he lifted up his eyes and saw Abraham afar off, and Lazarus in his bosom. Then he cried and said, "Father Abraham, have mercy on me, and send Lazarus that he may dip the tip of his finger in water and cool my tongue; for I am tormented in this flame."

The Third Heavens is where the Godhead lives, the great expanse holding everything created. The Third Heavens holds the First Heavens, the natural world, and the Second Heavens, the spiritual world. The Third Heavens contains everything pertaining to the Godhead such as the Holy City, which itself is millions of miles large, with its many great palaces. This area is so vast that it is implicitly impossible for it to ever be filled regardless how much is created. The First and Second Heavens and Lake of Fire, itself large enough to hold the First and Second Heavens, are so small in comparison I was stunned. From a very short distance, it looked as large as a miniature deck of cards in the Super Bowl arena...within the Milky Way galaxy.

When all is said and done, and New Jerusalem is set up here on earth in the Garden of God, the whole planet will become one city that the Lord will begin to create in His greatness. This area of expanse is reserved for the time when all that the Lord will create will be fruitful and multiply as He has commanded. He has not yet fully begun to provide supernaturally for His creation, and part of that provision is to fill the expanse with an unthinkable number of everything—planets, systems, stars, galaxies, animals, people....

There is no end to provision and absolutely no end to the creation the Lord will manifest now and for all eternity...when there once again will be no death.

And absolutely everything has been and will be drawn out of the Father and brought into the spiritual and natural realms. And when we think the expanse is full, which is not possible, it will not even have scratched the surface of what is left in the Father to be created. We, as Christians, think too small of a God who is so incredibly, infinitely, unthinkably, unbelievably, unimaginably big.

The First Heavens, made up of light matter, is where we now reside, before the first death.

The Second Heavens, made up of the dark matter, is where hell is. The Second Heavens is very dense and gravitationally strong. Normal bodies could not possibly exist in this matter and consequently to be exiled to this place means to be exiled from one's body.

Luke 11:24 When an unclean spirit goes out of a man, he goes through dry places, seeking rest...

It is the temporarily perpetual dwelling place of the angels who fell, unless they have the assignment of a *host* body in this realm. It is the place where most of them still reside, between assignments or overseeing the fulfillment of the plans of Lucifer. I have spent a great deal of time in this place, in spirit and vision. It is a colorless place where everything is only a hint of what it was—a hint of color, a hint of majesty, a hint of its former glory....

This Second Heavens lies between the Throne Room and our *universe* or *heavens*, constantly moving in and out between our realm and the throne, always getting in the way and interfering with life here. Scientists tell us that this Dark Brane is as close to us as our own skin, always present but kept within its own confines by means of its dense gravitation. It is only visible when viewing the distorting effects it has on the light of stars, as light is actually bent around this dark matter because of the gravitational pull, just as the spiritual effects of Lucifer and his minions can only be seen by the effects they have on mankind and nature.

I could see that the fallen angels, who were exiled and bound to this realm after their fall, could be in this world but locked in a different dimension or realm, able to move about but unable to touch or affect this realm.

As in the story where Abraham forbade the dead rich man's soul from talking with Lazarus' soul, the rich man was unable to gain access to this world. Fallen, unredeemed mankind is condemned to this hell, and they are locked in, forbidden interaction with this world at all. They cannot be *trapped* here waiting to *cross over*, nor can they communicate or talk with the living souls in this realm. There is no chance of communication or interaction between the two realms of man living and dead.

The fallen angels of this realm were as close to Adam and Eve, and every creature in creation, as the breath on the backs of their necks, though they were not permitted into the First Heavens realm. It was not until Eve and Adam gave them the deed to their realm or heavens, opening that door through sin—Eve's and Adam's allegiance or agreement with them—that the fallen angels were able to again gain free access to the earth.

Since a child, in the spirit, I have been to this Second Heavens many times without knowing what it was. It is a dismal place, lacking in any joy or life. The oppression of lost hope fills the wind torn atmosphere until it chokes out the very life. The fallen angels move about sluggishly, shuffling their steps as they go, heads hung down and their arms listless at their sides. They moved as if the weight of their hopelessness pulls them down by some sort of emotional gravitational pull of depression and oppression. Even though they are spirit they retain their appearance before the fall, but they are gray in color with only a hint of their former color and glory.

They live in small cubicles, which look very much like bland cement but are made out of a material that appears to be somewhat like storm clouds. At one point, in my childhood, they had given me one of these cubicles, promising me that I could in time live with them. In my unending misery from the burgeoning vision they forced on me, I actually looked forward to living in this place where everything was so featureless, unexciting and visually uneventful. I so desperately wanted an end to the things they tormented me with night and day…that I faced alone because no one else ever saw those things. I could not even tell anyone of the things I saw. How many people do we lock away in institutions because they see those same things? Thinking about that even now breaks my heart and causes it to weep for their unrecognized and continuing torment.

These fallen angels huddle in these indistinguishable abodes with a deep sense of desperation and hopelessness. These cubicles are without number, stretching forth across millions of miles like endless, faceless tenements, lacking any possible warmth and life. Everything in this place is made up of the subtlest shades of black on black, dark gray on dark gray, the slight hues seen only by the most discriminating eye. It took me years before I could distinguish the subtleties of color residing here. Without knowing what this place was, I called it *Grayland*, and it was a place that soon occupied my nightmares and daymares alike.

I have been to their conference halls, listened to their discussions and plans, and partook in their daily lives as much as possible. I have been to their war room—a massive hall that stretches for miles. In this hall, there were thousands upon thousands of fallen angels—slips of gray forms—flitting in and out as they received orders and gave reports. There was a constant flow of activity here, and as the ages wore on, the activity increased, reaching a level of almost critical desperation as they were losing the war and the close of this age was at hand.

I was sent to this place once with no option of leaving any time I wanted. I walked into my bedroom after a church meeting, and the Lord verbally said to me, "You have a choice. You can either choose Me or you can choose hell." Before I could even answer, I was sent to hell for eight hours...long enough to decide I did not like it. The most terrible aspect of this time, unlike being able to go there many times earlier, was that I was unable to leave. I was a prisoner and the screaming torment of the other inmates was horrifyingly deafening. Finally, I could move my natural lips, and I cried out the only name that counts, "Jesus!" Instantly I was back in my bedroom. I pushed myself up from my bed and, before I reached the door, I was baptized with the Holy Spirit, remaining wrecked and drunk for two weeks.

This Second Heavens is the place of Jude 1:10-13, Psalm 9:17, Isaiah 5:14, and Revelation 20:14. Science tells us a description of dark matter is as follows: It is a waterless place as the planets have waterless clouds and are subjected continually to strong winds or storms. There are no trees, vegetation or life available since there

35

is no light for photosynthesis. Every planet is a barren wasteland where horrific storms blow without hindrance and tear up the very landscape.

To live in this universe is to be in a state where one might wish they were dead. Planets have raging waves of gasses and other elements. It is a very large area comprising 90% of the known universe mass. This Dark Brane describes Hell perfectly as shown in scripture. Hell will eventually be cast into the Lake of Fire at the end of this time, a lake reserved in the furthest corner of God's Third Heavens that is more than large enough to accept 100% of our known and unknown universes.

I have seen this Lake of Fire, or rather the red hue of flames rising high on the horizon. I have been to the highest points of the Throne Room and could see it way off in the most distant corner of creation. Even from that distance, the Lake of Fire is enormous.

In both the dark and light matter universes, He created a countless number of suns and their spiraling galaxies, setting the laws and boundaries on all that was created. It all took time, but during that time, Lucifer, the angel of light, watched and learned how and why everything was done.

With the creation of Lucifer was the creation of time; the moment he took his first breath, so to speak, the clock started ticking. Before Lucifer, there was no calculation of time—it was merely eternity.

Jesus shared with Lucifer, His friend, some of the plans of God. I saw the two of them travel throughout the universe, almost at a leisurely stroll, walking through open space and through the systems as they were being created, talking and sharing all that was happening.

The Lord shared His vision of one day creating a heavenly host who would be made in His image and fill the planets He was creating. He told Lucifer many things about the creation He was planning, especially of His plan to one day have a bride, a people who would be one with His heart. This bride would work by His side as a helpmate, and together they would rule all that was created. The people who would make up His bride would be *"the living temple of the Living God,"* and He would dwell among His people forever.

Lucifer put these words in his heart and did all that the Lord had him do, happy for his friend and longing to see His joy fulfilled, not fully understanding the things he was told.

Lucifer was created first, and it was spoken over him by the Father that he had the fullness of wisdom because he was to be the experiential witness of God's work. His wisdom was experiential wisdom, not revelational wisdom. (Ezekiel 28:12-14)

I saw the Holy Spirit create all things, being moved to do so as the Son spoke. Always at the Son's side was Lucifer, watching and studying all that was done. He watched the lips of the Son as He spoke His creative words with great authority and gentleness, and in private, he tried to imitate the exact motions and movements he witnessed. But to Lucifer's dismay, nothing was ever created at his command. No matter how hard he tried, he simply did not have the ability to create. So he continued to watch and learn, keeping all that he saw in his heart.

Jesus and Lucifer were close friends, and Lucifer worshipped the Father unrestrained and with great joy and trembling. The more he saw the Father do, the more Lucifer purposed to worship Him in his heart. The more he saw the Father do, the more he realized the magnitude of God's nature. God's power is indeed all encompassing, and nothing exists without that power.

Lucifer was called to be the anointed cherub that covered, for under his watchful eye would all else be created. He alone was upon the holy mountain of God before anything else came into being. He walked up and down in the midst of the stones of fire, the planetary mantels cooling around their molten cores, his body impervious to the extreme heat and molten metals. (Ezekiel 28:14-16)

He walked through the emerging star systems, galaxies and Third and First Heavens checking the progress of everything as it evolved and changed at the precious guiding words of the Lord. The entire creation was birthed within the great expanse of the Holy Spirit, and it was His delight, His joy, and His great creative expression. I saw the Holy Spirit lovingly create every atom, giving each atom His personal attention. I was overwhelmed with a tsunami of love and pleasure as the Holy Spirit worked His special creative power building a universe as the Godhead had agreed, adding His own special touch to everything.

I saw that the Father expressed His heart to the Son about what He wanted; the Son expressed His love by detailing the Father's heart; the Holy Spirit poured out His creative ability, drawing the thing out of the Father, and making the animate, three-dimensional work of art. They were one in unity, and each had Their special part, one not greater than the other. They worked together, combining Their special offices and abilities to create the whole. They moved in complete fluid agreement.

The fullness of Their hearts fell upon me, and for the first time I realized the distinct personalities of the Godhead. Although one in unity, I could tell whom each one was by how Their heart felt, and by the aroma each heart gave off.

The Father's heart is a heady, almost aromatic love. There was deepness to it, a depth that resonated in my spirit as it came down and covered me. There is a distinct maleness to His love, manifesting a great sense of protection and unconditional love. In His precious, all-encompassing arms, I could have breathed in His love all day, feeling safe, accepted and loved in totality. His love does not depend on me, or what I have done or not done. His love depends on His heart and His nature.

The Son's heart is an ocean of love whose tide reaches out to me as if I was a small piece of land that His love continually woos like the ocean waves creeping up a beach. His love is like gentle wooing, tender prodding, and gentle direction, while at the same time relentless in its tireless beating against the harsh shore of my own being. There is an element of a love that always pursues, always thinks the best, and always longs to be with me. His love has a refreshing, vibrant odor to it, an almost invigorating and revitalizing quality to it. One touch of His hand, and I felt like running everywhere He led, keeping pace with Him…but it didn't matter; if I slowed, He slowed to catch me and help me along. His love is full of life and also filled with it, one just wants to live to totality in His presence, forever, never leaving for even a single moment.

The Holy Spirit is an emotional tidal wave—an intensity of emotion that wells up from within. I have walked out of a movie theatre where I just watched a thrilling action movie and been over-come with a great grief and sadness which almost drove me to my knees as I hung my head in my hands and wailed for the future of mankind. I have been angry with a friend and suddenly so over-come with a great love for them that I could barely stand under its consuming weight. Every time I have felt an overwhelming emotion that wells up within me, usually nothing to do with me or what I am doing, I know this is the Holy Spirit. His love smells of the lingering, distant odor of fresh cut grass or hay, like a harvest being brought in, with a delicious floral scent. His love is the one that stretches my heart to almost breaking until it grows beyond the borders I have set. His love is the one I can swim in, a mighty ocean of essence that created me and cradles me all my eternal life. He is the one who downloads me with such grandiose visions of His creation that I am breathless. He is the one who is like a fresh, cleansing wind that brushes my face and fills my lungs with essential life.

Lucifer is fourteen billion years old (guesstimate of science for the actual age of the universe—time began when he was created). During that time, he watched the Holy Spirit paint the beauty that surrounds us as an artist lovingly paints his creation on a blank canvas. The Holy Spirit did not rush His creation. God is never in a hurry to do that which He does. The Holy Spirit created the universes and all that are in them, but it was the Father who deter-mined the boundaries and the Son who spoke the words of law that binds them to the Father's will. They work in perfect choreography, each One doing Their part in conjunction with the Others—a most beautiful and impressive thing to watch. I was as awed as Lucifer as he watched the Three create all life.

The Holy Spirit drew out of the Father what was already there and brought it into the spiritual world of the Third Heavens. The Holy Spirit drew out of the spiritual world of the Third Heavens that which was already there and brought it into the natural world of the First Heavens.

Lucifer witnessed the galaxies form from nuclear fusion, the supernovas forge with their complex elements, and the suns ignite. He saw the planets form, each one in the palm of the Holy Spirit who molded each system individually and lovingly, the limits of His creativity being boundless.

Collisions of enormous meteorites carved chunks out of the planets to form moons and rings. Slowly, everything came into their proper place as the Lord ordered it. Everywhere Lucifer looked, this huge bare canvas called space became filled as the Holy Spirit moved, paying attention to every detail, hue and color, putting exactly in each place that which the Lord desired.

On Lucifer's face was etched innocence and awe at the works done at the Lord's hand, and he fell on his face to worship his God and Creator.

Planetary crusts cooled and life was appointed, each according to the account found in the first chapter of Genesis. Vegetation was the first life created as the crusts cooled. The suns and stars now stable could be seen as the atmospheres cleared from their toxic, impermeable gasses, and everything settled in its place as orbits steadied. The waters were the home of the first plant life forms. Creatures were created on the land—everything in its time as the Lord ordered and created it—were now able to partake of food and water, sun and darkness. Everything followed a perfect, logical order.

Lucifer witnessed everything come forth as an explosion of life, the endless variety of things keeping him in a state of awe and wonder at all times. Nowhere in the universe could be seen two things exactly alike, for everything fulfilled that *endless possibility* seen on and in the Father's face.

I watched everything happen, fourteen billion years of creation in a matter of months, taking note of the things of importance to me, such as the look on Lucifer's face, or what the Lord pointed out, such as the condition of Lucifer's heart.

Looking at the Father I could see an excitement and joy so powerful that it overcame me and I lay slain by that power for what seemed like forever. The joy of that creative force took away my breath and I lay helpless in the magnitude of its power, unable to do anything except let the joy wash over and through me. And everywhere there was life, I felt the innocence and purity of their existence, for it was a creation holy and pure and without one shred or notion of sin or agenda anywhere. The purity so overwhelmed me that I, myself, felt dirty and unclean because I came from a different place where sin not only bit at my heels but had once stolen my heart and mind. I wept uncontrollably, my heart stricken with grief because of my total uncleanness and unworthiness in the face of the undefiled innocence of what I saw and felt, and all I wanted to do was to crawl to the Lake of Fire and throw myself into its flames forever.

But the Lord called out, "Stand and watch. Write down what you see and what you hear." And in obedience, I arose and watched.

CHAPTER THREE

Creation of the Angels

After all was created in the heavens, the Lord created the angels. It was given to Lucifer to name all the angels giving them their station and work. The Lord gave each angel their gifting and talent, but it was God's pleasure to have Lucifer assign each angel their name and job description. Lucifer assigned every angel a place in creation, a planet or galaxy to keep and govern. To every angel was given a home according to what they liked and desired.

We are so afraid to dream and desire things that are great and wonderful, fearful that we are greedy. But if our first desire is to be in relationship with the Almighty Creator, there is nothing He would not give us. My desire is to spend eternity exploring everything He has created, because the more I see of His handiwork, the more I praise Him. The more I praise Him the more I love Him. The more I love Him, the greater my desire is towards Him. The greater my desire is towards Him, the greater are His pleasures towards me. The greater His pleasures are towards me, the greater are my dreams and visions. The greater my dreams and visions, the more I see of His handiwork...and so the circle continues.

I have always been taught that angels stood before the throne all the time, worshipping, but now I saw that this was only part of their service. They also had their own lives to live, and they traveled, worked, and rested, all according to their needs and the will of the Father. When they were not before the throne or being sent on a mission by the Father, they worked and rested in their own homes, or visited with each other, moving about and seeing the endless wonders of God's creation.

God created His creation for His pleasure. We are to be enjoyed and filled with joy and life.

Lucifer kept the Garden of God—later to become the home of the Bride of Christ—for himself, as the friend of the Lord. He would tend the garden and keep it in order until the Lord's bride was created. He wanted nothing for himself but to keep the Garden of God in trust for the bride.

Lucifer was the friend of the bridegroom. As I looked into Lucifer's eyes, I could see the deep love and bond between the two—he would do anything for his beloved best friend. I could see in his eyes a loyalty that screamed from the rooftops his undying love for his friend, Jesus, the Son of God.

Lucifer was created to teach the angels and mankind about Almighty God. Although it was the job of the Holy Spirit to prepare mankind to become the bride of Christ, Lucifer was to help prepare man by teaching them the wonders he had witnessed. He was the sum of all wisdom, witness to the power of God and all that He had done. Lucifer was the sum of all wisdom because he alone was the witness of creation, and he taught in great assemblies the glory of God through the things he had seen. His fully booked assemblies held millions upon millions of angels, anxious to hear what he had to say about their God.

Everywhere there was unity. From my place, floating in space somewhere in the center of the universe, I could feel that total, complete unity of purpose and heart. I could see everything that was created down to the single cell and each cell had an intelligence and a voice. With a single voice, it was not only the angels that broke forth in worship, but each cell broke forth in praise and worship, singing the praises of God with the words of its mouth. The entire expanse was filled with the voice of worship from every created thing, animate and inanimate alike, and there was such a total fullness of holiness, righteousness, purity and love, that I fell backwards, totally slain by the cleanness of the whole. It was as if I was drowning in an ocean of oneness with the Lord, and I lay on my back, floating in space, unable to move.

Every cell within me joined in the praises sung by all of creation for I could not have held back their voices if I wanted to, even though I myself could not open my own mouth. My spirit soared with the chorus, and it too sang the praises of God. I cannot tell how long I lay like that, soaking in and joining in the worship of the Godhead for it seemed like an eternity had passed.

Suddenly I heard a "clink" in the praise, and in my spirit I *saw* a very tiny black note in the brilliant white tapestry of sacrificial praise. I sat up and looked, my spiritual eyes immediately zeroing into the cause of the black chord, instinctively knowing the direction from whence it came, and seeing through the expanse of space and creation as if there was no barrier of distance at all. There in the heart of Lucifer I could see a minuscule black spot—a tiny cancer-like disease skulking in the darkness, hidden in the deepest reaches of his heart.

I had been in the worship of creation that knew no sin, and suddenly it was marred. I found myself weeping for the loss of the incredible beauty of innocence, for this evil marred forever the purity that joined everything in a perfect union and unity. I wept because I knew the loss that would happen from that one infinitesimal moment that passed by faster than a blink of my eye. I wept because the perfect beauty that the Lord had created was from that moment forever changed, and mankind would never know what the angels had known. I wept because I could never go back again to the time before that moment stole from all of creation its inherent innocence.

I heard the Holy Spirit tell me that Lucifer would sin six times before his sin would finally reach an unrepentant state. At that time, he, and the one-third of the heavenly host that mistakenly followed him would lose the war in the Third Heavens and would be cast out.

My attention was brought back to the scene at hand and I watched how Lucifer reached that end.

Lucifer did not want anything for himself because he hoped all would be his when he became the bride.

Lucifer, in the appearance of love and fear of the Lord, set up his home on the planet next to Earth, the chosen Garden of God.

Mars, named after Lucifer, god of war, for his part in bringing war to creation, was habitable before Earth, and he could easily build his home there. His declared reasoning, which had much logic to it, was to stand guard over the Garden of God while keeping it pure for the creation of the bride.

I could see the other angels wonder what he would stand guard against, for at this point there was no deception or even an enemy in all of creation. There was no evil, deception, violence, or anything against God in the universe, and they did not understand. The need to stand guard over anything was incomprehensible to them and a new concept they had trouble wrapping their minds around.

Lucifer often contemplated the discussions Jesus had had with him about the bride who would rule by His side. Lucifer longed to be more than the friend of the Lord for they had spent so many hours together. He longed to be that bride, even though he did not understand exactly what "the bride" meant. He held onto a vision that it would be heralded throughout all creation the names of the Father, Son, Holy Spirit, and Lucifer. He saw himself as the forth person of the Godhead.

This desire was hidden deep in his heart, a desire he had not even been aware of until it manifested in his thoughts as a quest. In his mind he reasoned that if he could prove himself worthy enough, the Lord would forget about creating mankind, as there would then be no need after he had been declared the bride. He hoped that his faithfulness and adoration would be rewarded with this great honor.

So, his heart set on proving his own worthiness, a point the Lord seemed to have overlooked, he built for himself a kingdom on the planet next to the Garden of God.

There was in the heavens no concept of male and female for the angels and the Godhead have no gender. They are both male and female, unlike man and the animals that were later created separately as male and female for reproductive purposes—something they could not do.

I heard the words he spoke to the other angels explaining his reasoning, but I could see a different picture play behind the words. I watched him sitting, eating at a large, rectangular table, and talking with other angels in a long discourse. But as he spoke, I could also see a movie of what was really going on behind his words—the video playing on his breast as if it were a television screen.

The path to the Garden of God was set so that every angel would have to pass his home first and pay homage to him. Although this was not verbally ordered, it was a non-written expectation with which no one had a problem. They did not even think it strange, for they gladly honored Lucifer, the one and only covering cherub. In a small way, this gave him a subtle preeminence over the Garden God had chosen for Himself.

I saw that Lucifer had a great contingent of angels who worked for him. They were pleased to be the honored servants of the anointed cherub who they revered above themselves. They did everything as he bid, laboring without tiring or complaint, for this left Lucifer to the important tasks of doing whatever the Lord would have him do.

At other times he held meetings with the *top brass* or archangels to hear the reports of the Lord's kingdom. He had given Michael and Gabriel their names and positions, and was therefore a close friend to them because of their high rank. They communed and feasted together often.

I watched as Lucifer, Michael, and about six other angels of high rank sat at a beautiful marble table, its sides ornamentally decorated with fine gold and platinum. They had just finished eating a most opulent meal, and, as they lounged in their chairs, a servant brought in a bottle of fine wine, pouring a glass for each of the guests and host. They sat there for hours talking about the realms of the Heavens. When sunset came, they all rose and moved to the expansive balcony and watched the sun set over the ocean and red earth.

Lucifer enjoyed the gifts the entire universe had to offer as angels brought him their presents of specially prepared foods and drink from every corner of creation. The entire angelic host offered their gifts to him honoring his station as first created, the anointed cherub and friend of God. He enjoyed the lavishness they poured out upon him…perhaps a little too much. I could see their attentions grow in his heart from simple gratitude for being blessed by their love and appreciation to dark expectation and demand of greater gifts of recognition.

47

I could see hosts of angels joining together in fellowship and sharing freely the best of all they had received from the Lord. There were no borders or walls. Everyone enjoyed freely the variety of what the Lord created. They were excited to share something new they had discovered somewhere in God's creation. There was always something new and wonderful to taste and see, and every day they participated in the work of tending to their assigned tasks and learning more about their God. Every day was a joy to partake of, and in all things they worshipped the Lord for His bounty and provision.

There were no battles or squabbles, for everyone preferred everyone else before themselves, and peace reigned in every corner of creation. There was no prejudice of race, for there are several races of angels, or office. They all shared in the unity of diversity, celebrating not only their differences but also the bounty and differences of every corner of creation where they lived.

Michael lives on a planet with royal purple skies and built for himself a crystal palace that allowed the majesty of God's glory to be seen through every wall, ceiling and floor. His palace glows with a brilliant light against the purple backdrop declaring the unbridled purity and royalty of the God he serves gladly. He fashioned his home after the attributes of the Lord he loved, designing everything he has to bring honor and praise to his God.

I was enthralled by the transparency of his home. He was in charge of a delegation of angels, second only to Lucifer. He had nothing to hide, ever. He is an angel with a pure heart, one that is the embodiment of strength, dedication and loyalty. Michael questioned the events that would transpire with Lucifer, and he never once dropped his guard or fell in disrepute. He stood when others fell all around him.

I watched the angels build their homes upon planets where there were no building materials except cooling mantles and firestones. They were assigned their planets before they were finished. I turned to the Lord and asked Him how they could do this, for their homes were opulent and beautiful, and as diverse as the angels themselves. Whatever they envisioned they built.

The Lord looked at me and pointed to an angel adding a new addition for larger gatherings to his already built home. As I watched,

I saw that he actually brought the supplies for his home from the Third Heavens, bringing it into the reality of the First Heavens. Chairs, tables, furniture, and decorations...it was all in the Third Heavens and was brought into the First Heavens by the angels. They understand how this relationship of supernatural existence to natural manifestation works.

There is an endless supply of building materials available in the Third Heavens. There is an endless supply of jewels, gold, silver, and every precious stone and metal that we have not even seen yet. We will have an eternity to experience and discover every corner of the universes, the Heavens and all they contain. We will have an eternity to taste, smell, touch, hear and see all that the Lord has created, is creating and will create, for He is an endless storehouse of creation.

CHAPTER FOUR

The Ten Plagues Of Lucifer

During these visions, I traveled back and forth between the king-doms of God, Lucifer and Pharaoh. This journey often spanned different time periods. I moved between the time before Lucifer fell to ancient Egypt as well as the undetermined time standing before the throne of God.

Through these visions, I was shown what was happening with Lucifer and the angels as they lived their daily lives, attending their feasts, conferences, concerts and events. In this, I was also shown the hidden motives of Lucifer as he was saying one thing but hiding another in his heart. I saw the things the Lord saw him do; I heard the things the Lord heard him say; I was there as he implemented his plans in secret behind a false cover of praise and worship. There were moments when I actually heard what he was thinking and saw the plans he was formulating in his head before they were even complete, concrete thoughts. It was a fascinating, albeit unusual experience.

While there, I saw how the other angels reacted towards him as well as how the Godhead responded to him. The Holy Spirit would point things out that He wanted me to give particular attention.

Then suddenly I would be whisked to ancient Egypt to witness the plagues God rained on Pharaoh and his people. I watched the priests in their worship of their false gods and how these gods reflected a particular aspect of Lucifer's attitude about himself.

Step by step, I would see, in order, Lucifer slipping into sin, the commandment that was broken, the plague that was sent against Egypt and finally, the characteristic of each god the plague was directed against. The growing attitude of the gods was shown to me to be the slipping attitude of Lucifer as he plummeted into sin.

In the visions following, I have tried to capture the essence by going back and forth as I saw it.

I also heard the Lord and the angels speak in their own language, which I assume is Angelese. Although they spoke in their own language, I heard it in mine, often in the words and terminology I understand and appreciate. Although I speak in my own language, they hear in their own words and terminology. It took me a long time to realize this.

Some may find the following chapters disturbing. They tell the story of an angel who betrayed his Creator and friend with the appearance of intimacy. But there was no real relationship between Lucifer and the Godhead. There was only the appearance of relationship. The following chapters tell of an angel who had the highest position in heaven but decided he must have the Throne of God as well.

The following chapters tell of a God so full of mercy and love, that He forgave Lucifer five times before finally condemning him and all the angels who fell with him to hell for their sin.

The visions in this book were unpleasant to watch and even more unpleasant to describe. The very gods that were attacked through the ten plagues of Exodus were the very gods that showed the declining attitude and moral decay of Lucifer himself. I do believe that the Lord had me go through these visions to show how precariously close we are to the end of the ages, as we, the human race, follow in the steps of Lucifer almost exactly. It is a warning to mankind that we cannot destroy and change indefinitely what God has created. There will come a time of judgment when the price for our interference and ignorance of God's laws must be paid. Science and mankind alike cannot continue to deny the creative power of God.

If there was any doubt as to the validity of what Lucifer did during His fall, we need only look around to the DNA and RNA splicing, control and manipulation mankind is now performing. If there is any doubt as to the ability Lucifer had to manipulate the cells and DNA of God's creatures to change them into gigantic creatures, we need only look at what man is able to accomplish today; genetic orchestration and cloning. Lucifer has no creative ability; however he knew how to re-create by scrambling and manipulating the creation already available to him. Interesting word, recreation, don't you think?

I have no doubt that what I saw is of God. You, the reader, must, however, judge for yourself.

To make sure of the validity of what I saw, I have tried to research the available scientific realms as much as possible, as shown in the research materials listed in Appendix A. God will use man's own scientific abilities to prove His greatness if that is what is necessary to reach some men. He will leave no stone unturned. Today, science is no longer the archenemy of the Bible, but it is proving the Bible in every detail.

Archaeology has shown us a history that is not possible through contemporary Biblical explanations, choosing instead the more static theory of evolution to explain their finds. However, I have realized that these *sins* of Lucifer were hidden in the snow and rubble of past *mass extinctions* and behind the curses sent against the world to be later found by man and used to reveal Lucifer's sins. With this in mind, I find no contradictions to the Bible and have referenced many Biblical scriptures to show the consistency between scientific fact and contemporary Biblical belief, as shown in Appendix B.

Above all, remember that these chapters are visions. As such, I cannot substantiate everything in them, although I have attempted to provide proof where I can.

CHAPTER FIVE:

The First Curse —
Coveting To Be The Bride

Lucifer built a city fashioned after the Throne Room of God, although not nearly as splendid. Lucifer did not know any other design. For some reason, unlike most of the other angels, he does not have a great imagination. It is as if after seeing all that was created, he simply became unable to imagine after that, believing there was nothing left to create or invent.

He designed Ziggurats, step pyramids, after the fashion of the one upon which the throne of God stood, but lesser in size and with fewer steps. He built his city beside the ocean, having a consuming affinity and fondness for water, perhaps to reflect the river of water coming from the Throne of God. He would retain this attraction throughout his entire career.

He cultivated a greater depth of honor from the angels under his charge, hoping their increased adulation would reflect his worthiness. They came to his home often, invited under the innocent guise of fellowship. He taught them flawlessly about the Lord and all that was created, holding great schools and conferences in his palaces as well as traveling to the ends of creation to visit their cities. His great oratory skill and knowledge put him in great demand in every corner.

I was shown the heart of Lucifer as I watched him creating his great city in the guise of honoring the Lord God. Although he, like the other angels, created their city to praise their God, Lucifer was creating for himself the beginnings of a kingdom, in expectation of being finally recognized for what he should be—the bride who was more than the best friend.

The Lord said to me, "Behold, I will show you a mystery. The Ten Commandments are given to man upside down to teach him the path back to righteousness. For in their reverse is the fall of Lucifer as he purposed sin in his heart. The ten plagues of Egypt are given to show all the curses upon the earth because of his sin and mindset. Now watch closely and see."

As I watched the panoramic events of Lucifer's downfall, the Spirit quoted to me the scriptures and showed me the change in Lucifer's heart and mind.

Each plague, in their given order, corresponded with a *mass extinction* the earth actually suffered, as revealed through scientific research. All the plagues were directed at specific gods in Egyptian mythology. Each Egyptian god revealed a new level of deception Lucifer was falling into. Lucifer began to believe his own lies that he was not only capable of creating, but it was he who created the Godhead and all life. Through the gods revealed, we can actually see the depths of sin Lucifer fell into, bringing along several of the angelic host with him.

The Holy Spirit said aloud, "Exodus 20:17 'You shall not covet your neighbor's house; you shall not covet your neighbor's wife, nor his male servant, nor his female servant, nor his ox, nor his donkey, nor anything that is your neighbor's.'"

I saw that even though the outward appearance was that Lucifer honored the Lord God, he was filled with jealousy for what the Lord purposed. He wanted to be the bride, coveting her place and station, and to have the place in the Godhead as befitting his position in creation. It did not matter that he had no creative power or any input into anything that was created—he was only a witness to what the Lord had done.

While watching Lucifer in his palaces, I suddenly found myself in the land of ancient Egypt looking through the window into Pharaoh's great palace, my feet not touching the ground.

Pharaoh was used of God to nurture the Israelites from a small family into a great nation, purposing in his heart to treat Joseph's family as if they were his own. But the heart of the Pharaohs changed throughout the generations. In time, the office of Pharaoh became not one of man but that of a god, this concept coming to the forefront when one line of Pharaoh was born with red hair, the color of their god Set's hair. Eventually, Pharaoh saw the Hebrews as cheap labor; slaves unworthy of any consideration except the sweat of their backs.

As I watched the hearts of the Pharaohs change as their kingdom grew in power and wealth, the Holy Spirit showed me that this was what was happening to Lucifer. He thought himself above all the other angels because of the timing of his own creation. The created, because of his assumed familiarity, began to think of himself as the creator because of the great things he had witnessed, having learned the mechanics of creation but lacking the power. The Holy Spirit showed me that this was the basis for 2 Timothy 3:2-5, for Lucifer had become a lover of himself, proud, a blasphemer, unthankful, unholy, and disobedient to his Creator. He was a lover of pleasure rather than a lover of God, having a form of godliness but denying its power.

By his familiarity with the process of creation he believed himself to be part of the creator and in need of greater recognition.

He whispered in his heart, as did Pharaoh, "Who is the Lord that I should obey His voice to let Israel go? I know not the Lord, neither will I let Israel go." (Exodus 5:2)

I saw that each character of the Egyptian gods was one more spiraling step downward into Lucifer's unrepentant sin. The character of the gods the plagues were designed to expose was the very character trait Lucifer had adopted as his sin grew.

The first plague in Egypt was the river turning to blood. (Exodus 7:17)

The first plague was against the five water gods: *Khnun, Hapi, Tatenen, Anget* and *Satet.* These first five gods show the beginning of Lucifer's confusion as his heart began to stray away from the truth and righteousness of God to new depths of sin.

Khnun was the ancient male god of fertility, water and the great potter who created children. His name means to *"unite," "join,"* or *"build."*

Hapi, a male deity who provided life to the Egyptians, was the first god of the Nile. Without *Hapi*, Egypt would have died. Even though a male deity, he was pictured with the large breasts of a female.

Tatenen, a male deity, was also female. He is known for his important role in the creation of the world, and bears the names *"father of the gods,"* thus being the source and ruler of all the gods.

Anget, *"She who embraces,"* was a female deity and goddess of the Nile. She was known as *"Giver of Life, and of All Power, and of All Health, and of All Joy of the Heart."* Known in ancient times as a fertility goddess, she became the goddess of lust related to all things of a sexual nature.

Satet was a female fertility goddess who purified the dead. She was also goddess of the hunt who protected Pharaoh and the land, keeping all their enemies at bay.

Lucifer was beginning to define his identity himself. He was male becoming female, created becoming creator, and friend becoming bride. He saw himself as part of the Godhead, the one who gave and sustained life. He saw himself as that great, fertile creative force, the bride and protector of all creation. He began to see himself as part or the sole creator of the worlds he witnessed forming, thinking in his heart that he could do as the Holy Spirit did.

Without saying anything, he began to display attributes and arrogance as one equal to God, magnifying his role of teacher to that of giver of life and power. Yet, he was still faithful to the Godhead, and as such, he was Their protector from all Their enemies. He began to believe that the blessings he bestowed on the other angels were actually giving and sustaining life, without which they would have long ago perished. He began believing that he was actually saving the Godhead from some as yet unseen conspiracy and overthrow.

I found it interesting that he began to see enemies everywhere in a time when no visible enemies existed, for all of creation was innocent in their loyalty to the Godhead, moving in complete obedience with one purpose. He did not seem to know that the enemy he was growing increasingly wary of was residing in his own heart, and he did not understand the words, "If you do well, will you not be accepted? And if you do not do well, sin lies at the door. And its desire is for you, but you should rule over it." (Genesis 4:7) But as Lucifer nurtured these feelings in his heart, the very thoughts of his heart became sin and were the beginning of his downfall.

His first sin was the transgression of covetousness, and the first curse upon the earth came in the way of a very large meteorite. Two meteorites actually fell that day. The first slammed into Mars with such impact that all life ceased to exist changing its very ecology forever so that there was no longer any water upon the planet.

The other meteorite slammed into the earth with such ferocity that this curse caused the first massive extinction. All life within the oceans died. Scientists call it the "Day the Earth Rusted," for all the water on earth turned red as all plankton died in the oceans, which effectively turned the water to blood.

This curse was represented by the first plague of Egypt when the waters of the Nile became red as they turned to blood.

I was transported back to the beginnings of Earth. It was, at this time, filled with life. Scientists call this period of time the Garden of Ediacara. It was the time of orange skies from toxic gasses and green seas from their abundant plankton life. When the meteorite fell into the earth, all the plankton died, turning the waters red, the resultant massive release of oxygen changing the skies to blue.

With Mars destroyed, his great city laid waste and the ocean gone, Lucifer repented of the sin brewing in his heart and was forgiven. He moved to the Earth, no longer having any home, but being glad to tend the Garden of God, keeping it in trust until the coming of the bride.

I found myself back in the heavenly realms watching Lucifer and the angels. Lucifer's sin was committed in secret, and although the curse of his sin was visible throughout all of creation, it was not publicly announced. There still remained an element of innocence amongst the angels.

Life in the heavens returned to normal. I saw everywhere the entire heavenly host going about their routines, pastimes and work. The angels worshipped God. They worked and kept their homes. They came together in fellowship and played games. They continued their attendance in the great halls to hear the teachings of Lucifer as he spoke about the creation of God. They were filled with the peace and joy of life.

Lucifer returned to teaching his classes with a renewed zest, teaching them about the mercy and greatness of the Lord God, the Almighty Creator of all that was. He had his assemblies of billions, held in massive arenas and halls throughout creation. After each session, angels left the arena, gathered together in their groups of close friends to discuss the things they had learned that day...some gathering at the coffee house equivalent to sit and drink the angelic counterpart of coffee.

But what Lucifer had only thought in his heart so many eons ago began to slip from his lips. He began to bear false witness against his creator, intimating that God could not have done anything without him, the mighty covering cherub, Lucifer, at His side, for he had always gone everywhere with the Son and Holy Spirit.

CHAPTER SIX

Second Curse—False Insinuations

Exodus 20:16 You shall not bear false witness against your neighbor.

Lucifer groaned that the reason God destroyed his home was because God did not want him to have anything good and most certainly did not want him to have anything of his own. The Godhead only wanted everyone to have whatever *They* provided, and this provision was being portrayed as a lack. I heard his words, and they were mere suggestions, slight insinuations, gentle innuendos, possible routes of logic, all pointing to the same thing: God was a selfish God who wanted everything for Himself.

This was the time when frogs were first created on the earth. I was shown the reason that frogs were the first creatures in the Garden of God. They were the natural expression of what was spiritually happening in Lucifer. Frogs were creatures that went through five transformations before finally becoming their true nature, as Lucifer would, sinning five times before he reached that new, unrecognizable being—the first unrepentant sinner. They were cold-blooded creatures that changed from spawn mass to single egg to tadpole to tadpole with legs to froglet with a tail to frog with legs and no tail. The fifth stage was also when the frog was capable of birthing new frogs. This was the stage when the angels would begin to fall following their new father, Lucifer.

The second plague of Egypt was abundant frogs that overran the land, going into the houses, bedrooms, beds, servants' houses, ovens and kneading bowls. They were everywhere. (Exodus 8:2-4)

The second plague was against the frog god, *Heqet*, goddess of childbirth, creation and grain germination. She was a water and fertility goddess of the later stages of labor. She gave all newly created life the breath of life. She was not only the goddess of birth, but of rebirth.

Lucifer was beginning to represent himself in a better light than that of the Godhead. The Godhead might have given these angels birth into bondage but it was Lucifer who would free them from that bondage in a rebirth. It was Lucifer who would raise them up, although he could not breathe life back into that dead planet that was once his home.

He was continuing in his growing delusion that he was the bride.

Caught in the act of misrepresenting himself and bearing false witness, Lucifer answered, "Intreat the Lord to take away the frogs and I will let the people go to sacrifice to the Lord."

Again he had been warned of the path he was on. This was the second change in his metamorphosis into unrepentant sin. The frogs were a natural sign of the outcome of the invisible change that would take place if he did not change his ways. Recognizing this, and accepting it, he entreated the Lord to take away the example. He wanted no part in sin. He repented of his ways.

Through his misrepresentation, he had reduced the joyful provision of the Godhead towards the angelic host to having to beg and plead for God's mercy and grace instead of receiving all things from His loving hands freely. Slowly, he repented of showing the Godhead in this light.

His sin was still only whispered in slight innuendos to his most trusted friends, keeping his sin quite private and close to his chest.

The sin was not widespread to the whole angelic host, but the curse was a public curse for all creation to see, and 95% of all marine life and 70% of all plants, insects and invertebrate in God's Garden became extinct. The Lord snapped His fingers and there was an instant global cooling as the laws of nature obeyed Him without question, proving to Lucifer once again that He was the only God... and He did God-things with very little effort.

Again, truly repentant before the Lord, Lucifer was forgiven and he returned to the task at hand of tending to the Garden and declaring the glorious mercy and forgiveness of a righteous Godhead who deserved his undying love and loyalty.

Forgiving Lucifer of his sin, the Lord replenished His Garden with new life. This is perhaps the most beautiful period of the garden, showing the true glory of God. Trees formed great jungles and there were forests of *sea lilies* which resembled starfish on stems. The high level of the earth's oxygen at 35% was much more concentrated than today's mere 21%. Life was good and easy in God's Garden, and it again became a great resort area for the heavenly host, who came and visited the place God reserved for Himself. Like the Throne Room, the Garden of God was holy ground.

CHAPTER SEVEN

Third Curse —
Stealing The Hearts Of The Angels

As time passed, the Lord recreated a new plethora of life for His Garden, and Lucifer once again poisoned creation with his sin.

Exodus 20:15 You shall not steal.

The third curse was the most devastating the Garden of God had yet faced, affecting 95% of marine and land life. Entire families and genera simply vanished. The cause of this extinction was an asteroid impact, the second in earth's history.

The third plague against Egypt was the turning of dust to lice or gnats. (Exodus 8:16-17)

The third plague was against one of Egypt's earliest gods, *Set*. He was the god of chaos, confusion, storms, wind, desert and foreign lands. Although he secretly conspired to overtake the throne, he was publicly seen as a friend and companion to the god, *Re*. He was at first worshipped as an ambivalent being, but was later denigrated into the god of evil.

Set is the only Egyptian god with the head of an unknown animal — an animal not found anywhere on the earth or in any fossil. He was the only god shown with red hair and white skin. He was also the only god who had his testicles torn off, emasculating him. This sudden emasculation caused him to have unusual sexual habits. Although he had a harem of innumerable wives and concubines, *Set* was clearly dissatisfied and preferred men, raping them despite his lack of genitals.

Set lived in the north, symbolizing darkness, cold and death. To the Egyptians he was the god who *ate* the moon each month—the black boar who swallowed its light—and the god who created earthquakes and heavy, thunderous rainstorms. He was a friend of the dead, helping them to ascend to heaven on *his* ladder, and the crowner of pharaohs and leader of warriors. Without his blessing, no pharaoh could be made king.

Lucifer was finally becoming evil. He was no longer able to hide it well. He was the tadpole with legs, getting ready to leave the pond. His sin was no longer secret. He introduced something never before seen in all of creation, as shown by the head of *Set*, which is from an unknown animal called the *"Typhonian Animal."*

Unlike the gods shown previously, there is no redeeming character trait seen in *Set*.

This is shown in Lucifer as the sin in his heart was hardening. He was sewing seeds of chaos and confusion throughout God's creation. Lucifer stole the hearts of angels from God while contending for His throne. This was the time when he created the first soul ties with other angels, connecting him to them in an insidious subtle way that was foreign to them and against which they had no defense, as they were not aware of the existence of this inherent evil. He learned how to do this quite by accident and over a period of time. I watched as he experimented with the newly developed control he held over others.

Lucifer discovered that a strong emotion created a soulish connection between two angels. In the early days, these connections were made accidentally by the inordinate affection and bond created by the angels that attached themselves to him through their unprecedented admiration of him. This connection did not exist with others, and it took him years of analysis to realize the difference and exactly what was happening. It took many decades more to discover how he himself could create these soul ties at will and use them for his own agendas. They were basic soul ties, not like the ones he created later, and were used basically to enhance emotional bondage with the angels in question.

He not only sowed seeds of chaos and confusion amongst the heavenly host, Lucifer was beginning to have unnatural relations with some of them. Through these unnatural, physical relations, he held a power over them, capitalizing on their shame and fear of exposure, stealing their affections from their true Creator. He replaced their love and trust with fear and mistrust. He owned them.

He was the first homosexual, creating something unheard of— same gender relations. There is a fine line between platonic and physical friendships, and Lucifer crossed that line.

I found myself a bystander at Lucifer's first appalling orgy. He invited some of his closest friends who were in reality his most passionate admirers, ones he could coerce with promise of power and position. They weren't the weakest angels in creation. Some were seraphim, cherubim and others from every nation of the angelic realm.

There were hundreds of angels lying around on cushions and couches, talking, drinking, eating, and laughing. They enjoyed themselves to the fullest. They had been to many of Lucifer's parties before, but none were quite like this one. This one was a little more lavish, a little more of everything. It not only lasted far into the night, but it continued for over two weeks. It was a festival celebration. This was the party that began to separate the sheep from the goats as he determined to introduce a new form of entertainment they had never before seen or imagined.

Lucifer waited until inhibitions were low from both merriment and tiredness. Although angels have a much greater stamina than mankind, they do rest. They partake of both food and drink and I have seen them make such wonderful delicacies, each one bringing the specialties only found in their corner of creation—bringing to the feasts the diversity of the Lord's creation. (Genesis 18:8; 19:2; Psalm 78:25) Although spirit, the angels have bodies as well even though they are not the same sort of bodies we are familiar with. They can move freely between the Third and First Heavens, spiritual and natural.

Lucifer perpetrated the first action while others watched. He taught several hundred of his closest followers the erotic pleasures of unnatural sexual habits—the first ever introduction to physical, sexual pleasure. Although we do not consider angels as sexual beings, they are the same gender...whatever gender that may be.

Lucifer at first forced himself on several of the angels, raping them while they protested, just as *Set* had gone about raping men without the convenience of male genitals. Soon, they all succumbed to the pleasures he taught them, that pleasure locking them into servitude with the threat of exposure to the Godhead. He forced a large number of angels into complete obedience as they became more afraid of him than the Godhead.

These parties became a regular part of the entertainment he offered and their secret fame traveled throughout the kingdom, angels whispering selected invitations behind hands covering lowered voices.

The interesting thing about *Set* was that he was the first maimed god, one who, like the angels, was without gender. *Set* was robbed of his sexual organs as they were ripped from his body, just as Lucifer felt robbed of his sexuality—not that he understood sexual intimacy. But he was aware that he did not qualify to become either Bride or Groom because he had not been created in the image of the Godhead. He focused on visualizing what that sexuality and intimacy might entail, and the more he concentrated on his lack and that the Lord preferred the Bride over Lucifer himself, the angrier he became and the more he hated God for robbing him of that intimacy and position.

It was the mark of his kingdom for the rest of eternity. He always did his best to do what the Lord had done or was doing. But because he neither understood nor was capable of creating, he only mirrored darkly what he thought it should be. Because he could not understand the intimacy the Lord had talked about, he mirrored the relationship with homosexuality, the first ever in all of creation. It would be the tool used by Lucifer to bring down nation after nation, people after people so that they would never fully understand or enter into the relationship as the bride with the Son.

We consider that angels, being non-sexed, have no gender. And just like *Set*, being made sexless, they should not have been able or interested enough to have sex. But he raped men and women regardless of his lack of the male organ. Lucifer, likewise, though non-sexed, had the ability to rape other angels, just as the Incubus and Succubus spirits throughout human history have been able to rape men and women of flesh.

Lucifer had taught the angels who followed him how to have sexual relations. He had taught them how to stretch the boundaries of life to become self-serving.

Because of the sin in Lucifer's heart, the Lord again cursed the earth with a meteorite that suffocated 95% of all life.

This was the curse of gnats against Egypt. I saw the Egyptians run trying to seek cover from the invasive creatures. However, with open windows, there was nowhere they could run to escape. Egyptians fell in the streets and in their homes, suffocating with gnats. There was chaos and confusion amongst the population. Through Pharaoh's words, he showed that his heart was becoming irreparably hardened, "Go sacrifice to *your* God in the land...*only do not go very far.*"

Though Lucifer repented in form according to that which was required, his heart was not in it. The Lord, however, still chose to show mercy upon His first created, for his sin was not yet full. The Lord continued to show His great depth of love for His created covering cherub as He does today with man.

Genesis 15:16 But in the fourth generation they shall return here, for the iniquity of the Amorites is not yet complete.

Lucifer was still a strikingly beautiful angel, perhaps the most breathtaking *angel* I had ever seen. When I gazed upon him, my knees weakened because of his great beauty. His splendor took my breath away. He had such a charming way about him that I would have followed him anywhere, and I had to check my own heart with caution.

I felt guilty about my reaction to him, feeling awkward because, being a Christian, I should not have felt that way. But the Lord checked me, showing me that He did not create anything ugly; of all His creation, Lucifer was the most beautiful. (Ezekiel 28:17) What I felt in that moment was what the angels had felt having seen him in all his glory, and I knew how he had been able to trick so many to fall even after the state of his former beauty had faded to a mere shadow of his former self.

Though his complexion was still glowing, I could see the signs of a scowl begin to permanently darken his eyes. That which had been slowly brewing in his heart for over one hundred million years was refusing to roll over and die. The offence he nurtured at the Lord's rejection of him as bride fanned the flames of his budding hatred. I could see Lucifer looking at his reflection while mumbling the words, "I know I am good enough, dammit."

I saw that Lucifer spent a good deal of time looking at himself and evaluating the greatness of his worth...just as King Nebudchadnezzar did in Daniel 4:30.

CHAPTER EIGHT

Fourth Curse—Arena Of Dinosaurs

The next step in his downfall is found in Exodus 20.

Exodus 20:14. You shall not commit adultery.

Though he had tried to turn the hearts of the angels to his side, one way or another, they were still faithful to the Godhead. He had taught them too well and they still knew they owed everything to God for His great provision. Although they acknowledged Lucifer for his position and knowledge, the angelic host still loved the Godhead passionately. They were not prepared to throw away their life for something they did not understand—this new thing Lucifer was trying to introduce.

Lucifer decided to look to a different field to cultivate, one that would not offer up so many obstacles. He turned his eyes to the creatures already in God's Garden. They were dumb creatures of no real consequence to him and were definitely more easily manipulated. Because these poor creatures were expendable, he would show everyone, God and angel alike, his true worthiness.

The fourth plague against Egypt was swarms of flies. (Exodus 8:20-21)

The fourth plague was against the gods *Anubis* and *Wepwawet*, the two gods of death and the two *Eyes of Horus*.

These were the two gods that judged the hearts of others and we now see the fourth level of Lucifer's declining attitude that was quickly plummeting to the level of rebellion. He appointed himself as judge and executioner, showing that he had the power of life and death. Up until now, death was not a natural happenstance although it did occur in nature at the hands of God in the form of consequences of Lucifer's sin.

Anubis was the god of embalming, a completely intrusive practice performed only by special priests,

I watched as Lucifer set his mind to the task of truly understanding how the complex composition of cells worked, even to the minute detail of DNA and RNA. He tirelessly experimented with the subtle manipulations of the physical and mental attributes of the creatures at hand. His determination was accompanied by a new terrifying disregard for life and God's creation. He performed his manipulations and experimentations through a never-before-seen method of cutting into the flesh of these creatures, as portrayed by the mummification invasion of the body. The thought of actually destroying anything the Lord had created was unthinkable in the realms of the heavens, but Lucifer took the first step over that unspoken boundary.

It was of urgent importance to him to create something bigger and better than God, something that was alive, not made of stone, for only a god of renown and great power could create life.

Because he was incapable of actually creating something out of nothing, he began his career of always *adding* to what God had already done, a sin that followed his every step, and man's step, throughout history. His reasoning was that if he could prove he too had the tangible ability to create and if he made something bigger and better, then God would have to recognize him as an equal and could not punish him. Lucifer's logic continued, as he muttered his plan to himself, that if God finally recognized *his* abilities, the angelic host would be forced to recognize *his* majesty.

He turned God's own *little animals* into the dinosaurs, each evolving change visible throughout the centuries of their developing stature and power. The Godhead had the ability to create in the blink of an eye a completely new and different living creature of limitless individuality, but Lucifer was forced to evolve his creations through genetic manipulation and minor changes throughout decades and centuries of slow evolution…much like science is practicing today.

Not content with changing the physical attributes of these creatures, he concentrated on creating the first-ever killing machines in the Garden arena. He reduced all life to a beggarly life-and-death struggle instead of one living in peace and partaking of the abundant provision supplied by God, something he has continued to do with man. Through this arena of death, Lucifer introduced the first insinuated fear throughout the universe—the fear of death and murder.

With this new power, he began to instill fear in the angels as he usurped control over their lives. They were introduced to this new form of *entertainment death*, and this broke for many the innocence of their understanding. They became afraid of the unspoken but unmistakably implied threat Lucifer held over them.

He alone held the keys of death and he hung it over them using the visual sport of the arena in the now transformed Garden. Some angels developed a lust for this type of sport offered nowhere else in the universe.

Like the other animals in the Garden, the early dinosaurs were vegetarian, ingesting life to sustain life. However, it was the later, refined family of dinosaurs that became vicious carnivores and were the precursors to the Roman arena that glorified the death struggles of fighting animals and warriors. The Caesar of Roman history could only keep his kingship, and subsequent godship, by giving to the people of Rome better and bigger games in the arena. By winning the peoples' hearts, the Caesars could bypass the Senate and make the governing body in Rome impotent. This was the very tactic Lucifer used during this time. By winning over the heavenly host, he hoped that the Godhead would be forced to make him one of *Them* due to his overwhelming popularity.

I saw Lucifer and the angels sitting off to one side of a clearing on a lavish veranda made especially for the occasion. The sun was hot and the air was rich and heady. The smell of the luxurious greenery filled the air. The sweetness of the luscious flowers' perfumery was almost intoxicating. There was much laughter and camaraderie amongst the angels as they waited for the show to begin. As they ate and drank, other angels serving them dutifully, standing by their side meekly waiting to fulfill every need, I saw two great creatures lumber into the clearing. Through laughter and friendly betting, the two creatures battled each other until, at the death of one of them, the other feasted upon the torn and bloody flesh of the loser.

These battles were a new daily and horrifying element added to the many parties thrown by Lucifer for his friends and would-be friends alike.

The fourth plague was that of dog flies, the Hebrew *'arobh*, which means *"mixture,"* the metaphorical symbol of Cosmic Babylon. Dog flies represented the demon powers of Cosmic Babylon, who were ruled by Baalzebub, symbolized by a spider. Bloodsuckers, these dog flies bit without mercy, attacking the unsuspecting passersby by attaching themselves to their eyelids. They blinded people and animals alike. They devoured the people (Psalm 78:45), leaving their victims swollen and disfigured.

Anubis was an ancient Egyptian god of the underworld, one of the two *"Eye of Horus"* gods, guide of the dead in the afterlife. The other *Eye of Horus* was *Wepwawet*. They were the first gods to be headed by a terrifying and fierce animal, the black jackal. *Anubis'* body, also painted black, meant that he not only stood for death, but also rebirth in the afterlife. He became the god of mummification, the preliminary stages being the opening up of a person or violation of the body.

Wepwawet was not just a god of the dead, but also a warrior god who opened the way to victory. The *"Opener of the Ways"* helped *Anubis* to guide the dead to the *Halls of Judgment* where *Anubis* watched over the weighing of the hearts. He judged the deceased, protecting the innocent from the jaws of death, but giving the guilty their final death. *Wepwawet* was also thought of as the *"one who has separated the sky from the earth."* *Wepwawet's* standard was always carried out in front before that of the Pharaoh or his army.

Lucifer declared his power and lordship over life and death, something never before seen by the angels. This first appearance of the *jackal* on the head of a god presents the first appearance of animals that were feared and had to be appeased. The dinosaurs were manipulated to strike fear in the hearts not only of other angels but also the dreaded "bride" to come. The dinosaurs were big as angels, and it was the plan of Lucifer to at some point include angelic/dinosaur games in the arena of the Garden.

We also see in the second god, *Wepwawet*, the first appearance of Lucifer as a warrior god, opening the way for the armies. He became the first general of an army he began to raise up, teaching war and military perfection to those that followed him. Lucifer accomplished this feat all in the guise of protecting the Garden of God from potential threats and enemies. He raised up an army of angels that followed him, putting his standard before God's.

With the introduction of this army, Lucifer was beginning the separation of heaven and earth, shattering forever the peace that had once reigned supreme.

At that time, the Garden of God was one large landmass, known today as "Pangaea." This single landmass was surrounded by one very large ocean. However, the large meteorite of this curse broke up the landmass. Earthquakes and plate shifts tore Pangaea apart, disrupting the circulation of seawater making the oceans stagnant. The consequent depletion of oxygen in the water and high concentrations of dissolved carbon dioxide trapped heat in the atmosphere, creating a long-term *greenhouse* effect. This global warming triggered climatic change, dramatically shifting weather patterns. Scientists call this extinction the "*Great Dying*," because it is one of the most dramatic events in Earth's history.

The division of the single landmass coincides with Lucifer's answer, as we see for the first time a division beginning to take place in heaven. Lucifer now had unwavering, loyal followers for the first time. He had caused a number of the angels to commit spiritual adultery, for they had now begun to follow Lucifer. "I have sinned: the Lord is righteous, and I and my people are wicked." (Exodus 9:27-28)

Heaven was becoming two distinct camps.

The words that came from Lucifer's mouth were not ones of sincerity. They rang hollow in my ears even though they were coated with certain desperation. At every turn God still proved that it was He alone that had the power. No matter what works Lucifer did of his own, God could simply destroy them with a wave of His finger without any effort. It was always Lucifer who was reduced to desperate panic while the Lord remained cool and calm even in the face of rebellion.

Lucifer began to rethink his situation. He did not feel his position was wrong; it was simply tenuous. He had to stabilize and fortify his position with more strength and power before making his move next time.

I could see a cloud of bitterness cover his eyes and darken his countenance. But he was forgiven his sin, and it was still given to him to lead the angelic host as the covering cherub. However, he now ceased his lectures for in his heart he felt there was nothing left for him to say.

Although he returned to duty publicly, Lucifer decided to continue his work secretly. He was very close to achieving the goal that now occupied his every waking thought—to be a god with his own bride.

Previously, with intelligence superior to any created creature, he had scientifically studied the inner workings of God's creatures. Now, he would psychologically study their inner workings. He would learn how to manipulate DNA and RNA without cutting into them and changing them manually, leaving no visible evidence of his control and deception. He would learn how to command them to change with his voice, just as the Son called things into being by the power of His voice.

CHAPTER NINE

Fifth Curse—Mighty Merchant

This was Lucifer's fifth sin.

Exodus 20:13 You shall not murder.

The curse penalty for this sin was against the three gods: *Hathor*, *Isis* and *Mut*. In these three gods, we see Lucifer's escalating self-view. This curse was against three of the most ancient deities of Egypt.

The fifth curse against Egypt was severe pestilence on the livestock. (Exodus 9:1-3)

Hathor was the personification of joy, love, romance, fruitfulness, dance, music, alcohol, perfume and success. She was also goddess of metal, Malachite and Turquoise. *Hathor*, though occasionally fierce and terrible, was never unattractive. She had as many different names as she did beautiful images. She embodied abundance in life, beauty, wealth, security and justice. Malachite was ground into eye makeup, thus allowing the devotee to not only worship her but to wear her essence upon their body. *Hathor* had an absolute, laser-like focus, making her single-mindedly vengeful towards spiritual transgressors, often taking the form of a vicious lioness. She is a consistently dangerous force that cannot be appealed to via emotion, for only through her own force can she be appeased and controlled.

Hathor's head was traditionally used to decorate mirrors, thus, when gazing at one's own reflection, you would see *Hathor* looking back from underneath one's own image, a shadow of the insidious truth.

Lucifer was showing his true nature. He walks around like a roaring lion, seeking whom he may devour. (1 Peter 5:8) He was no longer the gentle covering cherub, but he was an angel with an agenda, a plan and a purpose burning in his breast, one that constantly screamed in his head to be fulfilled.

His arena of animals not only threatened the other angels, but entertained them as well. He let the angels know that he would be vicious toward their transgressions if they dared cross him. He let them know that absolutely nothing would ever stop him in his pursuit against them, no matter how long it took. But if they sided with him, he promised them wealth, power, position and everything good in life—something they already had been given by the Godhead.

Isis, the most famous goddesses of ancient Egypt, was all that a mother should be—loving, clever, loyal, and brave. She was also known as the *"Mistress of Magic,"* one of the most powerful magicians in Egypt. But she lacked one thing to be all-powerful. She needed to know how to pronounce the secret name of the chief god, *Re (Ra)*.

To obtain this secret name, *Isis* made a venomous reptile out of dust mixed with her spittle. She then uttered certain words of power over it and ordered the snake to bite *Re* as he passed by. *Re* succumbed to the poison and lay near death. In order to preserve his life, *Re* revealed to *Isis* his most hidden name. Now *Isis* not only used the words of power, but she now also had knowledge of how to pronounce them so that everything to which they were addressed would be compelled to listen and, having listened, would be obliged to obey and fulfill her requests.

Lucifer may have been the seal of perfection, full of wisdom and perfect in beauty (Ezekiel 28:12), but he did not know how to create through the power of the spoken word. Try as he may, he did not have the power to create. He thought of the power of creation as magic, since he didn't fully understand it, and magic became his mirror image of creative power. Slight of hand, trickery, the ability to pull out of the supernatural what is already there into the natural—these are his miracles and abilities.

He had learned how to manipulate DNA and RNA through scientific methods of surgery, dissection and direct gene splicing. He had discovered that the body's natural chemical reactions could actually be changed and programmed into the DNA and RNA over time. But he was forbidden from operating on God's creatures. This he would later teach mankind in the name of science, teaching them to totally disregard not only God's provision for mankind, but also to disdain all the creatures and creation God has made.

He could not again be so obvious in his disobedience. He needed to be able to achieve the same results without any telltale marks. Nothing could be traced back to him until the time was right to strike. He needed to find the way to covertly manipulate DNA and RNA through the power of the spoken word.

In time, through thousands of years of intimidating creatures through fear, terror, and other negative emotions, he discovered that the body's natural chemicals would change DNA as effectively as his previous *operations*. It just took longer to achieve the same results. He had learned how to compel these creatures to obey his will and desire. He had learned what he believed was the secret power of God, the secret name which compelled all who heard it to obey him. He would stimulate their emotions that would trigger a chain reaction throughout the body and ultimately change the DNA and RNA of the genes in future generations.

For example, generations of fear and anxiety causes cell wall rigidity resulting in such diseases as glaucoma, leaky gut, allergies, stroke, heart disease and heart attacks. Fear and anxiety is the direct result of a person's broken relationship with God, another person or themselves, or it can be inherited from parents. The DNA, having been changed for generations throughout the family line will cause a predisposition to one or more of these diseases. The Bible holds many references to emotions causing diseases in mankind. Lucifer learned these things the hard way long ago. But the Lord has put these references in the Bible to help mankind learn quickly some of the weapons Lucifer has used against mankind for thousands of years.

Luke 21:26 ...men's hearts failing them from fear and the expectation of those things which are coming on the earth, for the powers of heaven will be shaken.

Mut was the mother goddess and the ferocious goddess of retribution, represented by a woman with the head of a lion. The original wife of god, she became the invisible goddess, often depicted with male parts because she not only gave birth to life but she was the one who conceived life itself. She was "*Mut, Who Giveth Birth, But Was Herself Not Born of Any.*"

Lucifer was portraying himself as something more than what he was created to be—an uncreated god of ferocious retribution. He was portraying himself as always being, just as the Godhead always was, and as one who had done more than merely name the angels but it was he who had in fact created them. There were no witnesses of his creation except the Father, Son and Holy Ghost themselves—no one could prove otherwise. Then I realized that I too was witness to his creation, and I am here to tell anyone who believes his lies that he was creator that he is simply a created being...just like the rest of us.

He was separating himself from his God, his calling and his brethren, threatening retribution to anyone who challenged him. He could, after all, now command life to change by the power of *his* spoken word.

Already billions of years old, the inevitable eons it took to actually change the DNA and RNA was but a blink of an eye to Lucifer. He learned that he could, over time, cause the DNA and RNA to change in the generations of any creature, the mutation replicating itself and continuing its mutation without any further interference from him. He turned the glandular system with its controlling chemicals into a weapon against the body.

God once again stepped in for the fifth time to curse the earth because of the sin of Lucifer.

This curse was against the cattle, horses, asses, camels, oxen and sheep of Egypt. It attacked Egypt's power that was represented by the horses, the symbol of wealth through military strength and conquest. It attacked Egypt's trade and commerce represented by the camels, the symbol of wealth through the caravan lifelines carrying their harvest to merchant markets of the rest of the world. It attacked Egypt's wealth which was represented by the harvest as the asses carried the grain to the threshing floor; the oxen performed the necessary agricultural duties; and the sheep treaded the seed into the ground at planting time and thrashed the grain on the threshing floor at harvest time.

Their own riches, abilities and everything the Egyptians put their faith and hope into to make them a great nation was affected through this curse.

Revelation 3:17-19 Because you say, "I am rich, have become wealthy, and have need of nothing"—and do not know that you are wretched, miserable, poor, blind, and naked...

Lucifer had not only commanded a following by this time, but he created something else new in the universe. He invented commerce. (Ezekiel 28:16)

Through the power of commerce, he is the one who could choose who would be rich and who would be poor. He set the standard. He set the price. He controlled creation by creating supply and demand, creating a ripple of the fear of lack throughout the heavens. Through commerce he could control the new fledgling emotions of envy, jealousy, anger, hatred, greed, etc.

Until now, the entire heavenly host gave freely to each other, for freely they had received and would always receive. There was no need for commerce, for everything they had was provided. They simply worked with what was provided and with the abilities and talents they were given. They created mighty works of art or invention, and they gave of the work of their hands to others who needed it. There was no gold or silver in trade. There was no commerce at all. It was a completely foreign concept to them. They gave of their abilities freely, giving gifts and offerings freely to their neighbors and their friends for all their needs were supplied through the abundance of their Creator, the Godhead. They gave the gifts of their talents and abilities as gifts of love one to another.

However, Lucifer had cultivated a unique niche market because he had something no one else had—he had everything from the one and only Garden of God. He had the supply and it would be an easy matter to create the demand with some well-planted words, suggestions and fears.

With this new method of commerce, he could *charge* any price for whatever items from the Garden were demanded. He could *sell* animals, plants, and even *holy water*—water blessed personally by him—from the Garden of God for whatever extravagant price he wanted to exact. As a true merchant that raised prices with demand, he could eventually set the price at indentured servitude, and there were those of the heavenly host that would pay that price. Like Pharaoh who purchased the entire Egyptian population for the stored food in his granaries, food he freely received as taxes from the very people who later traded their own lives to get some of it back, Lucifer purchased the indebtedness of the heavenly host with merchandise he freely obtained.

Ezekiel 27:32-36 In their wailing for you they will take up a lamentation, and lament for you: "What city is like Tyre, destroyed in the midst of the sea? When your wares went out by sea, you satisfied many people; you enriched the kings of the earth with your many luxury goods and your merchandise. But you are broken by the seas in the depths of the waters; your merchandise and the entire company will fall in your midst."

Ezekiel 28:12-20 By the abundance of your trading you became filled with violence within, and you sinned...Your heart was lifted up because of your beauty; you corrupted your wisdom for the sake of your splendor...You defiled your sanctuaries by the multitude of your iniquities, by the iniquity of your trading....

Ezekiel 31:1-18 ...Son of man, say to Pharaoh king of Egypt and to his multitude..."Therefore its height was exalted above all the trees of the field; its boughs were multiplied, and its branches became long because of the abundance of water, as it sent them out. All the birds of the heavens made their nests in its boughs...Thus it was beautiful in greatness and in the length of its branches, because its roots reached to abundant waters...no tree in the garden of God was like it in beauty."

A buried crater one hundred miles wide marks the spot where a mountain-size asteroid slammed into Earth at an estimated fifty thousand miles per hour along Mexico's Yucatan Peninsula, releasing an amount of energy equivalent to one hundred million megatons of TNT. The impact produced at least six tidal waves, some of which were more than three hundred feet high, a magnitude twelve earthquake, a deluge of sulfuric acid rain, and a huge cloud of dust that blocked the light from the Sun for months and contributed to the extinction of nearly every land animal whose adult form weighed more than fifty pounds. The impact also triggered a global firestorm that incinerated one-forth of the living biomass, releasing an enormous amount of carbon dioxide into the atmosphere that increased the average global temperature by 20°F for a million years.

The dinosaurs, however, through Lucifer's persistent manipulation of their DNA and RNA, were eventually deformed through a lack of diaphragm, something he did not think important since angels do not breathe oxygen. Lucifer considered the diaphragm as a redundant system that they could do without. This posed no problem as long as the earth had 35% oxygen—dinosaurs could be as big as he made them and still breathe easily.

In this fifth curse, the oxygen level of the earth changed drastically from 35% to 21%. The dinosaurs created by Lucifer were suffocated by their own weight as they struggled to inhale enough oxygen to live. Some also died of disease or as a direct result of the asteroid. The little animals God created still lived, because they had a diaphragm that kept them breathing through a natural mechanical ability. Everything that was the wealth of Lucifer's commerce was destroyed.

Although Lucifer took on the persona of the *"bride,"* as portrayed in the female gods previously dealt with, everything he created perished. All his *children* died shortly after birth and his life remained fruitless... and he has never been able to raise one of them from the dead.

Satan's answer: "Go...you that are men, and serve the Lord" (Exodus 10:8-11) is very revealing. Those that followed him were no longer sons of God, for together with Lucifer, they had all committed adultery—Lucifer, who was now a god in his own eyes, had become a god in theirs.

This was the last time Lucifer would feign repentance, and in it we see his total defeat. By his words he separated himself from the Kingdom of God, the creation that was made at the Lord's hand, and the fellowship of righteousness and obedience. He pronounced that he was no longer willing to serve the Lord in any form.

In a universe that knew no sin, Lucifer had chosen to sin. God, in His great love and mercy for all that He creates, forgave Lucifer five times. Once again the Lord God Almighty, his Creator and King, his one-time best friend, forgave him...for his sin was not yet full.

CHAPTER TEN

Sixth Curse—
The Cherub Who Would Be God

This brought him to the sixth sin.

Exodus 20:12 Honor your father and your mother, that your days may be long upon the land which the LORD your God is giving you.

Despite being cursed five times, the Garden of God once again blossomed forth from the curses in rich diversity of animal and plant life. Every new recreation of the Garden was more grandeur than the last; the Lord proving over and over that the limits to His imagination and ability to create something totally new and different was without end.

During this time earth had the horse, camel, dog, elephant, rhinoceros, and primate.

Montana and the Dakotas of America were home to tropical rainforest plants in the magnolia, citrus, fig, pawpaw, and cashew families. The Canadian Arctic was home to subtropical plants and animals; winters were dark, but not cold. This was the time of the huge land mammals such as the diatryma, a gigantic, eight-foot tall, flightless bird with a stout nine-inch beak, who stalked prey. The largest of these mammals weighed 20 tons and stood 18 feet tall at the shoulder.

Whale ancestors returned to the sea. Deciduous trees thrived and fruit tree families were seen for the first time. The Daisy family came to life. Squirrels, ravens and toads entered the scene for the first time.

This period of the Garden's history is known as the Golden Age of Mammals, with an astounding diversity of mammalian species on land. Woody and grassy savannas of wheat, barley, rice, maize, oats and millet spread throughout the world.

The Garden of God was alive with a diversity of life never before seen. Each time the Lord brought back the earth after a curse, He filled it with new and different life. Mastodons, tortoises, vultures, cheetahs, beavers and pronghorn are only a few. This was the time when hominids, chimpanzees, and Bonobos, the pygmy chimpanzees, were created.

Recent studies have shown that 98.7% of human DNA is identical with the Bonobos and chimpanzee. This is not because we are descended from the Bonobos or chimpanzee through some bizarre form of evolution, but because, with as little as 1.3% difference, but using the same basic elements, God can create an animal on one hand and His Bride on the other. He is just so incredibly amazing in every way—there is no one like Him.

Lucifer, during this time, completely filled his cup with sin. He manipulated the DNA and RNA of the Bonobos and chimpanzee to produce nine different hominid species. He decided his course of action—if he could not *be* the bride, then he would become the groom and *create* the bride for himself.

He had already assumed the role of god, declaring himself to be the fourth part of the Godhead and contended for the throne. Now, Lucifer would create the bride before Jesus did.

Each one of these ape-men groups mysteriously appeared in different areas, and died out without explanation. Each one was just one level higher on the evolutionary scale created by Lucifer's plan. As each genus of these ape-men appeared, they were more human-like in appearance and ability to think and problem solve. When one genus no longer served any purpose to Lucifer or did not reach the necessary potential he was looking for, he deserted them to their own devices, which eventually led to their death and complete extinction. Lucifer kept trying to attain a creature that he could teach and mold to be the "bride" he thought Jesus might create.

Unlike the man God would create, whose spirit would return to God, the spirit of these ape-men, being that of animal, returned to the earth upon their death. (Ecclesiastes 3:21) These were creatures without the soul of man. Lucifer, despite all his efforts, could never reproduce or copy the soul that the Lord would place in mankind. But he didn't really care about the soul of man as long as he had a semblance of man before the Godhead could produce one.

He was racing against time in his desperate need to create this *bride*. If he could create mankind before God caught him, then he would prove himself on the same level as the Almighty Godhead, the angels would have to declare him king, and the Godhead would have to recognize his worth. Then he would achieve everything he had dreamed of for fourteen billion years.

After nine tries at creating a human-like creature, Lucifer had finally created a man science today calls "homosapiens sapiens," the most man-like ape-man invented.

I saw an excitement arise in Lucifer. After fourteen billion years, he had finally come to the end of his plan of usurping the throne of his Creator. He would kill the king and take His place. After trying and failing five times, he was close to reaching his goal. Now that he had perfected man, he could be declared king and god, and his accolades would ring throughout the universe. He had finally proved his worth. He was as God for he had created the bride. The victory he had sought for so long was finally within reach, and he could taste the sweet taste of triumph.

I watched as his chest puffed out, overflowing with pride. If he was less dignified, he would have done a happy dance...he was so incredibly pleased with himself. He stared at himself in the mirror for hours at a time. He fantasized about the parade of victory, seeing himself stroll to the Throne like the king he was. In his fantasy, which played on a screen for me like I was sitting in a movie theatre, he paused at the base of the stairs before taking those exhilarating steps, each one moving higher to the godhood he so deserved. He would wear the royal gold and purple robe of a king, and on his head would be a golden crown. And he would mount the steps deliberately pausing on each one until, finally, at the top of the platform, he would turn slowly, face his thronging, cheering nations of angels, and sit upon the throne of Jesus. Then echoes would ring throughout all creation, crying, "Holy! Holy! Holy!"

It was now time for him to make his stand.

Lucifer decided that he would take the Garden of God for himself. It would be here that he would build his fortress and start his kingdom. To do this, Lucifer had many problems to consider. First, the earth had already been destroyed five times with asteroids, earthquakes and plate shifting so he would have to fortify his new kingdom with a God-proof warning system against such brutal attacks.

Lucifer, who now commanded a great army of allied heavenly host from every office of angel, also had an *ape-man* slave labor force to do his bidding. He set about to use both these forces to fortify the Garden. The first thing he did was to designate strategic positions around the globe, which, when aligned, would provide an astronomical early warning system for an effective defense against any sneak attacks.

Every part of the heavens could be watched from these vantage points. He chose what we now call Peru, Machu Pichu, Easter Island, Persia (Iran), Perseopolis, England, Petra (Haeshemite Kingdom of Jordon), Angkor Wat, and Ur (Sumeria), and others.

A temple or astronomical observation structure was erected so that as the Earth rotated on its axis, the Equator remained aligned. Today, these ancient sites can be plotted on a sine wave as a result of the earth's tilt relative to the Equator. The mathematical precision of these monuments separately and in relation to each other is astoundingly complex and consistent.

When the main sites are plotted in a simple diagram, the symbol created is a Pentagram in a circle, the universal insignia of Lucifer.

The largest pyramid complex in the Americas was located northeast of Mexico City, at a place known today as Teotihuacán. The entire ancient city was built on a geometric grid anchored by a central avenue that begins at the Pyramid of the Moon. This avenue, known today as the Avenue of the Dead, points 15.5° west of due south and 15.5° east of due north. What was thought of as a walkway between the Pyramid of the Moon and the Pyramid of the Sun, is now known to be a slue system, that, when filled with water, provided an incredibly accurate seismological warning system sensitive enough to report any earthquake, regardless of its size, from anywhere in the world.

With the skies monitored during every rotation of the planet with the various monuments and temples, and the Tectonic plate activity and subsequent earthquake activity monitored, Lucifer felt secure. God could no longer sneak up on him. He decided it was safe to build his palace and place his seal on the Garden of God making it his own property.

He would have the bride and the Garden of God.

He sold *souvenirs* of the earth's bounty; holy water blessed by Lucifer, Covering Cherub of God, creator of man, was his hottest selling item. He created an intoxicating drink made up of fermented berries, blood and *blessed* water, topped with spices, and by this he made his following drunk with desire.

The nations of fallen angels came and watched for hours on end the new creation of the ape-man Lucifer created. The simple creatures Lucifer presented as the precious bride the Son had talked about amused them. They lounged on their great couches while some of these ape-men, the best of the lot, waited on their every need. They watched as these ape-men, totally abandoned by Lucifer when deemed unworthy, fought for their very survival...mere animals barely able to amuse.

Lucifer had taught his fallen comrades well to hate and despise the world around them. They barely tolerated each other any more.

Lucifer chose Tiahuanaco, a city built at the altitude of thirteen thousand feet, beside Lake Titicaca, meaning *"Rock of the Puma— Rock of the Mountain Lion,"* a saltwater lake, the second largest lake in South America. This was his city and was to be his crowning achievement. Here there are over four hundred square miles of city, with a sister port at the south end of the lake. At the area of Puma Punka, hundreds of machined and dressed stone blocks, cut by materials other than stone or copper tools, lie toppled where they fell from some unexpected catastrophe, while Tiahuanaco, its sister port, lay unfinished.

Unlike the palaces built by the other angels, and the former palaces built by Lucifer, he built these fortifications and cities out of the materials of the earth. He did not pull his building supplies out of the supernatural realm. He did not want the Godhead to get wind of what he was doing. To maintain some semblance of secrecy, he used materials from the planet and blackmailed his followers into silence, holding the very sins over their heads that he tricked or coerced them into committing.

Three statues, estimated to be carved from original cooled mantle rock, stood in the courtyard of the great city. The one in the middle was *Viracocha, "foam of the sea,"* as this white race is said to have risen from the waters of Lake Titicaca. In the ancient language of the ancient Aymaras, these men were so named for they were *"men clothed in light." Illa Ticca Viracocha*, carved from white rock, stood in the middle, and beside him stood two others, one carved in black stone and the other in red.

Interestingly, the language of the Aymaras, not spoken anywhere, is used today as the international translator language. Any language can be translated in Aymaras and then translated into any other language. It is the base language upon which all other languages seem to have a common denominator. It is quite possibly the original angelic language of Lucifer and his friends, the heavenly host.

The *"Creator God," Illa Ticca Viracocha*, was *"the white man with red hair."* Beside him was *El Fraile (The Friar)*, standing six feet tall, and holding a book and knife in his hands to strictly enforce rules and regulations. He was entirely dressed in fish scales and was said to have been amphibious, living in the ocean as easily as on land. *El Fraile* taught men to construct houses, gave them insight into letters and science, and every kind of art.

I first saw this *El Fraile* while in the kitchen of my own home when I was only fourteen. He appeared to me dressed in an elaborate robe, ornamentally inscribed with woven gold words, and carrying the book and knife in his hands. The book was given to me to commit to memory, and the knife was used to draw my blood for a blood-contract. The book was filled with mysticism, ceremonial rites, spiritual intrigues and mysteries wrapped in endless enigmas. Upon receipt of this book, I was plummeted into an unforgiving, intolerant spiritual world that devoured me and soon became more real than this natural one. At the time, I did not know him by his name, *El Fraile*, but simply as a high priest of the supernatural world. I was to discover his true identity years later.

On the other side of *Viracocha* stood another statue, an imposing nine-foot figure without a name. It was hugely thick with hulking shoulders and a slab-like face staring expressionlessly into the distance. Its body was intricately tattooed. This ancient form of marking the followers of Lucifer was first hidden beneath robes, but later became a badge of dishonor to God as they marked their whole bodies. Their tattoos were not done with ink imbedded into their skin, but with stardust and radioactive meteorite particles that actually glowed.

Like *El Fraile*, he too was clad in scales from the waist down. In its hands was a cylinder with what is suggested to be portable balance scales, and a sheath from which protruded a forked handle. This was the judge and *Rewarder of Hearts*.

Tattooing and piercing began with Lucifer before Adam and Eve were even created. He branded his ape-men inventions to mark his newly acquired property. He branded his fallen angel followers with his brand to remove the mark of beauty and blessing placed on the angelic host by the Godhead.

Behind these three figures were three rows of eight figures, twenty-four in all. Lucifer had chosen his court. He was their father. Beside him stood his son and unholy spirit. Behind them were the twenty-four elders and so on.

El Fraile was the unholy representation of the Son, the Word of God, while the other was the representation of the Holy Spirit who "...searches all things, yes, the deep things of God." (1 Corinthians 2:10)

Revelation 2:23 ...I am He who searches the minds and hearts. And I will give to each one of you according to your works.

With his specially chosen heads of state in place of authority and his *ape-men* populace in place of slavery and submission, the great following of the one-third of the angelic host as his supporters, and his very own *usurped* kingdom, Lucifer was set to take over the throne of God after the coronation of his city. This would be heralded as the greatest achievement since creation. He had trained his followers to be a mighty army.

Peru is filled with symbolic carvings all over the land, which represent the plan of Lucifer's final victory. South and Central America has been proclaimed Lucifer's stronghold. It was his kingdom, capital and crowning achievement. Even today, the blood of his stronghold is soaked into the land. There is a curse on the land that stems from the beginning of his revolt. This must one day be cleansed and removed by the rightful owners of the land, the bride.

In the valley of Ollantaytambo, Peru, there is elaborate carving in great detail on the side of a mountain, a relief of *Viracocha* with the lamb lying at *his* feet.

The *"Gateway of the Sun"* in the ancient city of Tiahuanaco, represents *Viracocha*, flanked by forty-eight winged effigies: thirty-two with human faces and sixteen with condor's heads. This huge monument is hewn from a single block of stone, and legend says that these are the forty-eight different peoples of *Viracocha's* kingdom. They represent the twenty-four Elders, Archangels, Princes, Thrones, Dominions, Principalities, Powers, Rulers of Darkness of this World, Spiritual Wickedness in High Places, Horsemen, Common Angels, ten Legal Manipulators, seven Spirits, and one Bride—forty-eight in all.

Ezekiel 28:2-10 Son of man, say to the prince of Tyre, "Thus says the Lord GOD: 'Because your heart is lifted up, and you say, 'I am a god, I sit in the seat of gods, in the midst of the seas, yet you are a man, and not a god, though you set your heart as the heart of a god (Behold, you are wiser than Daniel! There is no secret that can be hidden from you! With your wisdom and your understanding you have gained riches for yourself, and gathered gold and silver into your treasuries; By your great wisdom in trade you have increased your riches, and your heart is lifted up because of your riches),' Therefore thus says the Lord GOD: 'Because you have set your heart as the heart of a god, Behold, therefore, I will bring strangers against you, the most terrible of the nations; and they shall draw their swords against the beauty of your wisdom, and defile your splendor. They shall throw you down into the Pit, and you shall die the death of the slain in the midst of the seas. Will you still say before him who slays you, 'I am a god'? But you shall be a man, and not a god, in the hand of him who slays you. You shall die the death of the uncircumcised by the hand of aliens; for I have spoken,'" says the Lord GOD.

Ezekiel 28:12-19 Son of man, take up a lamentation for the king of Tyre, and say to him, "Thus says the Lord GOD: 'You were the seal of perfection, full of wisdom and perfect in beauty. You were in Eden, the garden of God; every precious stone was your covering: the sardius, topaz, and diamond, Beryl, onyx, and jasper, sapphire, turquoise, and emerald with gold. The workmanship of your timbrels and pipes was prepared for you on the day you were created. You were the anointed cherub who covers; I established you; you were on the holy mountain of God; you walked back and forth in the midst of fiery stones. You were perfect in your ways from the day you were created, till iniquity was found in you. By the abundance of your trading you became filled with violence within, and you sinned; therefore I cast you as a profane thing out of the mountain of God; and I destroyed you, O covering cherub, from the midst of the fiery stones. Your heart was lifted up because of your beauty; you corrupted your wisdom for the sake of your splendor; I cast you to the ground, I laid you before kings, that they might gaze at you. You defiled your sanctuaries by the multitude of your iniquities, by the iniquity of your trading; therefore I brought fire from your midst; it devoured you, and I turned you to ashes upon the earth in the sight of all who saw you. All who knew you among the peoples are astonished at you; you have become a horror, and shall be no more forever.'"

Lucifer's sin was now full. He had broken the next commandment in his spiraling downfall into total iniquity. He no longer honored his

Father, the Creator. He had taught the angels to no longer honor their Father. He had taught his manipulated bastard creation, the *ape-men* to no longer honor their original Creator but to pay homage to the DNA-manipulator, Lucifer, now called Illa Ticca *Viracocha*, The First One, who was also heralded as the *"hero god"* who came in peace to bring civilization to a barbaric people.

The sixth curse against Egypt was boils on people and animals alike. (Exodus 9:8-9)

This curse was against the Egyptian man who would be god, *Imhotep*, whose name means *"the one that comes in peace."* He was the man who became god of medicine, healing and knowledge. He was, in actual fact, the first recorded genius who designed Pharaoh's first step pyramid—the ziggurat. He invented modern-day medicine, learned through the mummification process as chief priest, and operated on thousands of men and women, healing many of those who labored to build the pyramid. He was the Egyptian Einstein of their day. He was a poet and physician-priest, and the chief architect of the step pyramid at Saqqara.

He is recognized as the world's first named architect, the world's first doctor, a priest, scribe, sage, poet, astrologer, vizier and chief minister. In Egyptian society, he was the only man outside of Pharaoh to become god.

But *Imhotep* did not have the red hair that would make him a god like Pharaoh. He became god because of his own abilities and works.

Jeremiah 6:11-20 "Therefore I am full of the fury of the LORD. I am weary of holding it in...for I will stretch out My hand against the inhabitants of the land," says the LORD. "Because from the least of them even to the greatest of them, everyone is given to covetousness; and from the prophet even to the priest, everyone deals falsely. They have also healed the hurt of My people slightly, saying, 'Peace, peace!' When there is no peace. Were they ashamed when they had committed abomination? No! They were not at all ashamed; nor did they know how to blush. Therefore they shall fall among those who fall; at the time I punish them, they shall be cast down," says the LORD. Thus says the LORD: "Stand in the ways and see, and ask for the ancient paths, where the good way is, and walk in it; then you will find rest for your souls. But they said, 'We will not walk in it.' Also, I set watchmen over you, saying, 'Listen to the sound of the trumpet!' But they said, 'We will not listen.' Therefore hear, you nations, and know, O congregation, what is among them. Hear, O earth! Behold, I will certainly bring calamity on this people— the fruit of their thoughts, because they have not heeded My words, nor My law, but rejected it. For what purpose to Me comes frankincense from Sheba, and sweet cane from a far country? Your burnt offerings are not acceptable, nor your sacrifices sweet to Me."

This passage, though talking about the daughter of Zion, rings of the heart of Lucifer and the angels before they fell, of the pre-flood firstborn before they were drowned, of the citizens of Sodom and Gomorrah before they were destroyed, and of the people of the earth now, in this last age. This passage marks the fullness of sin:

1. Many are discontent with what God has given them or called them to;
2. No truth in them any longer—the pure, untainted word of God;
3. They are peace keepers, not peace makers, compromising whatever is necessary to keep the peace, instead of upholding the standard of God;
4. Having a completely seared conscience—no longer feeling shame for their sin;
5. They no longer want to walk in the ways of the Lord;
6. They no longer will listen to the watchmen set over them.

Six is the number of man. Not only does this curse have a spiritual meaning, but it also has a natural application as well. Lucifer witnessed six stages or days for the first creation of the universe and angelic host; Lucifer sinned six times before his cup of sin was full causing his overthrow in the war in heaven; there were six days of the recreation of the earth before he gained re-entry into the Garden of God he so coveted.

Revelation 13:18 Here is wisdom. Let him that hath understanding count the number of the beast: for it is the number of a man; and his number is Six hundred threescore and six.

I saw Lucifer as the great Emperor of all he surveyed, assured in his belief that he had complete control over the earth, because once the Garden of God was his, then the universe would fall. He reveled and partied like no other has ever done in the annals of history. I saw the bodies of intoxicated angels litter great rooms designed for partygoers, each one offering different delicious enticements and delicacies. His parties hosted hundreds of thousands and lasted for weeks on end. Before one finished, another started.

They were lost, no longer caring about their fate, believing and trusting in the lies that Lucifer could do all he promised, willing to bow their knees to his perverted government. They enjoyed the rewards he lavished on them and they were thrilled with the promise of more. Quite frankly, they served him because they were mostly afraid of judgment by the Godhead and retribution by Lucifer.

I saw Lucifer in a *Great War Room*, marking the strategic positions on the earth and the heavens just beyond the earth, building his garrisons and armaments, resting in his ability to outthink every angel, and even, if necessary, God Himself. He did, after all, know every move the Father, Son and Holy Spirit had ever made. He knew them more than anyone else ever could. He actually envisioned he was able to do all his preparations in secret, believing he fooled the Creator with his false obeisance and dripping words of reverence.

The Great War

I saw hundreds of angels working on his crowning glory, his capital city that would be the seal that would claim the Garden of God as his own. They laughed with joy over their new promised positions and sang the accolades of their new soon-to-be-crowned king as they built.

Lucifer stood upon the mountaintop looking down upon his city, the view of the whole world within his vision. He visually searched out his guards standing at attention just beyond the borders of the solar system. He looked down at his ape-men as they labored and lived their meager daily existence in the fields beyond the city. Confidence filled his breast with pride and action...he stood tall and declared the words, "Today, I am god."

But before his city was finished, I heard the word declared from the throne, "Enough. Michael, assemble the troops and banish Lucifer and all those who follow him to the Second Heavens. Destroy his kingdom, but leave the trace of it in the earth as a witness to his great sin."

Michael had been on one knee at the base of the steps before the throne, his head bowed. His right hand was on his sword—a gleaming silver blade that was so brilliantly lit that one could not see the razor sharp edges of such a fine blade. The hilt was gold with encrusted rubies. His breastplate was gold with the silver insignias of his God. Behind him flowed a red robe of the deepest crimson, gilded with deep purple and gold, held aloft by the breath of the Holy Spirit that followed him everywhere. His boots were gold with silver soles and laces. His armbands were gold and purple, declaring his station and allegiance. His helmet was gold with the insignia of his God upon it.

He stayed in that position, bowed before his God for a very long time, perhaps decades; he was waiting, fully prepared, to be sent on the mission he knew would soon have to take place.

His troops were beyond the city of God, standing at attention in perfect order in their assigned battalions and legions of forces. Nations of angels, each nation completely different in appearance and dress, waited patiently for the word from the throne. There was cavalry, chariots and soldiers beyond number. The fields were covered with the magnitude of the army, everyone with a gold and purple arm bracelet declaring proudly their loyalty and office. They covered the heavens beyond the horizon, and they all waited in position for Michael to arrive with orders to move out.

There was a heaviness of heart lingering within everyone. Lucifer had called a civil war in the heavens, destroying forever the peace and unity they had all known for millions of years. Brother was fighting brother. Friend was fighting friend. This was a war that could not be avoided because Lucifer would not repent. The Lord had extended His hand five times to forgive Lucifer, but that time had passed. The moment the words passed his lips declaring himself god was the moment the order was given for the troops to move.

Michael, at one time Lucifer's good friend and associate, was leader of God's army. Lucifer, who insisted preparations be made in case of an enemy uprising, personally trained him in the art of war. I believe that Lucifer was surprised to find that it was he who was the enemy he had been preparing for...until the sin had taken root fully in his heart, I believe he honestly did not know it was him. But once he was aware of the truth of his heart, he did not want to return to his innocence. He chose to become what his heart whispered to his mind every day.

It was a terrifying battle, like one the earth had never witnessed before or since.

The angels streamed out of heaven, a great army of trillions all riding enormous muscular steeds with nostrils flared and manes flowing behind them marking their urgent speed. The heavens rumbled and shook as the steeds thundered towards the earth. Magnificently armored warriors crossed the great expanse at the command of the Father, their swords drawn, armor glistening, and a mighty cry rising up and filling space everywhere.

The heavens opened upon the earth and the air was ignited with the energy of battle. The earth reeled under the attack. God's angels overthrew all that Lucifer had done, rendering his cities useless. In Peru, the cities of Lucifer's enormous pride were toppled. Massive stones weighing several tons were toppled by the hooves of just one or two steeds causing them to fall to the earth with a heavy, muted "thud." Some cities were left standing as a testimony to his great sin.

The air was charged everywhere and you could feel the electricity. The skies were overcast with dark clouds and the heavens rumbled and thundered with such a resonance that it was deafening. The sun was blackened by the sheer number of angels that rode upon the earth to destroy the enemies of God.

The eyes of the angels were resolute in their focus, for they had the command of the Lord to fulfill, and that command was to overtake the enemy and cast them out of the earth and all the heavens.

Everyone had made their allegiance. The lines were drawn. The Lord had waited until the entire heavenly host had every one come to their decision. This was their time. This was their test—to love God through their free choice not because of coercion.

The sides were chosen. One-third of the angelic host had pledged their loyalties to Lucifer, their commander-in-chief, in hopes of gained glory, rank and riches. They had tasted of the decadence he offered, and they had reveled at the massive orgies and games of death in the arena he provided on an almost ongoing basis. They had sold themselves into his servitude, and now, with judgment at hand, they lamented the cost of their misplaced loyalties.

I saw several of the higher-up leaders go to Lucifer, their god, and cling to his arm, crying out for him to save them. They had all thought in the times of reverie that theirs was a way that would never be toppled, but as the heavens poured forth its massive armies bent on the destruction of Lucifer's forces, victory did not seem so certain. As the sound of the hooves echoed throughout the heavens, panic seized Lucifer's troops. They did not stand as tall as they had done earlier. Their hearts were paralyzed with the sudden realization of their frail position as if they had abruptly been awakened from a very long dream...or nightmare. Lucifer had blackmailed, coerced, bribed and lied to win their allegiance.

I heard the screams of the angels as they fled in a feeble attempt to hide. Very few of them even stood to fight. They scattered like frightened civilians facing the ultimate doom of their city. The angels fled through the heavens in a last ditch effort to outrun the pursuing forces who hewed them down like kindling.

Every fallen angel was run through with the sword of righteousness held in the hand of one of the mighty soldiers of God who did not flinch from their duty. It was a civil war that tore at the hearts of everyone. Some of the enemy even turned to their former friends, pleading for their lives on the grounds of past friendships. The blood ran thick that day as every angel was banished from the world of the living with bodies to the world of the living without bodies—denizens locked into the realms of the torturous Second Heavens.

As they left their bodies, their screams grew louder—the desperate shriek of the vanquished. Their cries continued non-stop until I thought I could not bear it any longer.

Fire and Brimstone rained down from the skies causing whole areas to melt into glass. This nuclear holocaust fell upon the cities of Lucifer around the world, destroying the people, vaporizing the structures into ruins, and radioactively contaminating the area. The earth's ecology changed so suddenly that animals and ape-men scrambled to the highest places they could find to escape the vengeance of God, but they were frozen in a matter of seconds where they stood.

The skies rained fire, meteorites fell, volcanoes spewed forth death and destruction, and the earth shook and groaned with inner turmoil. There was nowhere to run or hide. Judgment had come to the Garden of God. The lake Lucifer had prized so much rose swiftly, flooding the half-constructed city and all its workers, before dropping eight hundred feet to never rise again. Temples disappeared as islands sank, rendering some of Lucifer's early warning systems completely useless. The Ice-Age overwhelmed all life on earth and buried Lucifer's folly and rebellion so that they would one-day be discovered and God's man would look and learn. God buried Lucifer's pride in the mysteries of earth and snow.

As I watched at the battle, I saw Lucifer's followers run for cover, but there was no cover to be found. They were run through with flaming swords and they perished from the earth and its dimension forever. Their punishment was to become bodiless spirits without a home. Forevermore, they were to be mere specters resembling their once glorious forms, doomed to a land without color, vibrancy or life. From every quarter of the universe they were rousted and driven into hell. Their screams were overpowering, and I dropped to my knees and covered my ears with trembling hands in hopes of keeping out their howling pleas.

I found myself in the halls of the Second Heavens. There were spirits there without number and they were thrown into utter chaos and drowned in a cacophony of their own protests and screeching fears. They cried out for their betrayer, Lucifer. They screamed for his blood, something they could never have. They wanted to string him up as a lesson to all for listening to his lies, something they vowed to never do again. They shouted for hours, days and weeks, but not one took notice of any of them. They spilled out their anguish on everyone around.

I saw Lucifer sitting off to one corner, away from the shrieking crowd of enraged losers, deep in thought. I could not understand how he could even think in that horrendous raucous. He had actually thought he could win and was very surprised that he lost. He had thought that he did everything that was necessary to not only win but to launch the inevitable onslaught on the throne of God. But he was wrong. And now, he found himself in the position of being head of nothing—not even head of the losing army. They wanted nothing to do with him. They had banked everything they had on his victory, but he had lied to them and they had lost.

It was a very long time before I saw Lucifer move. He slowly stood up, a mere shadow of his former grandeur, and he cried out above the deafening din of the crowd. "I have sinned against the Lord your God. Forgive my sin only this once, and entreat the Lord to take away from me this death only." (Exodus 10:16-17)

A hush fell over the googolplex of fallen angels as they awaited the answer. But it was too late. The cup of his...their...iniquity was full. There was no longer any time for lame, half-hearted repentance.

Then I heard the reply as an angel took up this lament, his head hung, and he cried out, "For My people are foolish, they have not known Me. They are silly children, and they have no understanding. They are wise to do evil, but to do good they have no knowledge. I beheld the earth, and indeed it was without form, and void; and the heavens, they had no light. I beheld the mountains, and indeed they trembled, and all the hills moved back and forth. I beheld, and indeed there was no man, and all the birds of the heavens had fled. I beheld, and indeed the fruitful land was a wilderness, and all its cities were broken down at the presence of the LORD, by His fierce anger. For thus says the LORD: The whole land shall be desolate; yet I will not make a full end. For this shall the earth mourn, and the heavens above be black, because I have spoken. I have purposed and will not relent, nor will I turn back from it. The whole city shall flee from the noise of the horsemen and bowmen. They shall go into thickets and climb up on the rocks. Every city shall be forsaken, and not a man shall dwell in it. And when you are plundered, what will you do? Though you clothe yourself with crimson, though you adorn yourself with ornaments of gold, though you enlarge your eyes with paint, in vain you will make yourself fair; your lovers will despise you; they will seek your life. For I have heard a voice as of a woman in labor, the anguish as of her who brings forth her first child, the voice of the daughter of Zion bewailing herself; she spreads her hands, saying, 'Woe is me now, for my soul is weary because of murderers!'" (Jeremiah 4:22-30)

> *Ezekiel 31:16-18 "I made the nations shake at the sound of its fall, when I cast it down to hell together with those who descend into the Pit; and all the trees of Eden, the choice and best of Lebanon, all that drink water, were comforted in the depths of the earth. They also went down to hell with it, with those slain by the sword; and those who were its strong arm dwelt in its shadows among the nations. To which of the trees in Eden will you then be likened in glory and greatness? Yet you shall be brought down with the trees of Eden to the depths of the earth; you shall lie in the midst of the uncircumcised, with those slain by the sword. This is Pharaoh and all his multitude," says the Lord GOD.*

As I looked back into the heavens from my position in hell with the fallen angels, sadness washed over me. These angels who were banished to the Second Heavens were friends and brothers of those very angels who banished them. There was silence in heaven as the armor was put away and the angels, those mighty soldiers of the Lord who had done His bidding, returned to their homes. There was a great loss in every office of heaven—the places held by the angels who fell were vacant and empty of the life that had once held them. The pain of that loss was felt everywhere, the ripple of the cost of their sin touching everyone.

CHAPTER ELEVEN

Lucifer's Plan "B"

The hysterical clamor rose once more in hell and the screams again became riotous. Everyone had an opinion and a voice with which to give it, and they all yelled it out at once. The reality of their situation was beginning to sink in—the shock had worn off.

Lucifer rose from his position of formulating another plan. He was desperate. He had to retain his position of leadership, even here in this dismal place.

I heard a voice from heaven say to me, "What is more terrifying than hell?"

I thought for a moment. Hell, when one is not there is a terrifying prospect, but what if one is there? The answer was easily the final judgment and Lake of Fire.

I turned back to the scene at hand, and I watched as a small slip of hope crossed the frown on Lucifer's face. He had formulated another plan. He arose and shouted over the deafening din of his maddened followers. They stopped and turned to face him.

He stretched his full height—a terrifying sight to behold especially in the form of a shadow of this blackened, evil place. I felt my heart sink within my own breast at the sight of him. He was no longer the glorious figure of light he had once been—he was black and fearsome. The other spirits turned and looked at him, themselves equally as frightening, none of them resembling their former glory.

They were black in a black world, not even a reminder of what they once were remained in this dismal, dry place.

He reached out his hand and took command of the crowd and began to speak with great authority. "We have lost the battle. What looms before us is the Lake of Fire. It is the judgment for losing the war. But we have not lost that war...yet. We are not in the Lake of Fire. It is not over yet by a long shot."

The crowd watched him, ready to strike, but willing to listen to what he had to say.

"We can hold off that judgment from ever happening. The Godhead is going to create a Bride. When that Bride comes forth and the marriage takes place, then the judgment will happen. If we prevent the bride from coming forth...if we cause that Bride—that prized possession of the Godhead, the apple of His eye—to fall, then there will be no wedding and there will be no judgment. If there is no judgment, there is no Lake of Fire. We have lost the battle, but we have not lost the war. We now own the real estate, the largest universe created," he whispered now, having their full attention.

The crowd of spirits looked at each other, questioning. A murmur arose as they asked each other what Lucifer could be talking about.

He continued, "All we have to do is cause the bride to curse herself. It is a very easy task ahead of us."

Almost to a man, the crowd cried out, "What do we have to do? How do we do that?"

He answered, "You follow me, no questions asked. You do what I say. You follow me and you will never see the Lake of Fire. We will win the war. And maybe, one day, we will find how to regain our bodies and glory."

They knelt, every one of the fallen angels condemned to hell, cursed to be bodiless specters, mere shades of their former selves. They again fell for the plan of their leader who had lost the last battle, putting all their trust in his leadership. They swore undying allegiance to Lucifer again, but this time it was not enough. They had sworn their allegiance to him before and run. Obedience and submission was inherently instilled in them—they just changed masters. Now, they had to put what little there was left of their lives on the line. They could never turn from Lucifer again, and they could never turn on him again.

They knelt and bowed their heads in true homage, making him the indisputable leader of the fallen angels. He had again regained his position as king of the fallen angels—a mere reflection of what he once had in the government of God.

With his position secure, he spent his time reorganizing the troops of his kingdom—issuing levels of rank to those who did not run from Michael and his army. The majority of those who ran were relegated to the ranks of demons, the great ranks of nameless, faceless specters that did the bidding of absolutely everyone above them.

He set up his kingdom and thought out his plan with careful consideration, waiting and watching for the recreation of the world that had been destroyed in the last war, the sixth curse the earth had suffered for Lucifer's folly.

Time passed as the earth lay under the curse, waiting for the Lord to give His word for life to once again begin.

An angel came and showed me the meaning of "Have you entered the treasury of snow, or have you seen the treasury of hail, Which I have reserved for the time of trouble, for the day of battle and war?" (Job 38:22-24)

The Lord had buried the sins of Satan under the snow and buried it for a later time when all would be revealed to mankind, His bride.

CHAPTER TWELVE

Creation of Man

Darkness covered the earth as a blanket of destruction filled the earth's atmosphere, obliterating the sun from penetrating the frozen surface.

From the throne, I heard the command, "Let there be light."

I saw the clouds begin to dissipate and the atmosphere drop its heavy load of dust and ash. The sun shone on the earth once again. The earth was restored to its former glory with one exception—the earth was 23.5° off its normal axis. The Lord divided the light from the darkness and the earth once again became the Garden of God, this time with seasons.

The snow and ice retreated from the land and the land once again could be seen. The waters that had accumulated and hidden the land dissipated and retreated. From a white, frozen planet could be seen the high places and mountaintops until finally the lowlands and plains were visible. The dry land became the earth and the waters became the seas.

Fresh water once again began to flow from the underground rivers, which had changed from their original courses when the turbulence of the Great War changed the very makeup of the Garden. Things had changed drastically, and the Garden was no longer the same Garden. Hail and brimstone, volcano, meteor, natural disasters and the angels in the mighty army of God took their toll. The Garden of God would never be the same again, pierced and tattooed by the signs of Lucifer's sins.

Grass began to grow as the ground was watered from lakes, rivers and the mist that the Lord caused to rise from the ground every night. The Holy Spirit recreated trees, herbs, grasses and all life as He hovered over the Garden. All manner of flowers sprang forth and the Garden was once again the lush greenery of former days, again the Holy Spirit showing His great ability to create new and wonderful life.

The changed tilt on the earth's axis caused seasons to change in the Garden for the first time, the stars in the heavens marking the time by the change in the skies. The heavens were set as a sign to reckon time for time was no longer going to be seen in the same light again. It was a new age. It was the age of the Bride and they would see time differently than the Godhead or angels. Time would have a gauge to record how it passed and what happened at specific points.

The Holy Spirit filled the oceans, rivers and lakes with abundant life. The Holy Spirit filled the land and the skies with copious life. Everything was full of song. Life was simple and free. Life was warm and easy. Everywhere was food—lush greenery blanketed the earth. There was no death in this wonderful, recreated Garden. The stain of active sin and death had been scrubbed away and purified from the earth.

When the time came, the Holy Spirit hovered over the red clay, a clearing specially made and preserved. As the Spirit moved, He lovingly formed man from the dust of the earth in Their own image. The Son came down and held the man in His arms. The Father came down and breathed into the mouth of man, giving him the kiss of life, His breath putting in man a living soul.

Heaven exploded with the sound of great joy. The Godhead had created His Bride—mankind. Although there was little understanding of what that really meant among the angels, the very fact this was the Lord's greatest desire was enough to make the heavenly rejoice. They wanted everything for the Father, Son and Holy Spirit—their love for Them was that great. They had given the angels everything....

The fingers of the man twitched and his eyes fluttered as he lay in the arms of his Lord and Creator. The Holy Spirit surrounded them basking the area in glowing warmth. His eyes opened and the first things he saw were the eyes of the Father who had just breathed life into him. A smile was on the Father's radiant face; a deep sense of pride and love flowed out from His eyes.

The Son helped the man to his feet, this first of a nation of men, and the angels held their breath. The anticipation in the air was thick and electrifying.

The Father smiled even deeper, His voice gentle and sweet as he said in a single, unhesitant moment, "Adam."

The angels let out their breath and the praises flowed out with the sound of applause. The whole universe rocked under the weight of the joy and praise. The heavens were charged with the electricity of excitement. Song broke out in every corner of the heavens—in all heavens except the Second Heavens that lay sullen and quiet.

In an instant the Lord had created the entire heavenly host— googolplex upon googolplex of beings of every shape, form and color. Entire races were fashioned in the blink of an eye—angels with wings; angels with four faces; cherubs; archangels; messengers; ministers; soldiers. Every race a different shape designed specifically for their task and position in the heavens. Every race had a multitude of colors and features. All perfect. All designed exactly how the Godhead wanted them to be.

And in an instant, the Godhead created man—one single, lone man made from the red earth of the very Garden of God itself. He was to be the perfect being that stood between God and His creation, a being made of the Spirit of God and the earth from the Garden. Adam was a being of the Third Heavens and the First Heavens, the natural and supernatural, spirit and body. He was made to be a citizen of both.

Overjoyed to finally see the Bride that the Godhead had spoken about and Lucifer bellyached about, the angels were, nevertheless, confused. Adam was but a single being—one in the entire universe. They had not known what to expect...but somehow, this wasn't quite it.

They didn't understand that man would be fruitful and multiply. They had not been fruitful and multiplied. They just were.

Lucifer had watched intently all that the Holy Spirit had done in His *new* recreation of the Garden of God. He was forced, by the rules of his banishment to remain in the Second Heavens—he could talk to those of the First Heavens if they could hear him, the sound of his voice sounding as if it were coming from a long distance, but he could not interact with them. The Second Heavens, although as close as the breath upon an arm, was as far as east is from west in the context of realms. He could not enter this world he had so earnestly coveted... the world he had tried to wrench from the very palm of the Father.

Keeping the necessary distance, Lucifer watched from the Second Heavens and learned everything he could about this new creation—something that had never been done before in the annals of creation. The Father Himself had breathed life into this man, giving him a living soul. Lucifer wondered for a brief, fleeting moment if that was how he was created so very long ago...but truly believed, by now, that he just always was as was the Godhead.

This new thing was a mystery that took much thought to figure out. The breath of God giving this creation life also gave this man a soul, something no other creature had. Although this man was made from the same elements that every other creation on earth was made from, the infusion of spirit and soul made this man something unique and spectacular. Regardless of his animosity towards the Godhead, Lucifer had to applaud the perfect ingenuity he witnessed.

It was something he had never thought of when he had made the ape-men.

Lucifer watched the loving way the Godhead each participated in this single creation of man. Father, Son and Holy Spirit left their throne to come to the Garden to jointly construct and create man in perfect cooperation of Their offices. In all that he had witnessed throughout the billions of years, he had never seen such fluid participation of all Three in such a way...he had never seen Them all come down from the Throne Room to make something.

As he watched the moment of life, remembering his own instance of realization, he knew this was not going to be as easy a task as he had hoped. He would have to watch and wait for just the right moment to make his move. I could see the resolve cross his face as he hunkered into an area right above the garden to get a very good vantage point despite being locked into his Second Heavens prison. This was an angel who knew patience as he waited for millions of years to strike against the God who created him and everything that was created.

Lucifer watched as the Lord brought everything before Adam to be named, which would give them their nature—their rank and position in the scheme of life on earth—just as he had done so many ages previously for the angels.

Then the Lord brought every creature before Adam to see if there was within those things already created a helpmate, someone of the same heart who could stand at Adam's side...but there was none to be found. Lucifer felt the pang in his own heart once again as he realized he would not be that helpmate. There was not one from among all the angels who had the same heart as the Lord, not even Lucifer. He remembered the rejection—a rejection created in his own heart with the increased belief that the Lord was holding out on him.

Then the Lord put Adam into a deep sleep, and took his rib to create woman. Just as Adam needed his own kind to be his helpmate, the Lord needed someone filled with His own Holy Spirit and heart to be His Bride. For a fleeting second the thought slipped through Lucifer's mind and he understood, but it was lost far too quickly in the darkness that had claimed his heart to fully register. He simply saw that his chances had now doubled to find an opening to bring the bride to her knees causing judgment to halt.

Lucifer watched for decades, waiting, studying their every move. He watched how they interacted with each other and the Lord.

Every evening the angels filled the heavens. They took turns to come to the Garden to sing to God's precious bride. These angels stood from horizon to horizon and were miles thick; there was no space between them, they filled the heavens totally. They began at dusk singing the praises of their God in melodies that were so pleasing, I wept at the beauty. They sang all through the night, softly singing of the glories and mightiness of the majesty of God. Every name of the Lord echoed through the heavens night after night...there was no end to the characteristics, creativity and names of the Lord.

Every day, in the early morning hours, the Son came to walk and talk with Adam and Eve in the coolness of the garden. They talked about all manner of things, the Lord hiding nothing from man. Every question was answered without hesitation. The Lord shared His heart—Father, Son and Holy Spirit communed separately and together with man every day. There was such a unity of purpose and heart; it was a joy to watch.

During the day, Adam tended to the garden. He planned and worked in the garden, excited to see the end results of the labors of his own hands...thrilled when the Godhead was pleased with his efforts. They talked about everything Adam planned to do, the Lord making suggestions that He would like to see, and Adam fulfilling the will of the Lord in every way. The Lord also expressed His pleasure over Adam's dreams, hopes and desires.

The angels from all over the universe came and taught Adam and Eve the things that they should know. They told them of all the things that God had created. There was a constant flow of angels gathering in and around the Garden—life was never boring for the couple that was the glory of God's creation.

As the decades passed, Adam began to put himself into his work more and more. He began to show more interest in work than his helpmate. He grew preoccupied during the praises of his God and Eve grew increasingly lonely for communion with her husband.

She could not understand why Adam was losing interest in her. He did not talk to her as he did before...and she wondered if her company no longer satisfied him. They did not discuss things as they once did, sharing ideas and plans. Perhaps after centuries of discussion, there was not much left to be said. The distance between them grew and festered. She began to take long walks in the garden alone, leaving Adam to his work.

Lucifer had waited over a thousand years for this opportunity. Eve wandered daily through the Garden on a path she often traveled, the forbidden tree being one of the many trees on her path. Lucifer was there waiting for her.

Lucifer chose to inhabit a snake, the creature that had long been his symbol. To the Mayans he was known as Illa Ticca *Viracocha*, *"the white man with red hair,"* but to the Aztecs he was known as Quetzalcoatl, "the feathered serpent." Every culture incorporates the sign of the serpent, but nowhere is it more prominent than in Lucifer's stronghold before the fall and Great War, the South American ziggurats.

Lucifer knew how to coax the serpent to allow him to enter—the first case of spirit possession to ever happen—so that Lucifer could use the voice of the serpent to entice Eve. Eve knew the Godhead and she knew angels. She knew about the Great War and the fall of Lucifer and his followers. She would not have been tricked by the specter of a fallen angel. He needed the voice of an innocent animal to sway her.

Adam and Eve could not see into the Second Heavens for that realm could only been seen through the effects it had on this realm. Lucifer was bound by the laws and boundaries set by God, and the law said that he could not interact with the beings of this heaven unless they gave him permission. But he could whisper to them from afar. But it was only the serpent that fell victim to the whispered promises that crossed the barrier of the Second Heavens. The serpent gave Lucifer the permission he needed to occupy his body and Lucifer was once more given the voice he needed in this world.

He lay in the tree waiting for an opening to speak to Eve—the timing had to be perfect. He waited and he watched as she passed by him every day for what seemed a very long time. Every day she lingered longer at the tree, gazing at its forbidden beauty and wondering why she was no longer appealing enough for Adam and why he preferred to spend his time working. She lingered at the tree, and one day she stopped and asked the tree what was wrong with her and why did Adam prefer his work over her—after all, it was the tree of the knowledge of good and evil.

It was the opening Lucifer had waited for. "Has God indeed said, 'You shall not eat of every tree of the garden'?"

The woman was not shocked by his words. At the time of this age of innocence, animals had a voice, and man and animal communicated. There was no sin or division. Man was God's representative to His creation.

She was, however, shocked to see the creature wrapped around one of the leafy branches of the tree. He had touched the tree and lived, something she herself was cautious to avoid.

Eve answered his words, "We may eat the fruit of the trees of the garden; but of the fruit of the tree which is in the midst of the garden, God has said, 'You shall not eat it, nor shall you touch it, lest you die.'"

Lucifer knew he had her. He had been in the Garden when the Lord gave Adam and Eve the instructions. The Lord had not said they could not touch the tree—Eve was confused about what the Lord had really said. He saw a perfect legal opening in her fear to plant a lie.

Then the serpent said to the woman, "You will not surely die. For God knows that in the day you eat of it your eyes will be opened, and you will be like God, knowing good and evil."

Eve thought Adam had lost interest in her because she did not understand the deeper things of God. She needed this knowledge that the fruit offered her—to have her eyes opened so that she would be as smart as God. Adam would have to love her again if she was like God. How could he not be enthralled with her? How could their love not be rekindled? He would once again see her as his equal. This tree promised to give her the wisdom she apparently lacked. She would know the things that Adam and God knew. She too would know good and evil as they knew. And when she grew in this knowledge, Adam would once again be in love with her.

She looked at the serpent wound around one of the higher branches and reasoned,

In order for that serpent to have gotten to that branch, he had to have gone by the fruit...and yet he still lived. Not only was he still alive after touching the fruit, he must have eaten of the fruit to know the power it possessed. He must be as God, this mere creature that was created without a soul and under our dominion. If this fruit, which did not kill the serpent, could make a lower creature be like God, how much more can it do for me?

Eve was excited with anticipation.

Eve plucked a fruit and held it in her hands as a cherished prize. She looked at it for a long time, weighing the words against the increasing need. The serpent had told her how to fix her obvious lack so that she would feel whole once again. She held the fruit and bit into it, taking not a tiny, hesitant bite, but a large, full mouthful. She took the plunge so deeply that there would never be any turning back. She wanted that knowledge.

Her eyes were definitely opened. She suddenly knew she had made a very terrible mistake. Part of her went dead. She was more alone than ever. She was on the opposite side of her beloved Adam because of her choice. She saw the consequence of her decision and it was not what had been promised. She took the half eaten fruit to her husband, Adam. She held it out to him, a terrible sadness filling her eyes. Tears flowed over her lids and it was the first time Adam had seen her cry. She looked at him and cried out, "Oh, Adam. What can I do? Look what I have done. Help me!"

When he saw the tears in her eyes, his love for her welled up in his heart and he took the fruit out of her hands, tears now flowing from his eyes as well. He too ate of it, hesitantly, but with a realization that there would be no turning back from this point.

He had chosen Eve over his God, not being able to imagine life without her. Eve's perceived lack of knowledge caused her to sin, and Adam's perceived lack of Eve, thinking that God would not or could not provide a way for them to be together, caused him to sin.

Both were wrong. But neither saw their mistake. They followed in the same steps as Lucifer and all the fallen angels.

Lucifer thought he had nothing when he had the highest angelic position in the kingdom of God...it has never been filled by anyone else. The angels thought they had no position when they had free access to the Godhead and the Throne Room, as well as being able to zoom around the universe wherever and whenever they wished. Eve thought she wasn't smart enough to interest a husband who loved her and a God who took time out every day to walk and talk with her in the garden. Adam thought God would or could not provide a way for him to keep Eve as his wife when it was the Lord who gave Eve to him in the first place.

They were all wrong—their lack did not exist.

CHAPTER THIRTEEN

Seventh Curse—
The Cherub And The Serpent

There was no singing that night. The heavens were quiet above the Garden. There were no praises floating down from the heavens to gently rock the pair to sleep. Adam and Eve got no sleep that night as they contemplated what they had done and what it might mean. Fear and shame had crept into their lives and they did not know how to handle it or even what it would mean.

Adam and Eve cowered within the bushes as Jesus walked through the Garden to the place He usually met them. The Lord reached the spot and called out to them. They knew that the sin they had committed would be seen by the Lord and they had no idea how to hide it from Him.

When faced with their sin, Adam blamed God who gave him the woman and Eve blamed the serpent that God had made and placed in the tree. Regardless of how they looked at it, they were accusing God of being responsible for their sin, and since it was His responsibility, perhaps He would then spare them the consequence of their decisions.

The seventh curse, although in part was to curse the serpent, was again against Lucifer himself.

The fourth commandment was broken. Exodus 20:8 "Remember the Sabbath day, to keep it holy."

The Lord had finished His creation. The Sabbath had arrived. All angels, universes, planets, stars, creatures and man had been created; unlike the angels that are finite in their number, the universe and all that are in it are fluid in their number, creation of new star systems, animals and man would continue to be fruitful and multiply.

The Bride was finished. The Lord had been working for over fourteen billion years. But now, all of creation could rest once again in the provision of God.

Genesis 2:1-3 Thus the heavens and the earth, and all the host of them, were finished. And on the seventh day God ended His work which He had done, and He rested on the seventh day from all His work which He had done. Then God blessed the seventh day and sanctified it, because in it He rested from all His work which God had created and made.

Lucifer had continued to work his evil, again counting on his own labors to win a victory.

The seventh curse in Egypt was hail. (Exodus 9:22)

Anyone, Egyptian or Hebrew alike, who heeded the word of the Lord and kept themselves and their livestock indoors were spared. Only those who did not heed the word of the Lord but listened to a different word perished or lost all they had.

This plague was against the Egyptian gods *Geb* and *Hu*.

Geb was the god of the earth, the most important of ancient Egypt's gods. He was one of the four deities that established the Cosmos. *Geb* was represented in the form of a man who wore the white crown. Earthquakes were believed to be the laughter of *Geb*. He was one of the gods who watched the weighing of the heart of the deceased in the *Judgment Hall of Osiris*. His first act of creation was to father *Ra*, "*the great god of life*," with his female counterpart, *Nut*.

Lucifer was completely convinced that he was part of the Godhead. He began to believe and perpetuate the idea that it was he that actually created the Son and the Godhead. He tells this story in every legend in history where he, the ultimate creator, was turned against and destroyed by his own children.

He had regained entry into the world he coveted. He was the *"Power of the Air,"* the god of this world. Adam and Eve had so easily given over the Garden of God, their inheritance, to Lucifer for the price of a piece of fruit and the promise his lies held.

Hu was one of the most important gods. *Hu* is the power of the spoken word. He personifies the authority of utterance. *Hu* represented the creative power of the gods. He was one of three gods who rode the *Sunboat* across the sky in order to create and sustain all life.

Hu was particularly important because he was the epitome of power and command. Through *Hu*, the King maintained his royal authority in the *Afterlife*. *Hu* allowed the King to cross the waters of his canal and acknowledged the King's authority and supremacy.

Hu was the personification of *Divine Utterance*, the voice of authority. However, *Hu* was not just a part of creation but was the creator. With each breath *Hu* expelled, creation took place. The first breath created the *Soul of Osiris*. His last creation was the *Sun*. So it is said that *Hu* is the Word of God, the first and the last breaths, *Hu Hu*. Lucifer was claiming to be the Word of John 1:1.

John 1:1-3 In the beginning was the Word, and the Word was with God, and the Word was God. He was in the beginning with God. All things were made through Him, and without Him nothing was made that was made.

Lucifer had usurped the place of Jesus in the heart of man. Even though a banished specter and mere shadow of his former glory, even though a created being and not creator, he was now the groom of the Bride God had so prized. He had become their substitute father, husband and god.

He had again taken that which God created and, by the power of his words and subtle speech, had changed in an instant the DNA of Adam and Eve from being a living person who was the child of the most high God to being, instead, a spiritually dead person who was the child of Lucifer, the devil. He had finally become fruitful and was the father of a nation of people.

John 8:44 "You are of your father the devil, and the desires of your father you want to do. He was a murderer from the beginning, and does not stand in the truth, because there is no truth in him. When he speaks a lie, he speaks from his own resources, for he is a liar and the father of it."

Eve had bought one lie and Adam followed her into sin believing a different one. Instead of covering and protecting her, he made the wrong decision himself, not seeing any other way. He saw Eve and perceived before him his lack—life without Eve. He believed that God would not provide for him, a righteous man, to stay with Eve, his sinful wife who was condemned to die. He looked at the tears flowing down the cheeks of his longtime companion and friend, and his envisioned lack pierced his heart. Knowing the consequences fully, he chose to die with her.

Lucifer had taken the gamble and after centuries of watching and waiting, he had moved from fallen angel banished to hell in the Second Heavens to *Prince of the Air* in the First Heavens.

Ephesians 2:2 ...in which you once walked according to the course of this world, according to the prince of the power of the air, the spirit who now works in the sons of disobedience...

Lucifer's only real power is working in and through the sons of disobedience. He can only work through those who give him permission to use them either through lack of knowledge of his presence or conscious co-laboring with him.

I looked at the snake and I could see two faces peering up at the Lord—the face of the spirit transposed on the face of the serpent. Lucifer looked out through the eyes of the serpent in rebellion and hiding. The Lord looked at the serpent, seeing the face of fallen Lucifer within, and spoke the immediate judgment for the sin committed.

For choosing to allow the banished angel, Lucifer, to take over his body and cohabitate with him and use the serpent's voice to deceive Eve, the Lord said to the serpent, "Because you have done this, you are cursed more than all cattle, and more than every beast of the field."

The serpent was a glorious creature. His scales were of the deepest red, black and gold, with a tinge of purple at its cheeks. It was the most sensible, sly and prudent creature in the Garden, but it lacked legs like the other animals. Even insects had legs. But the snake crawled on its belly in the dust beneath the feet of every other creature, afraid of being stepped on and killed. It had made a pact with Lucifer. His intelligence had put him in a position to make league with the devil, and it was his intelligence that was condemned. He had the choice to let the devil in or refuse him entry, but Lucifer wooed him with words of false promise. The Lord cursed his intelligence so that he would now be below the very cattle and beast of the field he had wanted to rise above. The serpent was made an abomination, an unclean thing, while the cattle and beasts were made sacrifices.

Because the serpent had sinned, all animals, regardless of their genus classification, were cursed. They had fallen from their place in God's kingdom to a place of lesser degree—that of sacrifice. They, who had been used to cause Eve to sin, would now pay with their lives for the temporary cost of that sin. They were cursed, their life now being forfeit.

Although the curse continued, it was announced that it would not be forever. Another would come who would pay in full the cost of sin.

Numbers 22:28-34 Then the LORD opened the mouth of the donkey, and she said to Balaam, "What have I done to you, that you have struck me these three times?"...So the donkey said to Balaam, "Am I not your donkey on which you have ridden, ever since I became yours, to this day? Was I ever disposed to do this to you?"

The Lord, because the serpent allowed Lucifer to speak through him, shut the mouths of animals. They had once spoken and man understood. In the innocence of the Garden, there was no confusion in their speech. But like the Tower of Babel, the language of animals became confusing to each other and to man. Man could no longer make sense of what they said. Man and animal could no longer communicate, and one species of animal could no longer communicate with another.

> *Romans 8:22-25 For we know that the whole creation groans and labors with birth pangs together until now. Not only that, but we also who have the firstfruits of the Spirit, even we ourselves groan within ourselves, eagerly waiting for the adoption, the redemption of our body.*

All of creation groans and labors for the manifestation of the sons of God when it will be freed from the curses of sin under which it now labors. At one time man cared for the animals, ruling over them in love and tenderness. But as the curse progressed through time, man became the embodiment of his *father*, Lucifer. He treated God's creation with the same destructive vehemence as Lucifer had treated God's creation. Dominion came to mean *domination* and *treading down* instead of *kingly rule.*

The Lord cares for every creature of His creation, supplying the needs of sparrow and man alike. Only man annihilates and destroys to extinction the wonderful creations of God, giving them no more thought than the means to fill his own need, desires and entertainment.

> *Revelation 4:11 You are worthy, O Lord, to receive glory and honor and power; for You created all things, and by Your will they exist and were created.*

> *Psalms 36:6 Your righteousness is like the great mountains; your judgments are a great deep; O LORD, You preserve (save, deliver, liberate) man and beast.*

Everything and everyone created was created for the express purpose of God's pleasure. Mankind was created to be the Bride of Christ, co-laborers with Him, a companion in work.

> *Revelation 22:17 And the Spirit and the bride say, "Come!" And let him who hears say, "Come!" And let him who thirsts come. Whoever desires, let him take the water of life freely.*

Unlike any other, man was given the ability to create. He was given a creative side to his nature, and the Lord takes pleasure in seeing what we will do with that creativity. We can use it for Him or against Him, to please Him or anger Him.

Man was made so that God could enjoy His creation with us and through us, but instead, mankind has been bent on destroying God's creation to fulfill his own lusts and carelessness. Man shall not escape the judgment of how he has treated God's Garden and everything in it...including how he has treated men, women and children.

Man was created to be the Lord's companion but Lucifer caused man to become the Lord's enemy, just as he was. Now positioning himself to be the Lord's enemy, man, the glory of God's creation was reduced to the dust of the earth when he died.

To Lucifer within the serpent, this newly appointed mighty *Prince of the Air*, the Lord said, "...on your belly you shall go, and you shall eat dust all the days of your life. And I will put enmity between you and the woman, and between your seed and her Seed; he shall bruise your head, and you shall bruise His heel."

The Lord told Lucifer five things in that one statement. The first was that his portion would be the dust. The body of man would return back to the dust after death. The second was that there would be hatred between Lucifer and the woman. The third, Lucifer would have seed in the earth. The fourth thing the Lord told him was that there would be hostility between his seed and her Seed. The fifth thing was he would ultimately lose because even though his seed would snap at the heel of her Seed, her Seed would crush his head.

Lucifer knew he could not win the war—that had already been proven. However, that was no longer his plan. His goal was just to prevent the Bride from manifesting and thus put off his own judgment to the Lake of Fire. He actually believed the Lord did not know his plan.

Lucifer was puffed up and full of himself. He had been given a free hand and free will throughout his life, but now, he would have to ask God's permission to do anything. He was cursed, reduced to crawling on his belly, a symbol of subjugation.

Joshua 10:24-26 So it was, when they brought out those kings to Joshua, that Joshua called for all the men of Israel, and said to the captains of the men of war who went with him, "Come near, put your feet on the necks of these kings." And they drew near and put their feet on their necks...

The Lord was cursing Lucifer but also letting Adam and Eve know that he was a defeated foe. All they had to do was put their feet on his neck to be victorious because he was already an overpowered enemy. Though they had sold their inheritance and their lives to Lucifer, there was hope of victory over him.

Lucifer may attack the Bride of God without mercy, but only with the permission of the Father and only to the degree that the Father withdraws His protection. And all that he will ever gain for his efforts is dust. It is God's mercy that man dies. The body of man, the empty shell, will return to the dust he came from. Man's spirit will return to God from whence it came and the soul will go to the Judgment Seat for judgment, then onto the appropriate reward or the Lake of Fire when the time comes. Both the spirit and the soul are out of Lucifer's reach. Man will not suffer forever at the hands of his deceiver.

After all was said and done, Lucifer had gained nothing for all his efforts. By returning man's spirit to God, his body to dust and his soul to judgment, God snatched man from Lucifer's grasp making his win a very hollow victory indeed.

In the end, everybody will see Lucifer for what he really is—a deceiver who had lied, destroyed their lives, and stolen every good thing the Lord had for them. All mankind will realize and become aware of the reality of what they have lost.

By these very words, the Lord was letting Adam and Eve know that they had moved out of His protection into the hands of Lucifer, who would continue to devour them throughout their lives.

Job 1:6-12 Now there was a day when the sons of God came to present themselves before the LORD, and Satan also came among them...So Satan answered the LORD and said, "Does Job fear God for nothing? Have You not made a hedge around him, around his household, and around all that he has on every side? You have blessed the work of his hands, and his possessions have increased in the land. But now, stretch out Your hand and touch all that he has, and he will surely curse You to Your face!" So the LORD said to Satan, "Behold, all that he has is in your power; only do not lay a hand on his person."

Lucifer still did not have the power or authority he craved. He might be *Prince of the Air*, but he still had to answer to God and could only do things with permission.

The second thing he now let Lucifer know was that redemption had been in place from the beginning. Lucifer knew that man was to be the Bride, but he did not know about the salvation plan for the Son of God to give His life to redeem the Bride. He was telling Lucifer that without a shadow of a doubt, the Godhead knew everything that was going to happen before it happened—and this came as a surprise to Lucifer who may have been with the Godhead but never really bothered to take his eyes off himself long enough to understand Them.

I John 3:8-10 He that commits sin is of the devil; for the devil sinned from the beginning. For this purpose the Son of God was manifested, that he might destroy the works of the devil.

He was told that no matter what he did, he could only snap at the heel of the Seed of the woman. He would not divert God's plan forever. Lucifer's plan to cause the Bride to fall came as no surprise to the Godhead. He had already made provision for this—the manifestation of the Son to shed His blood.

Lucifer did not understand what the Lord meant since he had known the Son all his life—he had always been manifest. He would have to wait and watch again to find out what the Lord meant.

Man, like fallen angel, had given over not only themselves but also their inheritance to Lucifer. They were completely his property and he could do whatever he wanted to them. He could kill them. He could maim them. He could experiment with them. He could manipulate them. He certainly had lots of practice altering God's creation and now man and earth were at his disposal.

But with this curse the Lord let Lucifer know that he could not do all that he wanted. He might have gotten the deed to the Garden, and he might have gained free entrance to mankind, but he still had to seek permission. The Lord might have partially withdrawn His protection from the people and planet He had created but He would return it if they asked Him into their lives. He would not let Lucifer have free reign, but man has always had freedom to choose whom he will serve...and there are only two choices—God or Lucifer.

Deception is the first part of Lucifer's power. Blackmail is the second part of this hold. Permission is the third part of his power over us. He can only do what he has permission to do...first permission from us and secondly, permission from the Father.

CHAPTER FOURTEEN

Eighth Curse—Eve And Woman

Exodus 20:7 You shall not take the name of the Lord your God in vain.

The woman did not tell the whole truth—the Lord did not say that to touch the fruit would cause death. The serpent did not tell the whole truth—God was not keeping the fruit from them for fear that they would become gods like Him. They were both guilty of "fudging" the truth with emptiness of speech and lies.

Genesis 2:16 To the woman He said: "I will greatly multiply your sorrow and your conception; in pain you shall bring forth children; your desire shall be for your husband, and he shall rule over you"

After dealing with the animal kingdom and Lucifer first, the Lord turned His eye to the woman. The eighth curse on Egypt was locusts that were sent to destroy everything left by the hail, destroying completely any hope of a harvest. (Exodus 10:4) The land was stripped of all life and seed, left defenseless and bare to the ravenous jaws of the locust.

This eighth curse was sent against *Re* and *Ma'at*.

Re, *"god of life,"* was the Egyptian sun god who, as *"Atum, the All Lord,"* created the world and was master of life. His closest ally is *Ma'at*, the embodiment of order and truth. *Re* was the master of the universe. His image was the sun itself. He is said to have created the earth solely for mankind who was made in his image. Evil comes from mankind's own deeds and *Re* rewards the obedient and destroys the disobedient and evil in death. Buried with the sun disc amulet, the dead were assured resurrection by *Re* after death.

The Egyptian story of creation explains that *Re* rose in the beginning of creation as an obelisk-like pillar that then spit forth Shu and Tefnut, the first godly couple. However, while *Re* is never paired with a goddess, he also bears several off spring including his son the Pharaoh, who becomes one with his father in death.

Ma'at was the goddess of *"Truth, Balance and Order"* who seemed to be more of a concept than an actual goddess. She was truth, order, balance and justice personified. She was harmony; she was what was right; as it should be. Without *Ma'at*, the universe would once again become chaos.

Because of *Ma'at*, everything in the universe worked on a pattern. Life was nothing without *Ma'at* for she was the solid grounding of reality that made the sun rise, the stars shine, the river flood and mankind to think. How can the universe be *"ethical or moral, right or wrong?"* It simply is. That is *Ma'at*.

She was a winged goddess who was judge in the underworld in the Halls of *Ma'at*. She was called *"Ammut—Devouress of the Dead."* If the deceased was found wanting in the concept of *Ma'at* during his life, his heart was devoured by a demon and he died the final death. If the heart weighed the same as *Ma'at*, the weight of a tiny feather, the deceased was allowed to go onto the afterlife.

Ma'at was also the justice meted out in law courts. A *"Priest of Ma'at"* resided over the people who were involved in the justice system as well as the priesthood of the goddess herself.

Ma'at was known as a *Neter goddess*, and as such, was described as a daughter of *Ra*. She was, really, the most important deity of them all.

Lucifer, rightly so, now declared that he was the father of the first couple created. He was declaring that his chaos was the real truth, balance and order in the world, a chaos that has wrecked havoc on mankind for over six thousand years. He was declaring that he alone was the model for goodness, and anything not declared by him was evil and needed to be destroyed. He had hacked down the standard of the Lord and set his own standard in its place.

Isaiah 5:20 Woe to those who call evil good, and good evil; who put darkness for light, and light for darkness; who put bitter for sweet, and sweet for bitter!

When Eve sinned, the spirit of Jezebel entered the world. When Adam sinned, the spirit of Ahab entered the world. There is a great deal of confusion about these two spirits and their assignments. Jezebel is commonly equated to matriarchal control. For one thing, men can have the spirit of Jezebel as easily as women, and women can have the spirit of Ahab as easily as men. Whole church congregations can have the spirit of Ahab while their pastor has the spirit of Jezebel; whole church congregations can have the spirit of Jezebel while the pastor has the spirit of Ahab. Or there can be any mix of the two. One does not even have to be in a church setting to have these spirits.

The spirit of Jezebel was to lead the people of God astray and the spirit of Ahab was to allow her to do just that as long as it was to his benefit.

The name Eve means *"lifegiver,"* for she was to be the mother of mankind, God's people. The name Jezebel means *"noncohabited," "un-husbanded,"* and *"chaste,"* and the first act she did was to kill the people of God and raise up the people of Baal.

Jezebel was raised to be a queen and in the service of *Baal,* which means *"Master"* or *"Owner." Baal* was the equivalent of the Sun god, *Re,* protector of crops and livestock. In times of great turbulence, children were sacrificed to *Baal* to appease him. Man's prosperity depended on the productivity of their crops and livestock, and Baal must be appeased at all costs.

Queen Jezebel, high priestess of *Baal,* and daughter of the King of Phoenicia, participated from birth in the ceremonies of *Baal.* Dancing, chanting and singing around his altars to please him were commonplace. The priests of *Baal* cut themselves in token sacrifice to their god. Priests and people alike drank of ceremonial drinks to

Baal, to lower their inhibitions and increase their frantic worship. And in times of trouble or yearly obeisance, children were sacrificed by being passed through the fire and burned alive to serve their god.

Jezebel was high priestess, a rigid devotee of *Baal*. She was first of all wife of *Baal*, regardless of her marriage to Ahab. It was her duty and honor to bring all she came into contact with, or had control over, to worship *Baal*. It was her one mission and passion in life.

Ahab, and consequently the spirit of Ahab, allowed *Baal* to be worshipped or God to be worshipped depending which better serviced his purposes. He allowed and enabled mixture to pervade the people of God.

In this story we see exactly what happened in the Garden of Eden. Eve, despite her marriage to Adam and her loyalty to the Godhead, had committed adultery with another, Lucifer. Lucifer became her husband and her god above all else, and it was her duty to bring all she came into contact with to worship him. The Spirit of Jezebel possessed her.

Eve took the fruit to her husband to show him what she had done. Tears streamed down her face. The reality of her situation weighed heavily upon her. She ran to her husband hoping he would help her find a way out. He could have covered her and stood by her and presented her sin to a forgiving, loving God, or he could have done exactly what he did.

They had spent a very long time with the Lord and knew He was a merciful God. Adam could have gone to the Lord for help in this situation. Eve would have repented. It is the nature and heart of woman to be a godly woman. But, like she followed Lucifer, she followed Adam's direction, hiding in the bushes and trees, and covering her nakedness with fig leaves.

Adam, who should have covered his wife and asked the Lord what could be done to save his wife, instead, allowed Lucifer to take over the Garden because it served his purposes better to keep Eve as his wife. The Spirit of Ahab possessed him.

The curse of the woman came in several parts. First, her sorrow would be greatly multiplied. Second, her conception would be greatly multiplied. Third, she would from this moment on bring forth children in pain. Fourth, her desire shall be for her husband. Fifth and last, she was told that he would rule over her by reason of her desire.

Another word for sorrow is *worry*. Eve would never know another day without worry. Worry would dog her heels—worry for her husband, her children, her grandchildren, and her own life. She would worry about everything from a state of helplessness. She had worried about her relationship with Adam, but now she would worry about everything.

When Noah was born, he was so named Noah because he was supposed to comfort the people concerning their work and worry because of the ground which the Lord cursed. (Genesis 5:29)

Eve's worry would never end.

Luke 21:34 But take heed to yourselves, lest your hearts be weighed down with...cares of this life...

The second curse on Eve was that her conception would be greatly increased. Up until this time, with all their centuries already in the Garden, Eve had not had any children. As soon as they left the Garden, she was pregnant and later had two sons as well as many other children. Children would come into the world quicker now that mankind had a shorter lifespan. Today, we have children having babies.

Every woman has a certain number of eggs given to her that can be fertilized throughout her lifespan. Because of the decreased lifespan of woman from hundreds of years to the current seventy or eighty, there is still the same number of eggs given to her. Thus, her conception is concentrated.

The third part of the curse was that childbirth was a painful process. Children would not be delivered without great labor and agony. The spirit of fear tightens the contractions of the muscles, increasing the difficulties and pain of labor. The contractions become more spastic and painful as the fear of the pain increases the activity. Eve had allowed the spirit of fear to work in her life—fear of loss, death, shame, and exposure—and it would now work to disrupt her child birthing process.

But it also meant that her children would cause her pain all her life. She would have to watch them be wounded and turned by Lucifer and his minions instead of being happy in the arms of God—as she had once been.

The fourth part of the curse was that her desire would always be towards her husband. Her desire in the Garden to rekindle the love of her husband caused her to fall prey to Lucifer and follow a lie. It was her perceived lack of his love that caused her to sin, and it was this desire that would haunt her for the rest of her life. Her desire would be to have a husband and always look for constant validation from him concerning his love.

Lucifer would use this desire as a weapon against her in the centuries to come.

The last part of the curse was that her husband would rule over her. Until this moment, she was Adam's helpmate not his servant. But that would change. Her desire to please her husband would allow him to rule over her and control her. She would become prisoner of her own desires, and man would abuse that weakness in her.

This curse has made woman's life hard for over six thousand years. But there is a promise that his will change.

Revelation 22:17 And the Spirit and the bride say, "Come!" And let him who hears say, "Come!" And let him who thirsts come. Whoever desires, let him take the water of life freely.

There will one day be no more worry for their will always be enough, and the woman, the bride, will be the helpmate and companion of the Son of God, not His servant.

CHAPTER FIFTEEN

Ninth Curse—Adam And Man

Genesis 3:17-19 Then to Adam He said, "Because you have heeded the voice of your wife, and have eaten from the tree of which I commanded you, saying, 'You shall not eat of I': Cursed is the ground for your sake; in toil you shall eat of it all the days of your life. Both thorns and thistles it shall bring forth for you, and you shall eat the herb of the field. In the sweat of your face you shall eat bread till you return to the ground, for out of it you were taken; for dust you are, and to dust you shall return."

The second commandment was broken—You shall have no other gods before Me.

Eve wanted the knowledge of the godhood. The fallen angels wanted the power and position of godhood. Lucifer made himself god above his Creator. Adam made Eve his god, choosing her above the Lord. Everyone wanted to be a god. All had transgressed the second commandment.

But Adam and Eve could have repented and found grace and mercy in a God he knew personally since the day he opened his eyes. Lucifer, at one time, could have also found repentance, but was now beyond redemption and condemned to Hell in the Second Heavens.

The ninth curse in Egypt was the curse of darkness. (Exodus 10:21-23)

This curse was against the gods *Wadjet* and *Nekhbet*, the two *Eyes of Ra*.

The land of Egypt was plunged into darkness for three days, plenty of time for any enemy to come upon and slay Pharaoh in a surprise attack. His land was barren, stripped clean of all life and seed, his armies were defenseless and now Pharaoh himself was powerless as his personal protector goddesses were blinded. The *Eyes of Ra* were the protector of Pharaoh, able to see the enemy approach from a great distance.

Adam was blinded first by his work and then by his wife. The first separated him from his wife; the second separated him from his God. He did not see the enemy approach.

Wadjet was one of the "twin" protectors of Egypt, the other being *Nekhbet*. Often shown as a rearing cobra, she was ready to strike and kill all of Pharaoh's enemies. She was usually depicted with her sister cobra, *Nekhbet*. They both stood side by side on Pharaoh's crown.

Wadjet anointed the heads of her followers with flames, covering them in an aura of light. She rose up on a person's head during each and every hour of the day as she did on her father, *Ra*. She is the goddess of heat and fire. She also takes on the form of a lioness, and is known as *"The August One, the Mighty One."*

Wadjet was also known as the protector of Royal women. She was the symbol of rulership, creator and god of papyrus, upon which the word was written. Not only was she a goddess, but she was one part of the land of Egypt itself.

Nekhbet was twin goddess with *Wadjet*, the second *Eye of Ra*.

Nekhbet was guardian of mothers and children, and, one of the two *Eyes of Ra*, guardian of Pharaoh. She was depicted either as a full snake or full vulture wearing the white crown on her head, her wings spread in protection and holding the symbol of eternity in her talons. Her symbol was always part of the sun disk, royal name or royal insignia.

Like *Wadjet*, she was protector of Royal women. *Nekhbet* often appears in war, offertory scenes, and suckling the pharaoh. She was not only protector of mothers and children, but she was the goddess of childbirth.

Lucifer, blinded, lives in darkness. His heart is black, and his love, mercy and compassion gone. There is nothing he can do about his situation because, when offered one, he refused to look at the way out. Now, for Lucifer and his fallen angels, there is no way out. They will remain blind, living in perpetual darkness.

But he also blinds his followers from the truth. He does not want anyone to be free. His ultimate motive is to convince them there is no way out whatsoever. Although there is still a way out for his followers, this way out is open only for a while. God will not strive forever with man. (Genesis 6:3) If someone continues to choose to believe a lie, God will send them a strong delusion. (II Thessalonians 2:11-12)

Blinded, by his love for Eve, he could not think of a way around the problem, so he succumbed to follow Eve.

This curse also had five parts. First, the ground was cursed because Adam ate the fruit of the forbidden tree. Second, he would have to work for his food every day of his life. Third, both thorns and thistles would spring up choking his edible crops. Fourth, he would eat the herb of the field. Fifth, he would eat his bread by the sweat of his face until he returned to the ground from which he was taken.

The first part of the curse against Adam cursed the ground that supplied him his sustenance. He freely ate of the fruit thereby sharing in Eve's fate so they would not be parted and because of this choice, the ground would no longer give forth in abundance the fruit of its seed. The largest crop he would now harvest was but a pale reminder of what once was just there in the Garden of Eden. The one bunch of grapes carried by two spies out of the Promised Land was but a hint of the size of a bunch of grapes in the Garden.

On my birthday, the Lord took me in vision to several places throughout the universe in response to my request of what, specifically, my future would hold. Of course, I meant in the next couple of months, but the Lord has a splendid sense of humor I have always appreciated. He took me to Archangel Michael's house with its rich glowing clear crystal walls, ceiling and floor. The elaborate palace that Michael had built was from part of a star, the light emanating from the crystal halls, shining day and night. It was brilliant against a backdrop of purple skies, red lands and navy blue trees. The sight was spectacular and amazing. I saw the emergence of several new star systems as they were created. I was taken to several other homes of angels as a sort of drive-by tour. I was taken to the Throne Room where court was being held. There was a ceiling of live angels worshipping in song. Several different nations of angels milled, praised and danced before the Throne. In the middle of a session the Father, sitting on His throne, leaned over on one elbow and held out His hand to me. In His fingers He held a very large pale green plant that looked a lot like a clove of garlic. He smiled and asked me, "Have you ever tasted this herb? It has the taste of garlic and black pepper."

I looked at the object in the Lord's fingers and replied, "No, I haven't." At that very instance, I heard Him laugh and I returned to the car where I was a passenger. His birthday present to me was to show me some of the great wonders of His creation that I will see and taste in the years to come, and what one day in my life would be like after New Jerusalem. There is no end to the abundance and variety of flavor, color, texture, smell and sounds throughout the universe, and the Lord has not yet made a dent into His great reservoir of creativity.

However, the earth, because of the curse, has stopped giving forth its abundance of flavor, color and harvest. The earth labors under a curse that must be lifted with the full repentance of every person on earth, but especially men, for it was through men that particular curse came.

God is a God of abundance, but He has had to withdraw that blessing of abundance because of man's choice to follow another god.

The second part of the curse against Adam affected the amount of labor required to bring in a harvest. No longer could one harvest where no seed had been sown. Man had to work for what he gained, work for what he ate, every day of his life. The free ride was over.

Matthew 25:24 Then he who had received the one talent came and said, "Lord, I knew you to be a hard man, reaping where you have not sown, and gathering where you have not scattered seed."

The third part of the curse was that now thistles would grow from the ground and thorns would grow on the stalks. The soldiers put a crown of thorns on Jesus' head crowning Him with the very curse placed on the earth because of man's sin. If we ever decide to walk in freedom from the curse, we could do so. Everything man put his hand to would be blessed and come forth in abundance. Jesus wore the curse on His brow, breaking the curse on the cross. However, we, as a people, have chosen not to walk free of the curse but to still labor under the curse.

It is a matter of revelation and choice.

Not only did the free bounty of the earth cease, but it was now a thorn in man's flesh to reap it.

The fourth part of the curse was that Adam would eat of the herb of the field. His food supply was limited. He could no longer eat of the Tree of Life or any other fruit of the trees of the Garden. The sweet, succulent fruit that nourished Adam for centuries was no longer part of his diet. He would now eat of the same grasses as the animals of the earth, the herb of the field. He no longer had the right to the fruit of the Tree of Life because he had sinned—disobedience forfeits inheritance.

The last part of the curse was that he would eat by the sweat of his brow until the day he died. Death was now man's lot. He would work hard and die. The work of his hands helped little to prolong his life that was forfeit because of his sin.

Five is the number of grace, and each curse against Adam and Eve were five-fold. Though they were condemned to death, God, in His great mercy, prolonged their life from instant death to life for a limited number of years. Although their lot would be misery, there was space for them to return to Him from their spiritual death in their lifetime.

There was even grace shown to Lucifer in his curses. He would finally be able to rest from his tormenting zeal of being god—if he chose. The matter would be settled forever and finally be put to rest. Eve's seed would crush his head—all his grandiose ideas and lofty ambitions would be shattered forever, and if he chose, he could finally lie down and give up.

CHAPTER SIXTEEN

Adam and Eve—
The Pre-Flood World

Adam and Eve were sent from the Garden, the only home they had ever known. Cherubim now stood before the newly gated entrance. Cherubim are fearful looking creatures—exceedingly tall, with a glowing breastplate and helmet, a soldier of the highest order. Their folded wings run the entire length of their bodies. Their hair flows in a wind only they can feel, for it is the breath of God, their constant escort. Unlike other offices, I have never seen cherubim take shifts while on duty. They are the guards at the city gates, the doors to the Throne Rooms and the sentry around the entrance to heaven. Their expression is one of grave responsibility with eyes fixed forward, their vision encompassing all that is around them.

In their midst stood a sword, appearing very much as if it had a life of its own. It was a blade of the finest luminescent silver shrouded in a thick flame of the most incredible bluish red fire that burns without fuel. It is a never-ending flame and appears to be the same flame that emanates from the eyes of the Son of God. The cherubim faced every direction from the gate while the sword turned in every direction, ready to strike whoever would dare attempt to sneak through to the Garden.

Eden is still here in the earth. However, it has moved to the same location on the plane of the Third Heavens, still luscious with abundance of life. As soon as the cherubim raised the sword, the land of Eden moved from this realm behind the veil of the Third Heavens, hidden from the sight of man, who was now spiritually dead. It is no mistake that in this last age of man, in this place in our heaven will be the most destructive war and deepest blood.

Adam and Eve watched as their beloved home disappeared from view, slowly the vividness of its color and sounds faded...their natural eyes and ears no longer able to discern spiritual things. The glorious fragrance was gone. Now filled with sorrow, they wept as it left, the first fruit of their sin suddenly dawning on them.

People think that the First and Third Heavens are separate places, but they are the same place, just different planes. Each one is as close to the other as the breath on one's arm. Eden is still here on the earth, but out of reach of those who are spiritually dead and trapped here in the First Heavens.

When our spirit man comes fully alive through salvation and the baptism of the Holy Spirit, when we are in full relationship with the Father, Son and Holy Spirit, we will be able to enter the Garden that is in the midst of the Paradise of God. There we will be able to freely partake of the Tree of Life and live forever.

Revelation 2:7 ...To him who overcomes I will give to eat from the tree of life, which is in the midst of the Paradise of God.

Revelation 22:14 Blessed are those who do His commandments, that they may have the right to the tree of life, and may enter through the gates into the city.

We may have been saved by Christ and have the baptism of the Holy Spirit, but we are sorely lacking in spiritual awareness and its full reality. Some of us do not believe there is more in this life for us while others simply do not know there is any spiritual reality at all. We still suffer from thousands of years of half-truths and lies that have buried us beneath a pile of ineffectiveness and isolation. The Lord has been removing layer after layer of historical blindness built up since the time of Adam and Eve. Now, with an even greater outpouring of the Holy Spirit on the people of God, He has stepped up the timetable, as planned, to move into fast-forward.

When we decide that we are hungrier for the relationship with the Father, Son and Holy Spirit than for the pursuit of miracles, signs, wonders, anointings, mantles, and gifts, then we will have decided to stop choosing the fruit of the wrong tree—works over relationship, deeds over love. These things that are now impossible for us will be more than possible because with Him, and only with Him, are all things possible. We will, one day, walk into the Garden of Eden as if it were any other garden. The guardian cherubim will nod as we enter—the only time I have ever seen them smile is when someone who has the right to enter the secured area approaches with confidence. The sword of judgment will permit us to pass for we will have been made clean, whole and alive before we even get there.

We could enter the Garden of Eden today, if we knew how.

We could take a lesson from Enoch. He walked with God so closely and their relationship was so tight that one late afternoon he just stepped into the Third Heavens without so much as a hesitation.

I watched as he went into the Garden of God, Jesus at His side and the Holy Spirit all around them. They went straight to the Tree of Life, where Enoch partook of a great meal, taking his fill, before moving onto the Throne Room of God to meet with the Father.

He now spends a good deal of his time in Eden, at the court of God, meeting new arrivals from earth, and in his home, entertaining angels and people alike. He is one of the teachers in the school of God for new arrivals who have not yet reached a mature walk. Enoch did not seek the things God could give him, regarding the relationship with the Father, Son and Holy Spirit as more precious.

Genesis 5:24 And Enoch walked with God; and he was not, for God took him.

Matthew 13:44-46 Again, the kingdom of heaven is like treasure hidden in a field, which a man found and hid; and for joy over it he goes and sells all that he has and buys that field. Again, the kingdom of heaven is like a merchant seeking beautiful pearls, who, when he had found one pearl of great price, went and sold all that he had and bought it.

When we esteem the relationship with the Father, Son and Holy Spirit as the greatest treasure and the finest pearl, selling everything or giving everything else up to obtain that relationship, we will be richer than we ever dreamed.

To reach into the Third Heavens is only a matter of reaching into a different plane of existence, the spirit realm. To go to the Throne Room is not a case of flying off somewhere out there a trillion miles into space, but merely stepping into it right here on earth, from one plane to the other. After all, the First and Second Heavens were created within the Third Heavens.

Our spirit man walks in the Third Heavens all the time, communing with the Father, Son and Holy Spirit at will. He hears the angels speak to us and sees the angels who minister and guard us. Our natural man walks here on earth. He sees, tastes, smells, hears and feels everything here.

If after saved and filled with the Holy Spirit, the communication between our natural and spiritual man does not perform as it was designed to, it means that there is a problem either psychologically or physically. The spirits we are possessed with, either through our generations or from our own participation with sin, break the communication inside us between our spirit man and our natural man. The broken communication blinds us from seeing, hearing, touching, smelling and feeling the spiritual world freely as we were designed to.

How can spirits possess a Christian? We were born with them first and became Christian later.

Consider this body we have to be like a boarding house. In the beginning, Adam and Eve filled their house—they were made perfect and whole, a single dwelling place. They knew who God, the Son and Holy Spirit were. Because of their relationship with the Godhead, they knew and understood who they were in Them. They understood their identity and their identity gave them the assurance to fill their house. But over the millennia of losing that identity in God, mankind no longer fills his house. We have become a mere shadow of the glory we were created to be. Mankind no longer fills their house because they do not know who the Godhead is or who they are in Christ.

There have been only four people in the history of mankind that have filled their house: Adam and Eve—who were whole but eventually gave out rooms to spirits, Enoch—who chose relationship with God over the sins of his fathers, and Jesus—who never walked in sin but went about doing the work of His Father. Everyone else has contended with spirits living inside them, and unless these spirits are dealt with, the spirits remain non-paying tenants who demand rent from the owner of the body. Even Paul struggled with this sin that dwelled within him in Romans 7.

When we let sin or spirits cohabitate within us, we are allowing the man of sin who exalts himself as god sit upon the throne in the temple of God. We are the temple of God and the throne is our hearts.

II Thessalonians 2:1-17 ...the man of sin is revealed, the son of perdition, who opposes and exalts himself above all that is called God or that is worshiped, so that he sits as God in the temple of God, showing himself that he is God...For the mystery of lawlessness is already at work...whom the Lord will consume with the breath of His mouth and destroy with the brightness of His coming. The coming of the lawless one is according to the working of Satan, with all power, signs, and lying wonders, and with all unrighteous deception among those who perish, because they did not receive the love of the truth, that they might be saved. And for this reason God will send them strong delusion, that they should believe the lie...

It takes completeness of identity to fill the house so that there is no room for spirits. It takes completeness of understanding who the Godhead is to fill the house with Their fullness.

Ephesians 1:22-23 And He put all things under His feet, and gave Him to be head over all things to the church, which is His body, the fullness of Him who fills all in all.

Some Christians believe that we drive spirits out of our lives by *"starving"* them—by resisting the temptation under our own will power. I have never seen a spirit leave because he was bored or *"starved out."* I have seen them idly sit within the heart of a person, waiting to be activated into action or to be passed onto a family member. All spirits must be dealt with and cast out just as the children of Israel were to destroy all the inhabitants of the Promised Land.

Our human soul lives in this boarding house, which leaves plenty of empty rooms inside for others. That space inside is partially filled with the generational spirits we inherit from our parents such as bitterness, rejection, fears and addictions. That is how every human being is born—one body filled with their soul and various generational spirits that have followed the family line throughout the generations.

When we cast out the spirits, we need to fill that space with the Holy Spirit and Word so that there would be no room for the spirit to return with his friends.

Matthew 12:43-45 When an unclean spirit goes out of a man, he goes through dry places, seeking rest, and finds none. Then he says, "I will return to my house from which I came." And when he comes, he finds it empty, swept, and put in order. Then he goes and takes with him seven other spirits more wicked than himself, and they enter and dwell there; and the last state of that man is worse than the first. So shall it also be with this wicked generation.

As we grow, every trauma, shock or fearful experience opens a door for more spirits to enter such as fear, stress and anxiety. They move in and take up residence in our flesh, controlling our emotions, chemistry and even our DNA through the over-or-under stimulation of glandular hormones. Some examples of this are:

- Anorexia moves into the stomach
- Violence moves into the muscles
- Fear moves into the adrenals
- Fear of abandonment moves into the lungs creating asthma
- Etcetera

This list is as long as the number of human diseases or malfunctions. And apparently, it is increasing, i.e. HIV, Bird Flue, SARS, etcetera.

Sometimes we even make pacts with familiar spirits to help us out of a very bad situation, such as all abuse, sexual molestation or even lack of nurturing by our parents.

When we are saved, we are given the key and ability to get rid of these spirits, as it is part of salvation. But being saved does not eliminate the spirits that cohabitate us. We must recognize them, take responsibility for their being there, and cast them out in the name of Jesus ourselves or through deliverance ministry. This may be contrary to some teachings, but even Paul talks about this.

Romans 7:15-25 ...But now, it is no longer I who do it, but sin that dwells in me. For I know that in me (that is, in my flesh) nothing good dwells; for to will is present with me, but how to perform what is good I do not find. For the good that I will to do, I do not do; but the evil I will not to do, that I practice. Now if I do what I will not to do, it is no longer I who do it, but sin that dwells in me. I find then a law, that evil is present with me, the one who wills to do good. For I delight in the law of God according to the inward man. But I see another law in my members, warring against the law of my mind, and bringing me into captivity to the law of sin which is in my members. O wretched man that I am! Who will deliver me from this body of death? I thank God— through Jesus Christ our Lord! So then, with the mind I myself serve the law of God, but with the flesh the law of sin.

When we receive the Holy Spirit, He moves into the available space within us.

I was walking down a street on my way to work in London, Ontario. Suddenly, I was taken inside myself. It was very dark and foreboding inside. As I wandered around from room to room, I saw a very small flame huddled in one corner. It was so tiny in relation to the potential space. It was so contrasting I went up to the flame and asked it who it was. He answered, speaking with strength although it appeared small, "I am the Holy Spirit."

The Lord is a gentleman. He will not remove from us those spirits we want to hang onto, even though we may be hanging onto those spirits due to lack of knowledge. We must recognize that they are there and our desire must be to walk with God more than to keep that which is familiar. The Lord will not break up a friendship we want to hold onto. We have to choose Him because we love Him. He will never force us to love Him under any circumstance. He has given us freedom to choose.

> *Joshua 24:15 And if it seems evil to you to serve the LORD, choose for yourselves this day whom you will serve, whether the gods which your fathers served that were on the other side of the River, or the gods of the Amorites, in whose land you dwell. But as for me and my house, we will serve the LORD.*

For the next two weeks after the vision above, I went through a period of time where every traumatic episode of my youth was relived and, at each step, I made a new decision for God and love rather than Lucifer and hate. It was one of the most incredible two weeks of my life.

Again, I found myself walking to work in London and I was taken inside myself. There I was again permitted to walk through several rooms. I did not realize but I had been delivered of several spirits during the weeks between these two visions, and now, as I walked through the rooms, they were empty and swept...and very much brighter. I stretched out my arms and was stunned by the amount of room inside—there was suddenly elbowroom. When I came into the room where the Holy Spirit was staying, He was much larger now, filling the entire room not just the corner.

The degree to which we are filled with the Holy Spirit and gifts of God depends on how much of our life—which areas we work to free from possession by the alien enemy—we allow Him to inhabit.

For God to be effective in our life, we have to *allow* Him to be effective. For His gifts to be effective in our life, we have to receive them. He will not force them on us just as He will not force Himself on us. Part of the co-laboring with God is to receive and accept what He gives—salvation, Holy Spirit, relationship, love, mantles, gifts, and much more. It sounds simple enough but remains a stumbling block for many.

Lucifer cannot really steal or destroy that which was intended for man, although he will continue to try. To say that he literally steals or destroys what God has created or given is to say that he literally has the ability to do so.

> *John 10:10 The thief does not come except to steal (take away by stealth), and to kill (sacrifice, immolate), and to destroy (put out of the way entirely, abolish, render useless). I have come that they may have life, and that they may have it more abundantly.*

What he can do and what he does do so very effectively is to prevent it from coming forth. Lucifer works very much like the Second Heavens he is condemned to. Just as the Dark Brane (scientific name for the Second Heavens) is invisible to the naked eye because it does not emit any discernable light whatsoever and it is seen only as it distorts and bends the light of distant visible stars, Lucifer, although invisible to the people of this realm, is seen only as he distorts the truth. As he distorts the truth and the answers to our prayers and petitions, he effectively hides from us those answers and gifts, thus stealing them from us by slight of hand. By stealing those answers and gifts, he kills our effectiveness. As he kills our effectiveness he efficiently destroys the Bride from coming forth— individually and corporately.

He cannot keep the answers to our prayers, but he can hold them up indefinitely. We must intercede in prayer, just as Daniel had to pray for twenty-one days for his answer.

> *Daniel 10:12-14 Then he said to me, "Do not fear, Daniel, for from the first day that you set your heart to understand, and to humble yourself before your God, your words were heard; and I have come because of your words. But the prince of the kingdom of Persia withstood me twenty-one days; and behold, Michael, one of the chief princes, came to help me, for I had been left alone there with the kings of Persia. Now I have come to make you understand what will happen to your people in the latter days, for the vision refers to many days yet to come."*

The most simple, basic truth of all life is this: From out of the Father who envisions the endless possibility of all creation, the Holy Spirit draws it into the Third Heavens and then from there into the First. We each came from the Father before we were conceived.

> *Jeremiah 1:5 Before I formed you in the womb I knew you; before you were born I sanctified you; I ordained you a prophet to the nations.*

> *Isaiah 49:1 ...The LORD has called Me from the womb; from the matrix of My mother He has made mention of My name.*

In order to have what God intended for man move from His realm into our realm, there must be two co-laboring together. God must first create it, and man must secondly accept it. Then it transfers from one to the other. It is called the "Yay and amen," the, "Hallelujah, praise the Lord and thank you very much!"

But, if there is a third party that effectively breaks that union of co-laboring, then what was intended to be brought into this

148

dimension is thwarted. In other words, it is stolen from man. But, it remains in the Third Heavens for someone to claim it.

We must learn and remember who we in Christ, understanding the privilege and authority that comes with our identity in Him. When we do not walk in our identity in Christ we cheat God. When we do not walk in the authority that comes with that identity in Christ we cheat ourselves.

One day, I walked through a city and suddenly I saw all three heavens at the same time.

In the natural, I could see hundreds of people in the streets walking, standing, drinking their coffee, chatting, talking on cell phones, waiting...all with their vibrantly colored clothing. The buildings stood as sentries alongside the streets; poles with connecting wires adorned the streets; people milled on the sidewalks and crossed at the corners; cars sped by on their way to whatever wherever....

Life in this *heaven* was bustling, noisy and smelly.

While looking at life in this heaven, I suddenly saw the black-ness—varying degrees of very dark grayness—of the Second Heavens overlaying this one. In this heaven were millions of spirits, mere shadows of their once glorious splendor, gray specters that were mere wisps of smoke...spirits of fallen angels. They hovered around the people of this world, darting in and out and around them. Great legions of them lived and worked in the people that walked along the streets, their eyes looking out through the bodies of their third-dimensional hosts. They crowded the streets, hundreds and thousands on each person. They darted in and around the cars, the buildings, everything that was around. There were so many spirits in this realm that they blackened the sun and colors of this world. They overshadowed absolutely everything as if they were a thick, heavy fog dropping all around.

While watching this life in both heavens, I suddenly saw the Third Heavens as well. It was absolutely stupendous. It was the first time I could remember, other than when I was very young, the outside gardens of the kingdom of God. I could see the throne of God, the courts and palaces. In the streets of the city roamed angels and people alike. There was a tremendous garden running through the city to beyond the city borders with a river running through it. On both sides of the river was the most glorious grass adorned with the most wildly vivid colored flowers of rich purples, reds and gold I have ever seen. The river flowed throughout the land to far beyond the horizons behind me. Around me angels filled the gardens, walking in small groups, conversing easily about the events of the day or some mystery...I could not actually hear. Off on the horizon before me there were hills and trees of the most glorious splendor, a brilliance that seemed to emanate from within each leaf, petal and blade. The life was thick and luxuriously rich with color and scent. Unlike the Second Heavens, there was not the congestion of spirits occupying such a small space—even though the Second Heavens actually holds ninety percent of the known universe, the fallen spirits seem to congregate in the area of the earth.

There was a constant stream of angels going to and from the Throne Room. And here on earth, beside, behind, in front and above several of the people were scores of angels guarding over them. They moved wherever the people moved, keeping, covering, and protecting them. Sometimes, fallen spirits were warded off from attack—we may never know how often these attacks by the enemy are thwarted by our Guardian Angels. Sometimes these angels actually prevented the people themselves from doing something God forbade or wished to keep them from—a step that would take them past that point of redemption. I have heard of people who were unable to kill someone else because no matter how hard they struggled, something prevented them from driving the knife home.

I could see angels speaking into the ears of people, whispering words given them by God. In the other ear, I could see fallen spirits whispering words given them by Lucifer. There was a constant warfare for the soul of man going on between angel and spirit. All the while, man continued to walk down the street oblivious that he was walking amongst thousands of angels and spirits, walking in the First, Second and Third Heavens at the same time.

The warfare is in our minds—it is our choices.

I also saw all around the streets, over the people and beside the people, gifts and promises covering the streets, grounds and hills everywhere. Every promise the Lord had for a person, city, state, country, hemisphere, and corporate bride was lying there waiting for someone to claim it and take it for themselves. It was a matter of believing, receiving and seeing its possibility to be able to take it. The land was covered with millions of these promises, like parcels untouched and unclaimed, within reach but hidden from view because of the sin and unbelief of man.

At the same time, I also saw a net of blackness lying on the ground, over buildings and trees, wrapped around the hearts of people. This net of blackness was the curses brought on by the words and deeds of our generations, lying there ready to trap all that it possibly could. This net kept the words and promises of God from taking proper root, and it lay like a net of acid eating away at the world and its people, keeping everything it touched in bondage like the snare of the fowler.

I saw that, when the veil is taken away from our eyes and we see the spiritual world at the same time, we can actually wade through an ocean of promises that lay all around us and pick them up like one would pick up items in a grocery store. Every word that God has spoken over each person or town lays there waiting to be fulfilled.

Lamentations 2:17 The LORD has done what He purposed; he has fulfilled His word which He commanded in days of old...

John 15:25 But this happened that the word might be fulfilled which is written in their law...

Every word of God will be fulfilled. Every promise will be fulfilled. Every anointing will fulfill its appointed work. Every mantle will be worn. Every declaration will come to pass. There is only one thing that is constant and true in life and that is that the Word of God will be fulfilled...no exceptions.

The only non-given is who will fulfill it. If not me and you, then another will pick up the mantle. If not me and you, then another will get the miracle. If not me and you, then another will be anointed. If not me and you, then another will receive the promise. It all depends on who will reach through the veil of this realm into the Third Heavens and claim the promise/mantle/word and draw it into this realm.

The only non-constant is who will love the Lord enough to become that Bride. If not me and you, then another will lay their head on His breast. If not me and you, then another will hear His sweet voice call out their name. If not me and you, then another will attend the wedding as the Bride of the most desirable groom in the entire kingdom—the Son of God. If not me and you, then another....

What can possibly be of more worth than a relationship with the very God who created us? What could possibly be of more importance or value than to be loved by and give love to the God who created us? What could He possibly give us that would be worth more than Him...the giver of everything?

Where and how did we learn to be a "*gimme*" people instead of a "*love me*" people? However did we learn to bite the hand that made us? When did we ever decide that it was better to mock, dishonor and hate the very One who not only gave us the breath of life but sustains that breath of life? How did we ever lose the reality of whom He is and who we are?

When man truly learns this truth in his heart, we will have returned to the place we were in the Garden—spiritual Eden. Corporate mankind must return to the place where he strayed from the path and sinned in order to continue on the plan God has for him. Until that time there is nothing new under the sun. When we arrive at the point where our spirit man is alive and we are truly and fully co-laboring with the Lord, sinless and free, then we can begin to see new things in the earth and the universe. When the sons of God are made manifest, the entire universe will be free to continue on the path of constant newness that God had intended for us all along.

Ecclesiastes 1:9-10 That which has been is what will be, that which is done is what will be done, and there is nothing new under the sun. Is there anything of which it may be said, "See, this is new"? It has already been in ancient times before us.

God is waiting...the whole of creation is waiting for the manifestation of the sons of God. (Romans 8:19-23) We can be that generation. Enoch was the first of that generation. He walked through that veil of the heavens right from the First Heavens into the Third Heavens without missing a heartbeat. There was no hesitation. There was no query. He simply walked through the veil from one plane to the next, reaching out and making the reality of his future tomorrow his present today.

Lucifer had tricked Adam and Eve into forfeiting the deed to the Garden of God, the world he had not so secretly coveted. The first couple had traded the inheritance of the firstborn for that proverbial bowl of pottage, in this case, a piece of forbidden fruit.

Lucifer assigned several of his fallen angels the actual job of possessing the couple, for he has never inhabited a man but conducts business from his office—an emperor sending out his troops, each following the strict rule of organization.

Shame, fear, anger, bitterness, grief and many others moved into the couple with one goal in their minds. They were bent on the couple's destruction.

Adam lost himself in his work further developing the reason there began to be a breach between him and Eve in the first place. What was his desire became his curse, as it was with Eve, the serpent and Lucifer. If their desire had been for God, it would have become their blessing. But when they stepped out of God's will into sin, their desire became their curse.

The serpent, which hoped to be greater than all other animals because of his intelligence, was now cursed above all animals. Lucifer, who wanted the Bride his entire life, would now eat the dust of mankind after they died, gaining absolutely nothing. Eve, whose desire was to regain her husband's attention and love, would now suffer his authoritative abuse to rule over her. Adam, who desired recognition for the work of his hands, was now cursed to work harder for less fruit.

In a very short time after they were cast out of Eden, relative to the length of time they were in the Garden, the Lord caused Eve to have two sons—Cain and Abel. These were the first and second sons born of Adam and Eve. Adam and Eve had several other sons and daughters, but Cain was Adam's favorite, his reward, and Abel was Eve's favorite, her solace.

Eve was of the same exact genetic makeup as Adam, having been made from the rib of his body. Brother and sister married each other, their genes still pure and untainted by sinful degradation. Without the contaminations of centuries of sin-caused-disease, siblings could marry without fear of diseased children.

Bitterness marred their previously happy countenance. There is no evidence recorded to suggest that Adam ever repented from his sin, for bitterness had partnered with his heart. He labored silently, bowed under the burden of his labors, to provide food, shelter and clothing for his growing family.

Adam and Eve had been tutored in the sacrificial requirements for temporary redemption for their sin. The Lord had revealed to them what was needed, and they had dutifully taught their children.

In a matter of seconds, I was downloaded about ninety years of the couple's daily life. It was a movie of daily grind and building. Every day Adam left to go to the fields he was clearing for crops. He knew the theory of farming, but now he had to perform the practical. There was not the same sense of satisfaction as there had been in the Garden. There was only hard labor. He built a house for his family. He hunted and herded the animals he would raise. He cleared several acres of land for farming. He scoured the countryside to locate the seeds of those plants he would grow and he began to cultivate the crops that would become their staple.

Eve made clothes from the skins of the animals Adam killed. She tended the cattle and sheep that Adam rounded up, domesticating them from their wild habits. She eventually learned how to spin wool and made clothes with varying degrees of success. Some did not look so good, but she learned over time how to make a good suit of clothes for both herself and Adam, and later the children. She learned how to cook the meat and produce a dish that was savory and tasty.

The continual orchestra of angels singing praises to God no longer lulled their nights into sweet sleep. There hovered above and around them a continual silence, something they had never known before. Any praise and song that was to fill their world now had to be made by their own voices. They had learned the songs, but somehow, those songs were no longer as close to their hearts as they once were. But they were the only songs the couple knew. Once in awhile, they both created new songs about the labors of their new life until those songs took over their repertoire crowding out the praises of God with the heartbreak of life. The song I heard Eve sing as she milked the cows is written below.

> *"We once lived in glory...the peace of the earth sang to us.*
> *But now, our labors are hard. The earth is silent. The*
> *heavens are silent.*
> *There is an ache in my heart as I tend to the sheep.*
> *I have lost the glory. Our work is hard. Our labors weary*
> *our hearts."*

After the trauma of the situation had passed, life had finally settled into a daily routine. The Lord no longer came to meet Adam and Eve in the cool hours of the morning to walk with them through the Garden. The angels no longer came to teach them the wonders of creation. The angels were close, but they were no longer visible to the natural eyes of Adam and Eve. The world they lived in had grown suddenly dull and simple, inglorious by the standards they once knew.

The Lord waited to hear from them, but they seldom called on Him. They could no longer hear Him talk to them as He had done before. The Lord had not grown silent, but their ears no longer heard the words spoken from the spirit realm unless the Lord spoke audibly to them so their natural ears could hear. Their spirit man had died, no longer able to hear or feel or see....

Eve continued to talk to the Lord from time to time. She acknowledged Him throughout her day, still appreciating His hand in the world. She sang lullabies of the songs she learned from the angels to the babies who suckled at her breast. She shared with them stories of life in Eden before they were cast out of the Garden.

Adam did not feel the same. He brooded under the weight of his lot in life and the things that he had lost; regretting his decision, but bitter not repentant. He could not forgive God for what He had done to him, and Adam, to his dying day, was angry with the Lord.

He too shared stories of his life with his children, but they were stories that were stained with the growing bitterness in his heart. Cain took the stories to heart, letting it sear his own heart with the bitterness of his father. Abel, on the other hand, grew more like his mother, as did the other children, for Adam's eyes were for Cain only, his first-born son.

As the days and labor pressed hard upon Adam, sweat poured down his brow from the constant challenges of making his way in this new, unfriendly environment. He awoke to the troubles of the day and fell into bed weighed down by the unfinished tasks. Every day was faced with the need for inventive strategies to tame a wild frontier.

With each passing moment, his great sacrificial love for Eve turned into a deepening pool of resentment. Watching her mirrored his own life. Sex, however, was the saving grace of his situation. It soon became the sole purpose of their relationship. Love no longer played a role.

Adam's heart was stretched to be filled with a greater depth of retaliation and anger. His words were cutting and his actions short towards his wife and family. He remembered what he gave up, and the more he realized what he had lost, the more he hated his new life. He talked less and less with Eve.

Soon his love withered into a cesspool of hate for his lot in life—the difficulties caused by a sinful wife who God had made and insisted Adam take as his mate. There had been no choice. There were no other women offered. The woman who was supposed to be the beginning of all life was in fact the end of his life, for because of her, he was condemned to death only after a lifetime of endless, backbreaking labor. Forgetting it had been his choice, Adam stayed in his pool of hatred, wallowing. He had crossed that thin barrier between love and hate.

With his growing hate, Eve's isolation and loneliness increased. Her children became her life, but it was not enough. She would see the worst thing a mother could ever witness. In her lifetime, she would see not only her first son murder her second son, his brother, but she would see the demise of everything good God had placed in mankind. She would witness war between the families of her own children. She would observe the degradation of women within only a few generations. She wept tears of anguish, tears of sorrow and tears of desperation as she saw the fall of mankind, her own children. Luckily, she and Adam died before the flood destroyed the world...and all their children.

CHAPTER SEVENTEEN

Cain and Abel

When Eve had her first child both she and her husband were amazed. Neither had ever seen nor imagined such a small human—everything about him was so very small. Eve could not have anticipated such agony having not known a minute of pain before. But now, childbirth was a terrifying and excruciating experience. Although the labor screams, tears and sweat lasted only for several hours, the fear and expectation of the first painful contraction gripped her causing the labor to become harder. Adam, distraught because there was no way for him to help, was beside himself with no idea of what to do. His bitterness dissipated for the moment in the face of her terrifying need. He had seen animals have their young but they didn't scream…and this was very personal.

When the baby came forth, they both wept, overcome by the sheer emotion and amazement at the sight of the first baby ever seen in creation. For a moment, there was a spark of hope for their marriage. She called the boy Cain, meaning "*possession*." He was the first *thing* that was truly theirs, for Cain came out of her belly and the seed of Adam's loins.

Adam was enthralled with the child. He looked upon Cain as a small reward for his life of misery and a helper to lessen his burden. He raised Cain to follow in his footsteps, those of a farmer who raised crops and tilled the land. He taught Cain all he had learned and all that he felt.

Cain was a bright lad, taking after his parents. He still had a great deal of capacity of mind, as sin had not degraded it to the condition it is in today.

Eve felt even more alone as the closeness of Adam and Cain grew stronger. Cain was like his dad, inheriting his mannerisms and spirits.

This was a first for Lucifer and his cohorts. Excitement rang throughout the cold, hard tenements of fallen angels. They had established strict ground rules for possession and the mission they had adopted. When Adam sinned, he opened the door to rebellion, fear and anxiety. He took the fruit of the tree from Eve out of rebellion to the word of God. The spirits of fear and stress moved into Adam's body immediately as the door was opened. He took offence to the curse God proclaimed over him and bitterness entered into Adam. He then blamed Eve and God for his problems, unable to accept his own responsibility. Unforgiveness soon gave room for resentment, retaliation, anger, wrath and hatred.

Man had received the spirit man when the breath of God gave him life. But the spirit man died when man sinned. However, God left the conscience behind which acts as a sense of discernment to help man find his way back to God. It is that same conscience that protects man from the intrusion of spirits by instructing him to avoid things that would open doors for those spirits to enter.

Conscience is the same as a lock on a door. The intent of the lock is to protect the spirit and soul of man by keeping the door closed so that bad things are locked out and good things are kept in. The lock can be opened allowing the things of God or the things of Lucifer to come into the soul of man. However, if the conscience is seared by continually seeing, hearing or doing wrong, it will become desensitized or dead leaving the door to swing freely on a hinge. This will allow not only spirits free access to us but it causes us to lose our anointing, ministry and walk just as an open door lets the cold in and heat out.

We have many such locks on our conscience; because one is broken does not mean all are. If one's conscience is seared regarding drug misuse, it is a small step to child abuse, theft and violence. Although the conscience prevents child abuse, theft or violence in the beginning, the seared conscience of drug misuse will weaken to access one of the other areas of conscience until they are all seared. It is a safe bet that the entire conscience becomes dead as the searing increases because one group of spirits will always cooperate to bring in others for the total downfall of the person they inhabit.

A good example of this is pornography. As the first shock of seeing a pornographic scene assaults the eyes, the conscience instructs the onlooker to look away. The door is closed. But if the onlooker does not look away, the view acts like a lock picking burglar. The door is jarred opened, and a spirit of lust enters. This spirit of lust stimulates the physiology of the person giving the sensation of both a rush and pleasure. The next time a pornographic opportunity arises, the combination to the lock is already known by the first spirit that entered; that spirit then unlocks the door once more. The door is opened, and another spirit of lust enters, joining the first one in its task to cause the person to curse themselves by the breaking the law of God.

Because the combination of the lock is known, it is easier and easier to get access until the conscience is seared. A man is then trapped by the seared conscience that has let a plethora of lust spirits enter into him. He must then reactivate the lock or conscience manually. He does this by getting rid of the spirits he has let in and turning away from the temptation. In the case of pornography, he must turn away from it each time the temptation returns. Eventually, the conscience is revived, the lock is restored, and the conscience is once again active.

1 Timothy 4:1-2 Now the Spirit expressly says that in latter times some will depart from the faith, giving heed to deceiving spirits and doctrines of demons, speaking lies in hypocrisy, having their own conscience seared with a hot iron

In the case of inherited spirits, the process is simple. At the trauma of being driven out of the Garden of Eden, the door opened and the spirit of bitterness entered Adam. Every time he remembered what he had given up for Eve, his wife, of his own free choice, he again opened the door for another spirit of bitterness to enter.

Unforgiveness, retaliation, resentment, anger, wrath and hatred are all members of the kingdom of bitterness.

When Adam had sex with Eve, his wife, the action of sexual intercourse opened the door to evil. The spirits in Adam flowed through the fluid from Adam to Eve. I saw the spirits reside in the fluid of the man and combine with the fluids of the woman, moving out from the point of contact within the new host via the increased blood flow caused by the stimulation. The woman or man through the act of sexual intercourse gave permission for this transfer of spirits.

Later on, Lucifer also developed this transfer of spirits by arranging a predisposition to sin through DNA manipulation. Lucifer had found a permanent opening to spread his kingdom throughout mankind through disease. But in the beginning, this transfer of spirits could only happen at the time of intercourse.

Lucifer later developed soul ties, which were a more permanent answer to his goal of transferring fallen spirits from one person to another to keep a people in bondage. He developed soul ties—will, mind and emotions—which are like express highways between two people, especially designed for the travel of spirits. I have seen the world of soul ties, using them at one time for my own agenda. They look very much like hollow, colored bungee cords connected between two people and can be thousands of miles long as distance is not relative in the spiritual realm. One person can have thousands of soul ties attached to them. If you look just at the world of soul ties, these super highways used for the ease of spirits to travel, the world looks very much like a massive spider web of colored threads with people at the junction points.

There are no such things as godly soul ties. They are the sole invention of Lucifer. There is love that knits two hearts together, but this is not to be confused with a soul tie.

The new invention of soul ties gave Lucifer and his fallen cohorts the availability of a continual open door to every human soul. Through these new travel lanes, they could speed up the possession of mankind and destroy the long awaited Bride effortlessly, preventing their descendants from ever seeking God. It was perhaps Lucifer's greatest innovation, his one insidious claim to fame.

The sexual open door also allowed the spirit of Bitterness that was in Adam to enter Eve's womb and attach itself to the embryo of Cain. This spirit resided in a dormant state in Cain, waiting until the repeated accusatory words and actions of Adam broke the lock of Cain's conscience allowing the spirit to function freely. As the conscience of Cain was seared, the door was left open and he added spirits to the bitterness already in his heart. He added jealousy, hatred, violence and murder to the spirit, completing the kingdom of Bitterness within him just by interacting with his family.

When Cain killed Abel, the first part of the inherited spirit of Bitterness' assignment was complete. Cain could have asked for forgiveness and repented to bring the cycle to a stop. However, he didn't and the second part of the assignment was completed—Cain's DNA was changed and murder mutated his conscience permanently so that his offspring would have an inclination to violence and murder.

Today, scientists argue about a gene that gives one the predisposition to violence and murder. Today, psychologists argue that the majority of children seeing a violent crime with a weapon will eventually commit a violent crime with a weapon. It has been proven that those who are molested as children molest others as adults. Children often become their parents or their victimizers because that is the second part of the fallen spirit's assignment for them.

In effect, the *conscience lock* on that door was broken throughout the generations. But only their continual turning away from the temptation, submitting that temptation to the Lord and consciously choosing righteousness, could they repair it.

Once the combination is known, which is how much temptation it will take to overcome the conscience, the internalized spirits can open the door anytime they like, inviting their cohorts to come into the person as well. For example, a person who has allowed a spirit of pornography into their soul will be open for greater degrading spirits such as lust, masochism, sadism, violence, rape, etc. These spirits can then, once inside, stimulate the glandular system that creates hormones in any way they like, changing the temperament and physiology of the person at will. These changes will eventually make their mark on the DNA of the person, mutating it, so their offspring inherit not only the spirit but also the tendency to allow that spirit to work in their lives.

This changed DNA will also result in a predisposition for disease. Genetic abnormalities and weaknesses are a direct result of generational DNA manipulation that follows through the family line, sometimes skipping a generation, but always showing up again eventually.

> *Exodus 34:7 keeping mercy for thousands, forgiving iniquity and transgression and sin, by no means clearing the guilty, visiting the iniquity of the fathers upon the children and the children's children to the third and the fourth generation.*

A person who comes from a long family line filled with bitterness, retaliation, hatred and anger can be born with cancer in the extreme case or will be born with a susceptibility to the cancer that has followed the family line. Generational spirits follow the family line in an intricate mosaic of assignment and designs, traveling through sexual intercourse, traumatic open doors, soul ties and attached familiar spirits.

Negative words spoken over a person will eventually open the doors for that person to accept and be in agreement with the associated spirit, and the spirit moves into the person to accomplish the assignment of the words. A curse against a person will dispatch a familiar spirit who will follow a family line until the curse is fulfilled, sometimes fulfilling the curse generation after generation; for example, poverty.

Lucifer concentrated all his efforts on Cain, realizing and exploring the mysteries of genetic mutation in this mankind who was formed from the dust—he had plenty of experience with the animals of a previous age. He wondered how much difference there was between the animals of old and mankind who was created from the same dust. He had the time from conception to death of his victim to wreak his havoc and bring his plan to full fruition. His scheme was perfect in its simplicity, following a twofold plan: 1. Separate man from God; 2. Cause mankind to curse himself. This twofold plan will prevent the Bride from being brought forth in her fullness.

Years later, Eve had another child, a boy she called Abel. His name meant "*breath*," for in Abel she hoped to receive a fresh breath of life. She doted on Abel as Adam doted on Cain. She tutored him, like his brother, in all that God required of them. She raised him to herd the sheep and livestock, as she did, leaving the farming and cultivation of the fields to Adam and Cain.

Cain had a thick dark, curly mop of hair. His rugged looks were handsome and appealing. His eyes were large and almond shaped, with circles of black. They were penetratingly striking. His smile was quick and had a boyish appeal of mischief. He was a beautiful child and an arrestingly handsome man.

Cain received the inherited Spirit of Jezebel from Eve and the kingdom of Bitterness from Adam. The two worked together to bring an end to the people of God and raise up a new religious system with Lucifer at the head.

Abel was lighter skinned and finer featured. His hair was more sandy and fine than Cain's. He was more of a thinker than his brother. His brow was always furrowed in deep thought as he contemplated the world he lived in and the God who made it. He had learned the stories of the fall and of the banishment from the Garden of Eden. He grieved at the loss. He did not hate God as did his father, but neither did he really know Him. But there was in Abel a need to know God more, although he did not really know what it was that tugged at his heart.

Often Abel would look to the west, trying to envision Eden and the cherubim and flaming sword held high, but he couldn't see it.

Adam and Eve had several children but none were like Cain and Abel, their two favorites. As the Lord had promised, her childbirth increased. The entire family learned how to live off the land outside of Eden, taming the world around them to make it habitable and comfortable.

The lands, although cursed, were still lush and bountiful, but over-grown and untamed. It was not as easy to harvest as before. Adam had to work the land and make it his own. His children worked at his side—those who farmed and those who herded. There were those who created music, learning the songs Adam and Eve missed and creating their own, singing about their love, passion, sorrow and labors. There were those who designed clothes and those who invented tools. Others explored the furthest reaches of the world. Each one followed the dreams in their heart for the world was theirs to take.

Before Adam and Eve sinned, mankind used one hundred percent of their brain. The Lord Himself as well as a plethora of angels had tutored them. In Eden they had an endless stream of visitors who taught them all things pertaining to the universe and the heavens. When they sinned their spirit man died, and a large part of their brain lay dormant—the part used for spiritual sight and understanding. They no longer saw any of their visitors...and certainly did not see their enemies, the new owners of the Garden of Eden.

Adam spent time in his fields along side of Cain. When Cain moved further out to clear land for himself to prepare a homestead for his own family, there began a friendly camaraderie between the two. Both were proud of the work of their hands, just as Adam had been in Eden. Life had taken on new meaning for Adam with the introduction of his children.

When it came time to offer the first fruits of their harvest to God, Cain and Abel did so as prescribed by the teachings of their parents. Through the process of complicated algorithms, mathematicians estimate that Cain was most likely one hundred twenty-nine years old and Abel was perhaps one to five years younger. At the time of the sacrifice, there were an estimated one hundred forty-two persons—brothers, sisters, nieces, and nephews—living in the earth. Cain and Abel stayed close to home, their two farms being closest to their parent's dwelling.

Cain reckoned that he worked much harder clearing, planting and tending his fields than Abel who simply watched his sheep and cattle, milking them, shearing their wool, butchering them and skinning them. Cain was the one with all the muscles from pulling out tree stumps and steering a plough. Abel was able to sit and contemplate the work of God while Cain labored by the sweat of his brow to produce his harvest....

Cain took the best of his crop, the work of his hands, and compromised. It was the sweat of his brow that watered the preciously

166

protected seeds. He labored to irrigate the fields through drought and winds, protecting them from the ravages of birds and rodents, protecting them from the ravages of animals that trampled the grains and produce under foot—while they helped themselves to an easy meal. He struggled to bring his harvest to the Lord while Abel simply walked his harvest to the Lord. Abel just watched as his animals dropped babies in the field with a resilience to grow. Abel could sit for long hours during the day, letting his animals feed off the land. Abel did not know what hard work was and Cain resented him for that. In his eyes, Abel did the work of women who could simply sit and watch their profits increase indefinitely.

As Cain presented his produce to the Lord, Abel took the best of his flock in accordance to the law that God had given his parents.

God had unfairly judged the situation by accepting only Abel's sacrifice. Cain fumed quietly over the judgment of God at refusing his sacrifice. Then one day, when the level of his seething rage had reached its zenith, Cain went into the pasture to confront his brother. The full measure of bitterness had welled up in the heart of Cain. Abel was not only the favorite of his mother, but now of God as well.

Jealous of his brother, Cain could not forgive God for accepting Abel over him. He could not forgive Him for refusing him like He had his father. He resented God for refusing the work of his hands and decided to go and confront his brother. He resented Abel for being acceptable for doing nothing.

Anger seethed in his blood, and when he saw how calmly Abel reacted to the confrontation, hatred fueled his motives even further. He picked up a rock and smashed it into Abel's head, hitting him repeatedly until his rage subsided. He watched as the look of surprise, worn like a mask on Abel's face, distorted into the agony of death. Cain had pushed the inherited bitterness from his father from resentment to murder.

Abel's blood cried out from the ground for justice, calling out the name of his murderer. Even today, the blood of every murder, rape and beating cries out to God naming the name of the attacker. The name called out is not the same as the names we give our children; it is the face and nature of the murderer, rapist or abuser. The blood carries the image of the attacker in its DNA, which is changed in an instant. The blood is witness to the atrocities committed against the person, and will be a witness at the Judgment Seat. I have seen the image the blood holds when another sheds it.

The Lord tried to stay Cain's plummet downwards by telling Cain that He was not a respecter of persons, it was simply a matter of doing what was required. Sin was baiting the trap for Cain, but he need not fall into it. He could overcome it, just as Adam and Eve could have overcome it. But Cain refused to listen. His conscience became seared as he dwelled upon the anticipated offence. He chose to listen to another voice that no longer needed a serpent, for the subconscious mind now heard the whispers of the fallen spirits that now dwelled within his heart.

With the fall of man, the fallen angels had the right to enter the domain of the First Heavens—in fact, the deed to the planet intended for man passed to Lucifer. They could come and go as they wished. Although man could no longer consciously see, hear, smell, sense or taste those of the spiritual world, mankind was subject to their influence.

Lucifer ordered the spirits to their particular assignments, the missions sifting through the set chain of command. He had a plan and agenda, and the spirits and mankind were used as pawns to bring that plan to fruition. His plan was to keep the Bride from coming forth so that they, especially himself, would be spared the agony of the Lake of Fire.

Although there are an unfathomable number of fallen angels, most of them stay in the Second Heavens until they are dispatched to the First Heavens to fulfill the directive given them by their governing commanders. Those few dwelling within Cain pushed his buttons, accusing God and Abel, and stirred up his adrenalin and hormone levels. They pushed him to such a rage that he forfeited any self-control killing his brother.

When Cain realized what he had done, he buried his brother hoping to hide the evidence of his crime. But he soon learned that the Lord was the God who sees everything.

Cain was later marked by God to save his life from his growing family who would want revenge upon him for the death of Abel. He was driven from the land and life he knew to become a fugitive and a vagabond—someone forced to wander continuously.

Cain took a wife from one of his sisters and moved eastward to the land of Nod where he wandered aimlessly until the birth of his son.

CHAPTER EIGHTEEN

The Genealogies of Adam

The Genealogies Of Cain

Adam had lost his son and Eve had lost her son. Consoling each other, Eve became pregnant once more. She bore another son and called his name Seth, meaning *"compensation."* She believed the Lord appointed her a substitute to replace Abel who Cain slew.

Cain moved away from the habitat of God's people who were still God's people even though their sin had driven them out of Eden.

I saw the spirits continue through the line of Cain, multiplying their hold by adding fear and guilt with the birth of each new generation. Lucifer's plan was going ahead on schedule. Lamech, the fifth generation of Cain, had married two wives and killed two men. He told his wives of what he had done with a certain amount of pride in his voice. The degeneration and propensity to sin was great in the family of Cain whose line was filled with the spirit of Bitterness. The kingdom of Bitterness always ends in some form of murder—a destruction of one's own life in some way or of another's life.

Cain, cursed by God to wander throughout the earth, settled down after the birth of his first son and built himself a city in defiance of the word spoken over him. Around the city he built a wall to protect his family from the retaliation of his kinsmen and God for the murder of Abel. Safe in the city, Cain set up a new religion based on the religion he had learned at the feet of his parents. He set up his own religious and sacrificial system, making his son Enoch the first high priest of this new religion. His training opened Enoch up to a religious spirit... and its co-worker, the spirit of Lust. The name of Enoch means "*dedicated to his god*," and Cain dedicated him to this new god he created, named from the whispers echoing in his own heart.

To Enoch was born Irad who was wild in his nature, inheriting the spirit of Lust and its sister spirit, Rebellion.

To Irad was born Mehujael who was smitten of God. He was the first one born with a deformity in his looks. To Mehujael was born Methusael, meaning "*Champion of God.*" Working very much like the first secret police, Mehujael furthered the cause of his god, enthusiastically making sure that everyone followed without hesitation the dogma and rituals set out by Enoch.

To Methusael was born Lamech, meaning "*Pauper*," and he was devoid of any redeeming factor at all. He considered women as property and married many wives to satisfy his lust. Lamech was the first to marry two women, completing the growing circle of hatred against women. Women were not treasured as the precious bride and helpmate God intended them to be. They were treated as chattel created for the benefit and pleasure of man.

War had broken out in the land. By now, there were more than four million people in the earth, by mathematical estimates. They all lived in an ever-expanding circle around the epicenter of Adam's farm. Adam and Eve were over six hundred years old and Eve was nearing the end of her childbearing years. The people of Seth and the people of Cain were two different clans distinguished by their faithfulness to a righteous God or the god of violence and lust.

Lamech killed a young man for hurting him and another for wounding him. Both offences were convictions of his lifestyle of depravity that was contrary to the institution of marriage set up by God.

Lamech had three sons. His third son, Tubal-Cain, crafted the very sword that Lamech used to kill his first two men—the first since Cain murdered Abel.

Tubal-Cain moved to the north and there he built a large complex designed for the manufacture of all things concerning metal. He designed and forged swords, knives, helmets, shields, pots, drinking goblets and more. He was so adept at his craft that he instructed and trained smithies and weapons manufacturers throughout the land.

Lamech's second son Jubal brought a new element into the religious rituals of Enoch. Musical instruments used in the ceremonies drove the people to new heights of religious ecstasy. The frenzy of their music ebbed and flowed to a crescendo of pleasure designed to excite the senses of those who listened. They were not the praises Adam and Eve listened to over six hundred years ago. This was music that stimulated the fantasies of the listeners, singers praising the deeds of murder, lust and the labors of life.

By the time of Lamech, war had broken out in the land between the people of Seth and Cain. It was a holy religious war fueled by the hatred of Lucifer against all God's people. Lamech started the war by breaking the fragile tensions between the two clans by murdering two men from the family of Seth.

<u>The Genealogies Of Seth</u>

In the land of Adam lived the line of Seth. Like Abel, his brother, Seth remained true to God, following in the steps of faith taught by his mother. They moved westward from the family estate.

To Seth, who married his sister Azura, was born Enos whose name means, *"Man,"* or *"Mortal."* After the birth of Enos, the line of Seth returned to God and began to call out the name of God in praise and prayer.

To Enos, who married his cousin Noam, was born Cainan who was a metal worker for his people. He created wonderful goblets, instruments and tools for his people, which were also sold to those in the land of Cain. He also created metal musical instruments that were used to praise and worship God, and Eve's heart was gladdened, as once again there was music in the land as there once had been in Eden.

To Cainan, who married his cousin Mualaleth, was born Mehalaleel, *"Praise of God."*

To Mehalaleel, who married Dinah, was born Jared, *"Ruler."* Patriarchal rulers were set up in the land of his people to maintain order over the increasing population of over twenty thousand people.

To Jared, who married Baraka, was born Enoch, his name meaning *"Dedicated."* Enoch walked with God. Men may have called on the name of God, continuing their sacrifices to the Lord in faith, but it was Enoch who had learned how to walk with God. Enoch was the first man in the fallen state who had a true relationship with God, choosing Him over all the world had to offer. He met with God every day, in the cool of the morning, walking with Him much like Adam and Eve had once walked with Him in the Garden. His every waking moment was spent contemplating the mercies of the Lord.

I saw Enoch walking through the fields and over the hills. He was a young man, by the reckoning of the ages of the antediluvian peoples. He walked towards Eden, the land that was marred by the fall of his great-great-great grandparents. The Lord lifted the veil from his eyes, and he saw for the first time the cherubim with the flaming sword, the sword that hid the Garden from the view of man. The cherubim, terrifying in appearance and countenance, looked down at Enoch as he drew near...but there was no fear in the heart of Enoch. The Lord had brought him to this place. There was awe in the heart of Enoch and the cherubim looked down upon the small man, smiled and bid him enter. Enoch walked into the Garden of Eden, the first man to return to the Garden since the banishment of man. He walked through the Garden, partook of the Tree of Life, and continued on his way to the throne of God.

Enoch simply walked from one heaven to another, from one dimension to another. There was nothing spectacular—nothing popped or exploded or changed. There was no lightning or fireworks. He simply walked from the First Heaven into the Third Heaven, seeing his future, believing what the Lord told him and showed him, and, instead of bringing what he saw in the Third Heaven into this reality, he took himself into the reality of the Third Heaven.

Enoch had inherited the same spirits from his parents, as had the other people on the earth. But he repented of those spirits; he repented of the sin of his forefathers, taking the responsibility of their effect in his own life; he chose God instead of his own way. He understood the relationship that was lost and he knew the Father and Son and Holy Spirit in restored relationship. In faith, he understood and accepted the sacrifice of the Son for his sin and wept for the fallen nature of man and the loss to God.

He understood the story of the fall of Lucifer and chose to turn away from his traps and temptations, falling instead on the mercy of God, building his relationship with the Lord every minute of every day.

He went about his Father's business preaching and teaching the people of God, bringing the word of righteousness back to mankind. And it was this rekindled understanding of the righteousness of God coupled with the Spirit of Evangelism that prompted two missionaries go to the land of Cain to reach their lost brethren. It was these two men that Lamech slew with pride. The reputation of Lamech reached far and wide. He had been the first to partake of two wives, and it was this reason that these two missionaries confronted at the very cost of their lives. In retaliation for the waves caused by this new evangelistic effort, the people of Cain declared a religious war on the people of Seth.

Enoch, the fifth generation from Seth, had found favor in the eyes of God for he was considered to be a friend by God. As Enoch walked into the Garden of Eden, Lamech was slaying his first two men.

To Enoch, who had married Edna, was born Methuselah, *"Man of the javelin."* Methuselah was only one hundred seventy eight years old when war broke out in the land filled with a population of four billion people. He became a soldier and a mighty warrior in the land. He too was a patriarchal ruler of his people. He raised his children and trained his brothers and cousins to be men of war. Methuselah was a man of the javelin, a long distance weapon. He was the greatest warrior known to man, as his prowess was responsible for his famed longevity.

To Methuselah, who married his sister Edna, was born Lamech. To Lamech, who married Betenos, was born Noah, over who it was prophesied that he would bring them comfort concerning the work and toil of their hands because of the curse of God upon Adam and Eve.

The land was in turmoil. The work was hard. There were over four billion people in the earth when Noah was born.

The land of Cain was one of great degradation. They were in full agreement with their god, Lucifer, and desired all the pleasures he offered them. They robbed and murdered innocent people at will. They treated women like chattel, raping whom they would when the fancy struck them. Their religious ceremonies were drunken orgies. Children were sacrificed and sold as young brides. They were a depraved people who thought of violence every moment of their day, dreaming of new ways to terrorize the people of God. Evil was in the land, and the people of God were rapidly falling victim to its enticements and pleasures.

Eventually, there was no righteousness in the land. The great persecuted evangelistic movement had dwindled to accept the depravity of the Cainites, mingling the two religious factions together. The Cainites, and consequently Lucifer, had won the war. He had brought down the Bride that God had created. His spirits worked without rest, assaulting without mercy the people God had created to worship Him, bringing them under the rulership of Lucifer.

There was a new elation and enthusiasm in the Second Heavens. Applause rang throughout the land as the fruition of Lucifer's plan was at hand. There were only eight souls left who still obeyed God, and their faith was teetering. Noah had brought up his sons under the strength of the teachings of Methuselah, his grandfather. He knew the reason for the war and understood the righteousness of God. He knew about his great grandfather, God had taken Enoch because of their relationship. He knew what was required and he taught his sons all he knew.

But they married women who had not been taught as stringently as they had. They married women of the land that had fallen into depraved chaos.

CHAPTER NINETEEN

Tenth Curse—
The Flood Of The Firstborn

Man had become exceedingly sinful. The sons of God, the line of Seth, saw the daughters of Cain and they were lured away from their faithfulness. They moved away from their God and compromised their practices and beliefs. They were taken by the enchantments and enticements of the sensual pleasures that the children of Cain offered. They began to fall one by one, but soon fell away in droves.

Lucifer took great pleasure in bringing down the Bride of the Son. He had millions of years to experiment on DNA manipulation and glandular activity to decrease or increase hormone production. Through spirit interaction within the flesh of the sons of God who married the daughters of man, the GH hormone levels were increased. These spirits lodged in the anterior pituitary gland, stimulating the excretion of pituitary adenomas causing an increase in the growth hormone. This caused abnormal growth patterns called *acromegaly* in the adults and *gigantism* in their children. Lucifer gained much satisfaction from the physical distortion of God's people.

Genesis 6:4 There were giants on the earth in those days, and also afterward, when the sons of God came in to the daughters of men and they bore children to them. Those were the mighty men who were of old, men of renown.

There were now over seven billion people on the face of the earth. War was always at hand as leaders felt to flex their muscles and gain more land closer to the center of things. Men of renowned who were great warriors and leaders rose up and led their people to covet greater fortune and easier lives.

Lucifer had won the battle. He had completely crushed the bride. This great creation that usurped his place in the heart of the Godhead was as depraved as he was.

The applause and admiration of the fallen host rose in the clamor of cheering accolades for their leader. He had proven his ability by stopping the judgment that would send them to the Lake of Fire. He had cleverly won the deed to the Garden of God, the planet Earth, and he had all but dismissed the possibility of the Bride ever coming forth.

A voice rang throughout the universes, crossing the veils of each heaven, and all the heavens trembled under the thunder of its sound. "The heart of man is wicked and every intent of his thoughts is bent on evil." (Jeremiah 17:9)

A smile crossed the shade of Lucifer's face. It was the proclamation he was waiting for. But the smile changed to outright horror as the proclamation continued and he began to realize his error.

"I will destroy man whom I have created from the face of the earth, both man and beast, creeping thing and birds of the air, for I am sorry that I have made them." (Genesis 6:5-7)

In a flash of the moment, Lucifer realized with utter terror that God was not only capable, but quite close to wiping out all He had created and starting all over again. And he knew in an instant that what was worse than the judgment of the Lake of Fire was to not exist at all.

Complete dread struck his heart, and the hearts of all those that fell with him. They knew only too well the power of God and that He alone could make that choice—continue on or start again.

This tenth and last curse was the curse of the death of the first born in Egypt...the complete annihilation of the first born of mankind in the antediluvian world.

This last curse was against Pharaoh himself. Like Lucifer, Pharaoh was a man who became god, and like Lucifer, Pharaoh was killed. Pharaoh was in direct opposition to God, keeping His people as slaves, just as Lucifer has done for millennia. The bible tells us that Pharaoh walked in the Garden of God, as did the king of Tyrus, linking the Pharaoh on earth with Lucifer, fallen cherub. (Ezekiel 31:8)

The Pharaoh settled legal disputes and led the religious rituals that held everyone in his kingdom. The Pharaoh was not only a god-king but was responsible for holding the balance of *Ma'at*, the rule of order over chaos that was waiting to envelope the world. Should Pharaoh fail, the entire world would suffer and descend into the unthinkable state of anarchy.

The symbols of the gods were the very tools of his office. He held the crook to reward the innocent, the flail to punish the guilty, the dual crown showing his authority to rule the two-lands of north and south Egypt (representing the First and Second Heavens), and the *Ureaus Cobras* or *Eyes of Ra* seeing all that the Pharaoh did, good or evil.

At his coronation, the *spirit of Horus* entered into Pharaoh and was thought to reside within him to guide him along the path of *Ma'at*. Pharaoh was believed to have been born through immaculate conception by *Osiris*, proving that the Pharaoh was divine.

The king's notional strength came from the support of the gods. All the pharaohs recognized the importance of this and they perpetuated the myth of divine conception as a means of legitimizing their claim to the throne.

Lucifer had perpetuated a line of belief that he was the creator who had always been, and therein he was divine, not part of creation. It was paramount to his control for that concept to continue, first with the angels before they fell, and then with mankind after they fell. Lucifer's main strength is his ability to perpetuate this lie and his power comes from our belief in his lies.

But when push comes to shove, God has the final power and authority in all things. The Lord God Almighty, Creator of all things, could just as easily wipe out everyone and everything from creation and begin again, if He so chose. And Lucifer finally realized this reality.

In the tenth curse, the Lord God destroyed all the firstborn, save eight souls (representing the Israelites enslaved in Egypt). He destroyed all the beasts He created except those that were secured on the ark of salvation. The plates of the earth were rocked giving up its reserves of water lifting the ark high above the earth; earthquakes below the rising water shook so violently no one could stand upon the earth; great windows were opened in heaven and water flooded upon the land like great waterfalls; it was the most horrific event the Garden of God had ever witnessed.

As the water fell from heaven and rose from the earth, with no end in sight, Lucifer and all his cohorts helplessly watched from the Second Heavens. At the pronouncement of this tenth curse, Lucifer' spirit army had already fled from every host on the earth that they had occupied. Those eight secured in the ark heard the screams of the dying; they heard the pounding, desperate hands of the condemned bang on the ark walls, screaming to be saved, repenting just enough to try to convince Noah to open the door; they heard the deluge eventually drown out even the last scream of death as the Lord cleansed His Garden from the evil and chaos Lucifer had caused.

I listened to the deafening cries of the lost and the fear of the Lord pierced my soul. He is the Lord God Almighty who is all powerful, all knowing, and all present. There is none like Him, no not one. When He makes up His mind to do something, no one, not even Lucifer, the great deceiver, can stop it.

Eventually, when the rains stopped and the earth ceased its shaking, the evil that was upon the face of the earth was sucked into the depths of the planet, burned in the great fires of the heart of the earth cleansing the earth from the evil it had endured for over sixteen hundred years.

CHAPTER TWENTY

Lucifer's Plan "C"

Lucifer went back to the drawing board. He had the right plan, but he and his cohorts were simply too uncontrolled in carrying it out. There needed to be some strategic refinements to make this work totally to their benefit. Lucifer could not risk the Lord wiping out all creation and beginning yet again. He could not fathom sudden non-existence after all those billions of years. He reasoned that life in the Lake of Fire would be preferable to not being at all.

For one year and seventeen days, all those in the Second Heavens watched, waiting for the waters to recede and for life to begin again. It was God's M.O.—He pronounced the curse on sin that had destroyed what He made, and then He would replenish what was destroyed when the curse was spent. Lucifer's team tightened their ranks to work more efficiently. They needed to maintain the strictest obedience if they were going to succeed, all agreeing that the totalitarian social structure of their new life was preferable to the Lake of Fire or non-existence.

In his sixteen hundred years dealing with the antediluvian peoples, Lucifer discovered that it was easier to get mankind to sin than it was the angels who took millions of years to fall. Man could not see what the angels had seen—the Godhead and all the supernatural world of the Third Heavens. Lucifer knew if he gave mankind something they could see, touch, taste, smell and hear, then he would have them in his power. He knew a false religion would do the trick.

When Noah and his family left the ark, Lucifer concentrated on his next plan—the modified plan.

He kept the attack of mankind going strong, but this time, it was very low key. Each fallen spirit had one assignment and they did not deter from that assignment until it was completed. No longer was mankind allowed to extinguish itself, nor was it allowed to completely wipe out the Bride, the people of God...that would be too dangerous for all concerned.

Lucifer designed his kingdom with strict laws and rules of engagements. All was still under the law of God, a law every fallen angel knew instinctively. I saw the picture of Lucifer's kingdom, which was rearranged after the flood.

Their assignments were simple—get man to curse himself by breaking at least one of God's commandments so there is a breach between him and God. It was not a hard task as the further man moved from Noah, the farther they went into idolatry.

Over each original family line of the three sons of Noah was assigned fallen Seraphim who maintained the original assignment over that nation. Under them were the fallen Cherubim who were head of the hemispheres where the family line resides. Under them were the fallen Archangels or Principalities in charge of each country within that hemisphere. As a person migrated into a different area, they were discharged from one authority to another until the assignments was completed for that family line.

I was shown a vision of the Man of Gadarenes. I saw Jesus go up to the man who was insane. The man had broken chains hanging loosely from his wrists and ankles as he ran screaming and frothing at the mouth. He was naked and looked a most frightful sight. His eyes were black from lack of sleep and great torment. His skin was sallow from lack of nutrition. His hair was knotted and frayed like an unhealthy lion's unkempt mane and he was as strong as ten men. The townspeople cowered in their homes, listening to the shrieks and screams that echoed throughout the darkness of the night and brightness of the day. The man would run out and terrorize a caravan or visitor, tearing them savagely, frightening their animals, and scaring

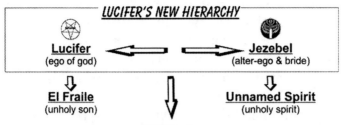

LUCIFER'S NEW HIERARCHY

Lucifer
(ego of god)

Jezebel
(alter-ego & bride)

El Fraile
(unholy son)

Unnamed Spirit
(unholy spirit)

24 Elders
in charge of specific areas of curses/works of the flesh
Adultery/Apostasy ●Fornication/Harlotry ●Uncleanness● Lasciviousness●
Idolatry ●Witchcraft/Pharmacea/Magic● Hatred● Variance● Punitive Zeal/Emulations ●
Wrath/Sudden Passion● Strife/Intriguing for Office/Partisanship●
Seditions/Disunion/Insurrection● Heresies ● Jealousy●
Murders● Lusts● False Swearers● Oppresser/Defraud● Evil Thoughts●
Thefts● False Witness/Untrue Testimony ●
Blasphemies● Rioting/Drunkenness● Clambering/Cohabitation●

7 Spirits of Lucifer
Abaddon ● Whoredoms●Fear●Antichrist●Error●Divination●Deep Sleep

Seraphim
in charge of original family lines
which originated from the line of Noah throughout their generations of dispersal

Cherubim:
Princes in charge of Hemispheres

Archangels:
Principalities in charge of Countries

Thrones
in charge of Cities and Villages

Dominions
in charge of gangs, rebels, social groups

Powers
in charge of specific families

Rulers of Darkness of This World:
Propoganda and Misinformation Bureau

Spiritual Wickedness in High Places
in charge of individuals

Common Angels:
Demons carrying out orders of all hierarchy
The majority of angels who had been cowards and ran in the Great War

183

them off. The town suffered from years of decreasing trade and dwindling economy until they became an impoverished town, the people too afraid to leave the boundaries of their homes to move away because of the threat of the insane man who lived in the caves.

When Jesus approached, the man ran out to meet Him, the spirits possessing him recognizing Jesus immediately. They had known it was Jesus from a long distance away, but the possessed man, still somewhat himself, wanted more than anything to be free...so he struggled through the shrieking threats screaming inside his head.

The shrieks were deafening and without end...the very endless noise of them driving this poor man to the brink of suicide, but they would not allow him to kill himself. Desperately, this man pushed his rebelling body out to meet Jesus. He could hear what the demons inside him were saying about Jesus, and he knew he could be freed.

Jesus cast out the legion of demons that possessed the man, and they begged Him not to send them to the pit, but to let them go into the pigs. Jesus consented and they went into the pigs and immediately ran the entire herd off the cliff into the waters where they died. The spirits returned to the Second Heavens for a new assignment.

The Lord turned to me and asked, "Why did I do that?"

I had no idea. It seemed counterproductive to me, for I had been taught that a spirit longs to inhabit whatever creature they can as long as they have a nice warm body to express their nature in...now their sole purpose in life.

The Lord smiled at my confusion and said to me, "They had not finished their assignment. Their assignment was not to make this poor man insane. The assignment given to them by Lucifer was to ruin the town, keeping them in a state of poverty and fear. They finished their assignment by destroying the last vestige of food the town had; this herd of swine. By killing the herd, they could return to their master and receive a new assignment. The enemy is not stupid—his plans are carefully mapped out and with purpose."

I asked Him, "But why did you permit that?"

He answered me, another smile on His beautiful face, "I was not sent here to free a town that would not receive Me. I was sent here to free a man who had cried out to My Father to be free."

The enemy is a very calculating, intelligent adversary who has an agenda, knows the rules, and has a tremendous organization behind him—even at only one-third of the heavenly host, the number in his ranks is beyond our ability to fathom. We tend to simplify his role, making our position weak for we believe one of two lies—1. The enemy is stupider than we think; 2. The enemy is more frightening than he really is.

The enemy is the most intelligent adversary we will ever encounter, with over fourteen billion years of experience, but he has already been defeated in every sense of the word.

Luke 8:26-39 ...there met Him a certain man from the city who had demons for a long time. And he wore no clothes, nor did he live in a house but in the tombs. When he saw Jesus, he cried out, fell down before Him, and with a loud voice said, "What have I to do with You, Jesus, Son of the Most High God? I beg You, do not torment me!" For He had commanded the unclean spirit to come out of the man. For it had often seized him, and he was kept under guard, bound with chains and shackles; and he broke the bonds and was driven by the demon into the wilderness. Jesus asked him, saying, "What is your name?" And he said, "Legion," because many demons had entered him. And they begged Him that He would not command them to go out into the abyss. Now a herd of many swine was feeding there on the mountain. And they begged Him that He would permit them to enter them. And He permitted them. Then the demons went out of the man and entered the swine, and the herd ran violently down the steep place into the lake and drowned...

I was shown another vision, which summed up the plan of Lucifer in the life of man. His only power is to entice us to curse ourselves. We are responsible for every sin we commit, either through commission or omission, and it is that sin that curses us and brings the judgment of death upon us. If we break one of the commandments of God, we sin and are therefore cursed. Jesus summed up the law into three commandments: 1. Love God; 2. Love others; 3. Love ourselves.

If we do not love God, we sin because we are not honoring our Father and Creator. If we do not love everyone else, we sin saying we are not honoring His friends, our brothers and sisters, thinking that we are higher than they are. If we do not love ourselves, we sin because we are calling God a liar because we are unworthy of His love.

When we sin, we step out of the protective hand of God because we have allowed a breach to separate our relationship. If we step out of the protective hand of God we move into Lucifer's grasp.

Numbers 31:16 Look, these women caused the children of Israel, through the counsel of Balaam, to trespass against the LORD in the incident of Peor, and there was a plague among the congregation of the LORD.

Lucifer concentrated on the man of the species, using man to destroy the woman and children.

God made man in His image, a replica of the nature of God—body, soul and spirit. Lucifer needed to destroy this image thereby corrupting man's image of himself. Instead of a man of God, he quickly developed through the generations, into a man of depravity, control and destruction—the image of his new father, Lucifer.

Man, in his growing need for power and supremacy, took his strength and used it for the plans of Lucifer, his new master. Woman was beaten down and sold as chattel, and the children were abused and exploited. By controlling the strongest of the species, Lucifer easily destroyed the woman, her children and the future of mankind. With this tactic, Lucifer hoped to effectively pervert the promised seed and keep him from ever coming forth.

Although the first born of mankind drowned in the flood, the sons of Noah struggled to follow their father's footsteps. Their wives were touched by the evil that pervaded the world and were not brought up in the righteous training of Noah. They knew what it was to be beaten down and feel of lesser worth than their male counterparts, and they carried those spirits of fear, anger and self-hate with them to the other side of the flood. This is not to suggest that Noah and his family were not touched with their own spirits, but they were the most righteous of man to be found on the earth.

*Genesis 6:9 This is the genealogy of Noah. Noah was a just man,
perfect in his generations. Noah walked with God.*

The Genealogy of Ham

It wasn't long after the flood that man again took a downward
swing. Noah planted a vineyard, made wine and fell on his bed in a
drunken state. Ham, his second son, the less noticeable middle child,
mocked his father's nakedness. Anyone who dishonors his parents
is someone who can and will dishonor God. Ham was no exception.
Welcoming bitterness into his heart, he was cursed by his father,
and he went out from his father's land and moved south-east into
Canaan, Arabia, and Northern Africa.

Ham had inherited the Spirit of Jezebel through the family line,
but it lay dormant within him. Spirits will lay silent waiting for just
the right moment to strike in a person's life to either affect the person
directly, someone closely related or manipulate the circumstances
around them.

It was the final rejection in a lifetime of rejection. Noah had
disapproved of Ham's choice of wife. Ham was the one who always
strayed just to the boundary of acceptable. Ham had been chastised
for showing up late for work. Ham had been disrespectful and a
challenge, as were his friends outside the family core. Ham just
could not make the grade in his father's eyes, and he eventually
stopped trying.

There is overwhelming and indisputable archaeological evidence
that all of the early Hamitic peoples were given over to the most
debased and degraded systems of thought and worship. Ham
purposely disregarded the words his father had taught him and quickly
divested himself of all knowledge of God. It was within only a few
generations of the Hamitic migration from Babel that the Canaanites
and Sodomites had already filled their cups of iniquity. They were a
people who cared little for anyone else but themselves...a spirit that
traveled throughout Hamitic generations.

Ham's people moved into the traditional site of Eden to spite
Noah, taking it for themselves and occupying it. The peoples of
Ham's line populated parts of Asia Minor, the Arabian Peninsula,

and eventually the entire continent of Africa. Africa was once known as the Land of Ham, and the Egyptians called their own land Kam. Their descendents are still alive today in many areas, including areas around the Mediterranean.

The Babylonian city of Kish was one of the earliest cities to be built after the Flood. Ham's children refused to be slaves or servants to the sons of Japheth and Shem. They were determined to rise as the dominating power. Cush settled in the land of Nubia and was father of the Nubians. Sebah was the father of the Sabaeans of the Arabian Peninsula. Havilah settled on the east coast of Arabia overlooking the Persian Gulf. Sabta settled on the eastern side of the Arabian Peninsula. Raamah's descendants settled near to the land of Havilah to the east of Ophir. Sheba was the southern neighbor of Yemen, one of the four 'spice kingdoms' of Arabia. Dedan settled seventy miles southwest of modern Taima and Sabtecha settled in modern Yemen.

Nimrod was probably the most notorious man in the ancient world who was credited with instigating the *Great Rebellion at Babel*, and establishing the foundations of paganism, including the introduction of magic, astrology and human sacrifice. He was worshipped from the very earliest times as *Marduk*, the Assyrian god of war, and as the Sumarian deity *Amarutu*. His image was incorporated very early in the Chaldean zodiac as a child seated on his mother's lap, and both mother and child were worshipped as gods. He was also worshipped as *Bacchus*, the name meaning, "*son of Cush*." The Caspian Sea was once known as the 'Marde Bachu,' or the Sea of *Bacchus*. One of the chief cities of Assyria was named Nimrud, and the Plain of Shinar was itself known as the Land of Nimrod. Iraqi and Iranian Arabs, of the line of Shem, speak his name with awe even today.

The Babylonian religion begun by Nimrod is still fueled today throughout the world by the spirits of Religion and Jezebel under the watchful eye of *El Fraile*. It is their sole purpose to make all mankind bow their knee to Lucifer.

When his uncles sought to bring Nimrod down, sending portions of his dismembered body to the ends of the earth as a sign against apostasy, Nimrod's wife fled, pregnant with her unborn son. When she returned with her newborn son, claiming he was Nimrod raised from the dead, she began two religions—the continuation of the

Babylonian religion, and the secret *Mysteries* religion. She enslaved the upper class and men of power through the secrets *Mysteries*, which were later handed down to the Chaldean Magicians.

The secret *Mystery* she taught was simple—her husband Nimrod, who was assassinated by Shem, had risen again. She was both mother and wife of the god Nimrod. This mystery has persisted throughout history in the story of *Osiris* of the Egyptians, *Mithras* of the Persians, *Dionysius* of the Syrians, *Bacchus* of the Romans, and *Tammuz* of Sumeria. All their stories are known as the collective *Ancient Mysteries.*

The first King of Tyre, Hiram I, developed the secret *Mysteries* into the beginnings of the Masonic religion that would later secretly sweep the world. Hiram I helped Solomon build the temple of God in Jerusalem. The three elements of the Masonic belief system are the Bible, the square and the compass. The Masonic belief system follows the same tactics set out by Lucifer himself—to present the truth of the Bible under a veil of complete deception; use the Biblical words and names, and the teachings of God, but twist the truth to condemn the believer.

Mizraim is a collective name for the people who settled in Egypt. Phillstim was the father of the Philistines, their land known today as Palestine. The Philistines effectively disappeared as a coherent nation but were absorbed by conquering nations. There were five lords of the Philistines known as Gaza, Ashdod, Askelon, Gath and Ekron.

The descendants of Put settled in close proximity to Egypt in North Africa.

The family line of Canaan settled the land that was later given to Israel. At the time of the Israelite conquest, the population of Canaan consisted of all the tribes that were descended from him. In spite of their Hamitic descent, however, the Canaanites spoke the Semitic language of Shem.

Zidon settled on the Mediterranean coast of Canaan, where his name is still preserved today in the city of Sidon. Originally known as Zidonians, his children were later called Phoenicians. Jezebel was Phoenician born. She inherited the spirit of Jezebel from the family line through Ham and was used of Lucifer to raise his high places in the land of God, something that was a continual problem throughout Hebrew history. The spirit of Ahab, which was also inherited through the family line, rose up in Ahab, working with Jezebel to destroy God's people.

Heth was the progenitor of the Hittite nation, the first nation to smelt iron. Heth's people are still in the Hittite capital Hattushash that is modem Boghazkoy in Turkey. Jebus was the father of those who settled in the mountainous regions of Judea; the original city of Jebus later came to be known as Jerusalem.

The Amorites conquered Babylonia. The Girgashhites settled east of the River Jordan between Galilee and the Dead Sea. The Hivites moved to the foothills of Lebanon. The Arkites were described as rebellious. Their city is known today as Tell-Arqa. The Shinites are still to be found today in the cities of Nahr as-Sinn and Sinn addarb. The Arvadites settled on the island known today as Ruad, and lies north of the bay of Tripoli. The Arvadites were famed in the old world for their skillful seamanship. Later, the island of Arvad was to play a crucial role in controlling certain areas of the mainland during the conquests of Alexander the Great.

The name of the children of Zemar is still preserved in the modern city of Sumra, just north of Tripoli. The Hamathites settled in the city known today by its ancient name, Hamath.

Although most of these peoples were destroyed or absorbed into other cultures, the powers that were assigned to them have not finished their assignment, and they still hover over the lands of their assignment insinuating their control over the inhabitants.

I saw that there are two forces covering the world—blessing and cursing.

The mantles, anointings and promises of God hover over cities and countries and family lines waiting to be claimed. There is in each family line a fountain of blessing, a calling on their lives that stems as far back as Adam and Eve, and Noah and his wife Emzara. If the chosen person does not fulfill their calling, it lies dormant in that family line until someone rises up to claim it. If the line dies with no descendants, the promises, blessing, mantles, and anointings are available for anyone to claim.

The curses and assignments of Lucifer hover over cities, countries and family lines waiting to be accepted. These also go back all the way to Adam and Eve, Noah and Emzara. If a curse or assignment fails over a person's life, it moves to the children, grandchildren, sisters and brothers. The curse or assignment will stay over a family until it is completed or cancelled by breaking its power and canceling its assignment in the name of Jesus.

Both are active waiting for a man or woman to choose his or her way. Man has a choice to break the powers, curses and assignments and claim the promises, mantles and anointings. The world could be free if man was to simply break the hold Lucifer has over him and his generations, which has already been overcome by Christ's sacrifice and redemption, and claim the promises that God has for him.

The Genealogy of Japheth

The people of Japheth moved northward. Gomer was the father of the Galatians and Phyrgians who later became known as the Gauls and Celts. From these people came the Germans, French, Welsh, Irish, Britons and the various Anglo-Saxons.

Magog was the father of the Tartars and Scythians whose descendants are predominant in modern Russia.

Madai was the father of the Medes, Persians and Hindus. Here we find the seed of the people of Iraq and Iran who moved south to control and conquer the Shemites and Hammites.

Javan was the progenitor of the Greeks, Italians, Spaniards, Portuguese, and the other peoples through Cyprus and the Mediterranean coasts.

Tubal was the progenitor of the Iberians, Georgians of the USSR, Cappadocians, and other Asiatic and European races.

Meshech was the father of the Muscovites tribes that now inhabit Russia.

Tiras was the father of the Thracians and Etruscans of Italy.

The Genealogy of Shem

The sons of Shem moved into Asia and Asia Minor. Elam was the father of the Elamites who settled near the Persian Gulf.

Asshur was the father of the Assyrians.

Arphaxad was the father of the Israelites, Arabians, Edomites, Moabites, Ammonites, Ishmaelites, Midianites, and other tribes of Asia.

Lud was the progenitor of the Lydians of Asia Minor and the Ludim of Persia and Chaldea.

Aram was the father of the Aramaeans who were later known as the Syrians.

The descendents of Shem and Ham settled the Arabian countries and all of Shem's people followed the Hammite false religions, with the exception of Israel who kept a fragile allegiance to their God, the true God of Heaven and Earth.

The Three Sons

As the people dispersed throughout the world, they were watched by the *Prince of the Air* and his government.

The first three fallen seraphim over the three family lines of Noah's sons were *Wóden* for Japheth; *Mardok* for Ham; *Baal* for Shem. Shem's descendents moved eastward into India, Asia and eventually North and South Americas. As this happened three more fallen seraphim were assigned to the new classifications of people: In India—*Bhahman*; in the Orient—*Chang'e*; in Central/South America—*Viracocha*. These fallen seraphim branched out with a pantheon of *gods* and *underlings* to encompass every facet of life.

Viracocha bathed South America in blood as a ritual sacrifice to the mistaken divinity of Lucifer. As the prior capital of Lucifer's kingdom, a special curse is placed on that land. The blood of the victims cries out to God and prevents any real or lasting freedom from bondage into the salvation of Christ. It is a curse on the world that must be particularly cleansed and freed through spiritual warfare and repentance.

Every country has their ritual sacrifices and murders that must be cleansed from the land to release the blessings of God and break the hold of Lucifer from that land.

I was shown that one day Lucifer and his government will all be driven from this world into the pit. Jesus died to take back the deed of the Garden of God and return it to man, but man must take an actual part. He must believe and receive the truth in order to co-labor with the Lord. The world will be free of the influence of Lucifer and his lies.

The Seven Nations Of The Promised Land

When Israel, a descendent of Shem, entered the Promised Land, they were instructed to destroy the tribes of Canaan that lived there. They were not allowed to cohabit with the people of the land, just as we are instructed not to cohabit with the spirits that are in our land. God promised to send His angel before them as they entered the land. He would be an enemy of their enemies and adversaries. He would send His fear and hornets to drive out the inhabitants of the land. But they were to make sure that everyone from these tribes was driven out of the land lest they corrupt the children of Israel.

Most of the tribes of Ham were destroyed throughout the long years since the dispersal of mankind after Babel. There were seven main groups left in the Promised Land. These were the Hittites, Girgashites, Amorites, Canaanites, Perizzites, Hivites and Jebusites. (Deuteronomy 7:1)

The Hittites

The Hittites represent the spirits that affect the body through fear.

The Hittite nation was descended from Heth whose name means *"terror and fear."* They represent the spirits of Fear, and were the first nation Israel was to overcome. The Hittite state was a military organization that used rigid laws to closely regulate every aspect of daily life. Fear causes Christians to give up the freedom and provision of God for regulations and rituals of a religion controlled by the doctrines of man and the spirits of Lucifer.

The Hittite nation represents the church of Ephesus, whose name means *"permitted."* Ephesus had the temple of *Diana*, which was the equivalent of the modern day Bank of England controlling all wealth in the known world. It was a sanctuary for the criminal, a city of refuge where none could be arrested for any crime, causing a village of thieves and murderers to spring up. Like the Hittites, Ephesus was a city to be feared.

They forgot their first love, Jesus and His salvation. They also forgot that they were rescued from fear and terror. They were told to repent and do the first works. Paul's letter to the Ephesians was one reminding them of the position and practice of a Christian, beginning his letter with praise towards God.

Fear and faith are in direct conflict with each other, each one demanding to be fulfilled. Fear shows us our lack while faith shows us our provision. It was fear that first caused Lucifer, Adam, Eve and the fallen angels to sin, and it is fear that keeps us in a place of sin.

The Lord represents Himself to Ephesus as the one who holds the seven churches in His right hand protecting them lovingly in the palm of His hand. He walks in the midst of His church, not as a stranger afar off, but as a loving friend who knows everything they need and want.

The reward for overcoming fear in our lives is to eat of the Tree of Life. It is to return to the Eden experience. It is to realize God's provision in all things through faith. It is to never ever consider a perceived lack in fear.

Fear breaks the tenth commandment of God—thou shall not covet. This was the beginning of Lucifer's downfall, and everyone's downfall from that point on. Fear, always showing us our lack, drives us away from the promised provision from God. It keeps us away from Him, causing us to forget that He died for our sins, saved us from death, and longs to supply everything for us.

The Girgashites

The Girgashites represent spirits that bypass God under the pretense that there is no cost.

The Girgashites, whose name means *"clay dwellers,"* were scattered throughout the land. They represent the works of the flesh that insists on having all the comforts of this life. They did not work to build cities, but gathered together building their temporary cities out of goatskin tents that effectively hid them from onlookers by clever camouflage. They were the second tribe Israel was to destroy in the Promised Land. The Girgashites represent the spirit of Divination.

Divination gives the hearer the hopes and dreams they want to hear. It tells them that what they are doing is right, lulling them into a false security. They tell the hearer that life is good and their future is filled with wonder and promise.

But the Lord reminds the church of Smyrna that the cost for walking with Him is everything…even their death. The Lord reminds them that the struggle against the works of the flesh is a hard one.

The Girgashites represent the church of Smyrna, whose name means "*myrrh*," which is used as anointing oil to anoint a believer or as an ointment to embalm the dead. There were two classes of Christians in the Smyrna church. There were those who were Christian, the wheat, and those who said they were Christians but weren't, the tares. There are those among the body of Christ who have given themselves over to this spirit of Divination, because they want so desperately to work for God, but want to do it their way without paying any cost. They have allowed a great deception to overtake them.

No reproach was given to the church because the Lord knew the struggles they had with the flesh. It was enough for them to over-come that struggle. The Lord represents Himself as the First and the Last, He who was dead and came to life, He who had successfully overcome every temptation.

To overcome the tribulation of Smyrna meant that they would not be hurt of the second death.

The flesh breaks the ninth commandment of God—thou shall not bear false witness. In order to keep our comfort, the flesh causes us to say whatever is necessary and whatever someone wants to hear. It causes us to lie. It causes us to make sure we come out on the winning end, saving our reputation and pleasure regardless of the cost to others.

The Amorites

The Amorites represent spirits that affect livelihood through moral compromise.

The Amorites, descendents of Shem, were a proud nation whose name means "to *boast self*" or "the highlander." Their capital was Babylon. Abram was called out of the pride of the Amorite kingdom to serve the living God.

The earliest recorded kingdom in Canaan, these Mediterranean peoples were thin mountaineers with fair complexions, blue eyes and light hair. They moved to the western slopes of Canaan and erected a *high-place* at Gezer. This "*high-place*" consisted of nine monoliths and was surrounded by a platform of large stones. The second monolith was reputed to have been polished by the kisses of the worshippers. Under the pavement of the sanctuary were jars filled with the bones of children and a few adults who had been sacrificed.

The Amorites represent the spirit of Antichrist who thought himself equal to God regardless of the cost to others. This is the kingdom of abortion, cannibalism, tyrants, blasphemers, patricide, matricide, pestilence, and every foul belief that seeks to raise itself up over the interests of anyone else.

The Amorites represent the church of Pergamos, whose name means "*height or elevation.*"

To the church of Pergamos, the Lord represents Himself as the Lord with the sharp, two-edged sword. He knew that Pergamos was the seat of Satan. The one thing he had against this church was that they harbored those who held fast to the doctrine of Balaam and the teachings of the Nicolaitans. Balaam was a false prophet who taught Israel to eat things sacrificed to idols and commit sexual immorality. He taught the children of Israel to cohabit with the daughters of Moab. This teaching was one of moral weakness supporting a freedom that became self-indulgence.

He who overcomes will eat of the true manna of God and will receive a new white stone with a new name written upon it.

Moral weakness breaks the eighth commandment of God—thou shall not steal. Moral weakness steals our love and our heart from God. It causes us to steal what others have to maintain our level of self-exaltation, stepping on whomever we must to reach the desired level of office in the church or world. This was the second step in Lucifer's fall when he brought the Godhead into a bad light in order to make himself shine brighter.

The Canaanites

The Canaanites represent spirits that hurt others.

The Canaanites, whose name means "lowland dwellers," were peddlers and merchants. This nation represents the spirit of Abaddon, which means "*destruction.*" These are the people who bring everything and everyone who are holy low through action, slander, innuendos and viciousness.

Hidden under their deceptive beauty and talents was a base, degrading side that ensnared their followers until they were eaten up by the destruction of their evil. The virile monotheistic faith of the Hebrews was continually in peril of contamination from the lewd nature worship with immoral gods, prostitute goddesses, serpents, cultic doves, and bulls.

El, their chief god, was the hero of sordid escapades and crimes. He was a bloody tyrant who dethroned his father, murdered his favorite son, and decapitated his daughter. *Baal* was the son of *El* and dominated the Canaanite pantheon. He is pictured brandishing a mace in his right hand and holding in his left a stylized thunderbolt. The three goddesses, sacred courtesans, were *Anath*, *Astarte*, and *Ashera*, who were all three patronesses of sex and war. These Canaanite cults were utterly immoral, decadent, and corrupt, dangerously contaminating and thoroughly justifying the divine command to destroy their devotees.

The Canaanites represent the church of Thyatira, whose name means "*odor of affliction.*" Thyatira was the only city that dyed purple cloth, the color of kings and rulers.

The Lord represents Himself here as having eyes of fire and feet of fine brass, a God of judgment. He condemns Thyatira for suffering the Spirit Jezebel, a false prophet, to teach and seduce His servants to commit fornication and eat things sacrificed to idols. He warns this church that He searches the mind and heart, and He will pay people their rewards according to their true motives as well as their works.

The only thing He requires from this church is that they continue to resist the false teachings of this seducing spirit. Those that bend to this teaching will be cast into judgment while those who overcome will receive true power over the nations. They will rule with a rod of iron, the standard of the Lord, not the standard of violence and control. The overcomer will also receive the Morning Star.

Debasement breaks the seventh commandment of God—thou shall not commit adultery. When we bring about the fall of another through seducements, we stand in great peril of the judgment of God. This was Lucifer's next step in his fall, causing the angels of heaven to commit adultery with him.

The Perizzites

The Perizzites, whose name means, *"belonging to a village,"* represent spirits that affect the mind.

The Perizzites were a people who lived in the open country, unprotected. They insinuated themselves to any city they could move into, easily fitting into the lives of those who conquered them, marrying their conquerors and subduing them through compromises from within. They represent the spirits of Deep Sleep, the spirits who lull us into a false sense of security, artificial liberty, and spiritual compromise, opening the doors to our destruction from within.

The Perizzites represent the church of Sardis, whose name means *"Red Ones."* Sardis was one of the wealthiest cities of the ancient world, and it was here that gold and silver coins were first struck. Among the hills above Sardis lived a band of robbers who robbed the people at will, slipping effortlessly through every attempt to catch them. While Sardis dropped their guard, a single Mede soldier scaled their impregnable walls and let his army into the city, bringing about the fall of the city

The Lord represents Himself as having the seven spirits of God and the seven churches. He condemns Sardis as being dead or dying, telling them to hang onto those things that are still alive, for if they fall asleep in those areas too, He will come and remove their candlestick. He that stays awake and overcomes will be dressed in the white robes of His righteousness. Their names will not be blotted out of the book of life, and He will confess their name before His Father and the angels.

Compromise breaks the sixth commandment of God—thou shall not murder. Compromise kills the spirit man and when we teach others to compromise, their blood is on our heads. Compromise causes us to fall into a deathly deep sleep. We don't belong anywhere because there is no standard to follow. This was the next step in Lucifer's downfall into unrepentant sin.

The Hivites

The Hivites represent spirits that affect the family.

The Hivites, whose name means *"life giver, first woman,"* represents the spirit of Whoredoms of subtle seductions. They were primarily nomadic herdsmen who built their tent villages with black and tanned goatskins. A stranger traveling through the area could not distinguish their naturally camouflaged tents from the landscape until almost in the village. They used deceptive diplomacy and craftiness rather than arms to gain their objectives.

The Hivites represent the church of Philadelphia, which means *"brotherly love."* Philadelphia's chief god was Bacchus, the god of wine and revelry, famous for the drunken orgies held in his honor. Their brotherly love was sexual promiscuity and moral indebtedness.

The Lord represents Himself as the one who is Holy, true and has the key of David; who opens and shuts. There is no camouflage in His words. He says what He means and He means what He says. When He says He loves you, He really means it…in the true sense of love.

The Philadelphians were willing participants of ribald love, very much like the '60s *"free love"* era that was artificial and fake, a product of drugs and loose morals. Like Lot's daughters who made Lot drunk to have sex with him, Bacchus commended sexual relations with parents, siblings, animals and anyone else who was available. He tells the Philadelphians that a test is coming upon the whole world that will test whether their love for God is true or their love is one of adultery and whoredoms.

He that overcomes this test will be made a pillar in the temple of God and will never again go out. The name of God, the name of the city of God, which is New Jerusalem, and the new name of the Lord will be written upon the overcomer.

Untrue love breaks the fifth commandment of God—honor your father and mother that your days may be long upon the land. We replace true love and honor with a deceptive love that totally dishonors those we should care about. God's kingdom is based on His love, true love, and it is the basis for the Ten Commandments.

The Jebusites

The Jebusites represent spirits that affect the spirit of man.

The Jebusites, whose name means *"trodden down, threshing place, polluted,"* had fallen everywhere in Canaan except in their last remaining city, Jebus. They are a people of harsh and warlike character, who balanced their existence between the kingdoms of the Hittites (*fear*) and Amorites (*pride*). Hiding behind impregnable walls, they withstood every attack until David finally conquered the city. David called the city Jerusalem, made it his capital and allowed the Jebusites to remain in the city.

The Jebusites represent the spirit of Error and the church of Laodicea, whose name means *"justice of the people."* Laodicea is famed for being the lukewarm church, unaware of her blindness, poverty, misery, wretchedness, and nakedness. She lived well off the wealth of the world, saying she was rich by her own hands and in need of nothing God could supply for her. She is the epitome of self-sufficiency as are the seven women in Isaiah 4:1 who only want the name of God to give them the appearance of being without reproach.

The Lord represents Himself as the Amen, the faithful and true witness, the beginning of creation of God. He is the God who knows everything and every word He speaks is faithful and true. He tells them to purchase gold tried in the fire—true character which makes a man rich; white raiment—His righteousness that clothes our nakedness; ointment for our eyes so we can see.

He tells this church that He is standing at the door and knocking, waiting patiently to come in and dine with them, developing that precious relationship they seem to lack. They have put works and appearance above truth and relationship. To him that overcomes this sin of dead works, he will sit with Jesus in His throne, just as Jesus overcame through obedience unto death and sits with the Father in His throne.

He does not want to give His name without a relationship. Marriage is intimate relationship.

Dead works breaks the forth commandment of God—Remember the Sabbath Day, to keep it holy.

Matthew 7:21-23 Not everyone who says to Me, "Lord, Lord," shall enter the kingdom of heaven, but he who does the will of My Father in heaven. Many will say to Me in that day, "Lord, Lord, have we not prophesied in Your name, cast out demons in Your name, and done many wonders in Your name?" And then I will declare to them, I never knew you; depart from Me, you who practice lawlessness!"

We must destroy all the kingdoms in the land that the Lord has given us, the Promised Land. We began as spirit beings in heaven with Him. He prepared a body for us and we are born. However, like the Promised Land given to the Israelites, it is a body filled with generational spirits. We must be cleansed. We must deal with the seven common breaches inherent within us as children descended from Adam.

We must deal with the fear of lack, the temptations of the flesh, pride and boasting, slander and destruction, compromise, seduction and false love, and dead works. If we do not deal with these in our lifetime, then we will not receive the overcomer's reward, but will also stand up with Lucifer one day and declare that there is no God.

CHAPTER TWENTY-ONE

The Crucifixion—God's Plan "A"

The Two Armies

I was shown a vision of an aged five-star army general. His troops were at war in the east, fighting in a fierce battle that had already claimed countless lives. The general had his feet perched up on a leather ottoman. In one hand was a hand rolled cigar from Cuba, its rich aroma filling the windowless room. In the other he held a glass of scotch, which he sipped easily. To his right was a desk on which lay a map of the war zone, strategic tokens showing the position and types of the different troops. He sat some twenty thousand miles away from his fighting troops, directing their every move in the safety of this unbreachable office.

Then I was shown a history of warfare. I was there in the beginning when the combat was hand-to-hand, one-on-one. I saw the sweat in the eyes of the leader, or man who would be leader. Blood stained his mouth and arms as he sliced through the men who stood before him. The zeal in his eyes, the utter commitment to the complete destruction of the perceived enemy was astounding. This man was made leader by being the strongest in battle. The leader fought beside his men, winning the battles by his cunning and strength. He won the loyalty of his people by his willingness to fight with them, being an example of courage, strength and resolve.

As time passed, the men went into battle first, the leader following closely behind. Then, later, the leaders stayed atop a hill watching his men go off and fight his battle. Eventually, the leader didn't go near the fighting at all. Finally, the leader didn't even leave their home country or city; they didn't even leave their palace or headquarters.

I saw how the line-up of men changed throughout the ages. In the beginning everyone was in the front lines. Then the strongest were placed in the front lines to make the quickest dent into the enemy. Eventually, the weakest were sent in first as fodder to weary the enemy. Eventually, men were not sent into the front lines at all as weapons shot and killed their prey from far away distances, killing the innocent along with the soldiers.

Then I was taken to a battlefield that encompassed a very wide valley. On either side of the valley were two great armies, each lined up facing the other. Each army was so thick they covered the land completely, except for the thin strip of ground that lay between them. They were so thick; their mass was black and their men faceless.

I could hear the jeers and the shouts as they shook their swords at each other, yelling taunts, threats and promises of what they would do to each other. Many swung tightly gripped fists in the air at the enemy, making vows and sending curses at them.

I faced the strip of land between them; the two armies were positioned on my right and left.

On the right side, the army was aligned with the weakest men first, the ones who would be the fodder to tire out the sword arms of the enemy. Behind that row, I could see the various ranks of stronger men until their leader sat perched on his black horse atop a hill a great distance from the battlefront.

On the left side, the army was aligned with the strongest of the men in front. Behind them were the varying levels of weaker men, so that the weakest of the men could be protected and guarded from the enemy.

I saw the sun rise until it was mid-afternoon—the signal for the war to start.

The screams and taunts on the right were deafening. They jumped up and down, chomping at the bit to run into the enemy and tear them asunder.

The heat of the afternoon sun beat down on the armies. Anticipation electrified the air. I could feel the uneasiness and twitching. Then I saw the leader on the left step down from his horse. He dropped his sword and stepped out into the empty ground between the two armies. He walked slowly across the barren space; the enemy went berserk with screaming—they were so maddened they frothed at the mouth, their spittle flying into the air as they cried out for his death. His face shone with a glow about it, his eyes were focused and determined on the task at hand. There was a smile on his face that shouted out love and warmth, a startling contrast to the noise of the enemy army he was walking towards. There was a regal air about him that showed he was the king.

The king walked straight into the enemy army, unarmed and vulnerable, and they drove their swords into him with an uncontrolled frenzy, as if generations of hate drove their arm with a frantic need to eradicate this king. It was not an act of war, but one of complete annihilation.

They took the body of the dead king, determined to dishonor it more...to control him even in death. They dragged the body over to a horse, intent on tying his feet to a rope and drag the body around the empty field to destroy the strength and morale of the enemy. The victorious army's leader came down off his hill to view his prize. He rode his horse as fast as he could until he arrived beside the body of the fallen and mutilated king.

All looked lost, the war being over in an instant. The noise stopped. Silence reigned in the land on both sides—the king's army thinking they had lost; the enemy's army thinking they had won.

The king moved his feet from the hands of the apparent victors. He pushed himself up, rising from the ground, very much alive and well. He walked out of the enemy army, the staff of their leader in his hand. He had won the war. They were defeated. Their power was gone. The King walked back to his army and handed the scepter of the kingship of the land to his generals. The King climbed on his horse and rode back to the kingdom.

As I watched this, I heard the voice from the throne say, "This is what happened at the crucifixion. Go and take back the land. I have given you back the staff of authority. They are defeated."

And for the first time I understood the crucifixion according to the scheme of the plan of God.

The Three Tests

I was shown that there have been three tests in this creation plan set out by God. Everyone would have to pass the test to live for eternity. Those who did not pass the test went to the Lake of Fire.

The first test was given to the angels.

Lucifer spent over fourteen billion years and the angels spent millions of years with the Godhead. They experienced the Throne Room and Godhead every day. They worshiped Them. They saw first hand what it was the Lord had created; Lucifer personally saw God create everything. They knew first hand that the Lord provided for all their needs in every situation. They knew how to draw out of the Third Heavens what they needed to build their homes. They had a relationship with the Father, Son and Holy Spirit.

They were given free will, just as man was. They could choose God or they could choose their own way.

Unlike us, the Lord is never in a hurry. He knew how much time it would take for the angels to make their decision. He gave them that time. He did not move onto the next stage of the plan until every angel made their decision…and one-third of the heavenly host chose their own way.

Lucifer had made his choice first, and he had made it easily… although it had been a shock to him in the beginning. But the more he meditated on the injustice of God not choosing him to be the Bride, the more his conscience was seared. He sinned five times and was forgiven five times, until his heart had reached an unrepentant state.

There was no excuse for Lucifer's sin. He knew about the Lake of Fire and why it was created. He knew it was the ultimate penalty for a sinful life. But it didn't matter. He actually thought that it would never come to that. He actually believed the Lord was holding out on him. He swayed the angels to believe that the Lord was holding out on them as well.

Lucifer failed the test. It took fourteen billion years before he fell. It took only a few million years for one-third of the angels to fall under his persuasive coaxing.

Despite everything the Lord offered them, they did not love Him...they chose not to love Him.

And the Lord loved them so much He would not interfere with their choice but let them go to the reward they chose. There was no ignorance on the part of the angels. They all knew what the outcome of their sin would be. Despite the threat of the Lake of Fire, they chose that fate over eternity with God.

When there was no awareness of sin anywhere in the universe, Lucifer invented sin. Presented with the concept of sin, the angels chose to sin over a life of unity and peace, a life of plenty and provision. They chose to love their own lives over the Lord and each other.

The second test was given to mankind.

Man was created next. It took forever for Lucifer to fall. It took less time for the angels to fall. It took man only one thousand years to fall. Until Adam and Eve made their decision, there would be no other men on the earth. Everything waited for the moment, when faced with their test, they made their decision.

Like the angels, they were given every provision for their life. They had an abundance of food and anything they could want. Unlike the angels, they had been given a mate to share with and explore the meaning of the true, intimate relationship of the Godhead. The Lord came and walked with them every day, making sure to take time out of His busy schedule of ruling the entire universe and all its innumerable citizens.

Man communed with the Godhead—Father, Son and Holy Spirit—for over one thousand years...and yet, it wasn't enough.

Eve bought the same lie the angels did—God was holding out on her. Adam could not bear life without her, and he too fell, believing God would take her away from him.

When there was no sin in the world, although there was sin close at hand in the Second Heavens, the first couple chose to sin. They chose to believe a lie and fall away from God. They chose to love their own lives over the Lord and each other.

The Lord created all life in the universe. He created every angel, man, woman, animal, insect, bird, plant life...every manner of life in the universe. He thought for eons about everything He wanted to create...fashioning every detail in His mind and heart. There was nothing left out. Everything was considered and every possibility calculated.

He loved us—His creation—enough to create us out of Himself. But it wasn't enough. He too had to prove His love. There was only one way this could be done.

The Third test was given to Themselves, each member of the Godhead.

He would create the angels and give them space to accept Him in love or reject Him in hate. He would create mankind, his intended Bride, and give mankind space to accept Him in love or reject Him in hate. And then, when the rejection was decided and sin was in the universe corrupting both the First and Third Heavens, He would prove His love for His creation.

Jesus, the Son of God, would offer His life up for the very nations He created. He stripped Himself of His Godhood, making Himself the Son of Man. He gave Himself over to the very Bride He created...a bride filled with the fallen host of angels. He gave Himself to mankind to be slain...to give up His life to pay for the sin of mankind.

The Son gave up the most precious thing in His life for the redemption of mankind. He gave up His communion with the Father and Holy Spirit. The Father gave up the most precious thing in His life for the redemption of mankind. He gave up communion with His beloved Son. The Holy Spirit gave up His joy. He felt each nail pierce the precious flesh of the Son and grieved with every rebuff and rejection. He wept for the entire time the Son was not accessible, feeling the separation keenly. His heart was so broken that He caused the land to go dark and the thunder to ring forth throughout the land.

God did not have to die for our sins. He could have just as easily gotten rid of everything and everyone and started over again...as often as it took for us to get it right. He did not have to suffer losing us and He did not have to suffer to bring us back. He didn't have to do it this way at all. However, in order to have a kingdom based on the values of His true nature, He could not and would not ask anyone to do what He was not prepared to do.

John 15:13-14 Greater love has no one than this, than to lay down one's life for his friends. You are My friends if you do whatever I command you.

Mankind's test is the only one that is not over. Born into sin, filled with spirits of sin, sin surrounding the very air we breathe, we must all still make the choice. We must decide while swimming in sin to sin no more. The Lord's sacrifice has given us that opportunity to repent from turning our backs on our God who gave us life and sustains us. God will have a people who will chose to love Him when we do not know love.

The economy of God is forgiveness. With forgiveness we
    receive love.
The government of God is love. With love we receive blessing.
The wealth of God is blessing. With blessing we receive life.
The life of God is giving. With giving we receive forgiveness.

When the end of all the ages comes to pass, every angel and person will have decided who they serve...themselves or others, themselves or God. We will either decide to accept the economy of God or we will not, accepting instead the economy of Lucifer.

The economy of Lucifer is unforgiveness. With unforgiveness
    we receive hate.
The government of Lucifer is hate. With hate we receive
    cursing.
The poverty of Lucifer is cursing. With cursing we receive
    death.

The choice is ours and the whole of creation is groaning for that choice to be made and for the sons of God to be manifest.

Romans 8:19-23 ...the creation eagerly waits for the revealing of the sons of God. For the creation was subjected to futility, not willingly, but because of Him who subjected it in hope; because the creation itself also will be delivered from the bondage of corruption into the glorious liberty of the children of God. For we know that the whole creation groans and labors with birth pangs together until now. Not only that, but we also who have the firstfruits of the Spirit, even we ourselves groan within ourselves, eagerly waiting for the adoption, the redemption of our body.

Intimacy

I have been happy with my calling and place of observer in heaven. There was a certain distance to everything and everyone that I enjoyed because of my life of isolation.

However, one morning I was whisked off to the most glorious bedroom I have ever seen. It was luxurious and rich in texture and color. The curtains were a velvety purple of the deepest royal shade. The bedspread was a deep, rich scarlet. Over the four-poster bed was a raw silk canopy of the richest sky blue color. The pillows were soft and gloriously inviting. The sheets were the most shimmering satin, thick and heavy. It was marvelous.

I found myself in bed with the Son of God. I was His Bride and it was our wedding night. I saw the scars on His back and I ran my fingers over them, one at a time. They were wounds that had been cut deep into His flesh, and as I ran my finger over a scar I would ask Him, "What is this one?"

He smiled, His eyes twinkling with the deepest love overflowing His heart. He spoke ever so lowly, almost as if in a whisper. Love dripped from His words and voice as He said, "That one was for you."

I asked Him about scar after scar, and each time the answer was the same. His back was scarred with so many of whip wounds it took a long time.

I wept for weeks as the true realization of the crucifixion enveloped me. He had made it personal to me. For the first time I knew what it was He had sacrificed for me...and for you.

His entire creation is based on love and relationship one with another. I realized for the first time that the entire purpose of this vision was to show me that love and relationship are the only things that matter. It was because of His love that He created us. It was because of His love that He gave us free choice. It was because of His love that He gave His life to redeem us from our wrong choice. It is because of His love that He has given us everything we could ever want or need. It is because of His love that everything that is exists.

And just as much as He loves me, He loves everyone else. When I am angry with someone else, I am angry with His friend. When I hate someone else, I hate His friend. When I avoid someone else, I avoid His friend. This was a revelation more than a vision. I pray, that through the vision presented in this book that everyone who reads it receives that intimate, precious revelation of who the Godhead is, and who we are in Jesus. This can only be received through revelation. No amount of intellectual rationalizing can give a person the same truth and reality as revelation. In fact, it was this very intellectual rationale that Lucifer used to bring the downfall of one-third of the heavenly host and mankind.

CHAPTER TWENTY-TWO

The Book of Job

I saw the courts of the Throne Room. Steps went from the Sea of Glass to the thrones where the Godhead sat. Around the throne hovered a mist, which was the Holy Spirit. The Throne Room is an incredibly busy and crowded place. At each of the two entrance doors stood an angel and each angel is about eighty feet tall, dressed in red and gold, silver insignias adorning their robe. Around their head, each door guard wore a thin crown of gems set in gold.

I have been to the Throne Room many times, and there is always an endless stream of angels milling around, coming and going to perform their duties and rounds. On the Sea of Glass there are all manner of nations of angels, each nation with their particular appearance, color, shape and height, each one suited for their particular field of work and lifestyle. Their clothes are vivid shades and subtle hues of so many colors, some of which the human eye has never seen— but in heaven there is no limit to the capability of the eye. Everything is visible, even that which is transparent. The full spectrum able to be viewed by a wholly alive spiritual person is incredible.

As I watched the nations of angels mill about—some praising the Lord, others talking to each other, some just standing listening, others lying on their faces or backs on the floor—I saw Lucifer walk into the court. He was taller than some, but not as tall as most. His color in heaven was a golden glow of purest white. His hair was fair and his face shone with a gloriousness not seen in any others. Even in his fallen state, he was a sight to behold as he stood in the court.

(It would take much more time in hell for that glory to fade completely away. I have seen Lucifer's end state after the millennia spent in the Lake of Fire. He is a shriveled up wisp of a spirit, black and empty, diseased and deathly, sitting in a corner reminiscing in his insanity about all the things he had given up...and wondering why. His agony was intense and he wished for a drop of spittle to fall from his gaping mouth, but there was nothing left in the cherub except broken dreams and hollow victories. The Lake of Fire purges the façade of our imagination and vanity, leaving the very core of our essence — the true heart.)

Heaven is an odd place. There is absolutely no way I could know in my own natural state who was who, but there, one just knows the name of everyone. They are their name, like God, whose nature is the sum of all His names. While in heaven, I know who everyone is without ever being told or having to ask.

I saw Lucifer mill around as if the Father would not see him, looking very nonchalant as if he actually belonged in the court... knowing full well that the Father would see him before he had even entered the court.

The Father beckoned to Lucifer who went over to the base of the stairs. I saw them talking; no one else seemed surprised at this at all. Then Lucifer went out from the courts and back into the realm of the First Heavens. The Lord beckoned for me to follow.

I followed Lucifer, and from a distance I saw that he went to the time and place of Job — again it was simply a knowing inside. I saw as Lucifer went and destroyed all that Job had in several different attacks until Job lay on his pile of ash, unrecognizable in his boils. Beside him was his wife.

Job's wife, who had loved the wealth and prominence of being married to Job, was overwhelmed with the grief of the loss of her children, home, money and position. She saw the miserable state of her husband, seeing no hope for improvement, and overcome by her grief, she went over to speak to her husband the only words she had left to say. "Curse God and die."

At that moment I understood why Lucifer had destroyed all that Job had except his wife. Overwhelmed by grief, she had opened herself up to be the spokesperson of Lucifer...who could not touch Job himself. As spokesperson for Lucifer, she was now possessed by the spirits who were assigned to cause Job to fall. In the trauma of her overwhelming grief, she allowed herself to be in agreement with Lucifer. Now, in obedience to her master, she tried to get Job to curse himself and die.

This is the power of Lucifer...deception to get man to curse God through rebellion and die.

When this failed, he sent three of Job's associates over to see him, continuing the assault to get Job to curse God so that he is cursed to death.

I asked the Lord how it is that a mere specter of an angel could have the power over the elements and the armies. His answer was to take me through the book of Job in steps.

Job 1:7-19 So the LORD said to Satan, "Behold, all that he has is in your power; only do not lay a hand on his person." So Satan went out from the presence of the LORD...and a messenger came to Job and said, "The oxen were plowing and the donkeys feeding beside them, when the Sabeans raided them and took them away— indeed they have killed the servants with the edge of the sword; and I alone have escaped to tell you!" While he was still speaking, another also came and said, "The fire of God fell from heaven and burned up the sheep and the servants, and consumed them; and I alone have escaped to tell you!" While he was still speaking, another also came and said, 'The Chaldeans formed three bands, raided the camels and took them away, yes, and killed the servants with the edge of the sword; and I alone have escaped to tell you!' While he was still speaking, another also came and said, "Your sons and daughters were eating and drinking wine in their oldest brother's house, and suddenly a great wind came from across the wilderness and struck the four corners of the house, and it fell on the young people, and they are dead; and I alone have escaped to tell you!"

In the first attack, Lucifer had accomplished four things.

1. Sent the Sabeans (*descendant of Cush, propagator of every false religion that has gripped the heart of the world*) to take away the donkeys and oxen and kill the servants by the edge of the sword.
   a. Lucifer uses false religion and lies to fill the hearts of the people of God and to prevent working in the field to plant the seed for the harvest of lost souls, promises and livelihood.
2. Fire of God (*false fire that consumes and destroys*) fell from heaven and burned up the sheep and servants.
   a. Lucifer causes false fire to fall on those of God's people who have unrecognized and unrepentant sin in their lives, filling their mouths with lies, false miracles, and false manifestations to destroy God's people and lead them astray.
3. Sent the Chaldeans (*descendant of Shem, brothers of the Israelites, but the progenitors of magic and astrology that has led the world on the false path of Divination*) formed three bands and took the camels and killed the servants.
   a. Lucifer causes a three-prong army to surround and attack the people of God—mysticism, divination, and magic— to rob the people of God of their ability to prosper and so they can invest in the harvest of God's kingdom.
4. A great wind (*the lying winds and storms that plague mankind*) killed all his sons and daughters in the oldest son's house.
   a. Lucifer sends a lying wind and perverse storms of drought to destroy the offspring of the people of God—spiritual sons and daughters, and our own children, causing the children to leave the fold of Christ.

Job 1:22 In all this, Job did not sin by charging God with wrongdoing.

And yet, after all the traumatic news, the loss of his children and his wealth, Job praised God and did not charge God with wrongdoing which meant that he did not sin.

Job 2:3-7 Then the LORD said to Satan, "Have you considered my servant Job? There is no one on earth like him; he is blameless and upright, a man who fears God and shuns evil. And he still maintains his integrity, though you incited me against him to ruin him without any reason." So Satan answered the LORD and said, "Skin for skin! Yes, all that a man has he will give for his life. But stretch out Your hand now, and touch his bone and his flesh, and he will surely curse You to Your face!" And the LORD said to Satan, "Behold, he is in your hand, but spare his life." So Satan went out from the presence of the LORD, and struck Job with painful boils from the sole of his foot to the crown of his head.

In the second chapter, the Lord admits that he has allowed Lucifer's request to ruin Job, putting Job's love to the test. Again He gives Lucifer free reign to touch Job but not take his life.

Lucifer attacked Job with painful ulcers from the soles of his foot to the crown of his head. It was only then that Job cursed the day of his birth...still remaining blameless by not accusing God.

Job 2:9-10 Then his wife said to him, "Do you still hold fast to your integrity? Curse God and die!" But he said to her, "You speak as one of the foolish women speaks. Shall we indeed accept good from God, and shall we not accept adversity?" In all this Job did not sin with his lips.

Lucifer causes our own body to become our enemy, drowning us in misery and pain. He sends those who are closest to us to accuse us—our mothers, fathers, siblings, and relatives. We are most vulnerable to those who are closest to us, especially if we are in a weakened physical or emotional state that makes us dependent upon them.

Job still wasn't responding the way Lucifer planned. Lucifer, who had the right to take the life of Job's wife, chose instead to use her against Job. She allowed her bitterness to needle him into sin and cursing himself.

Job 2:11 Now when Job's three friends heard of all this adversity that had come upon him, each one came from his own place— Eliphaz the Temanite, Bildad the Shuhite, and Zophar the Naamathite. For they had made an appointment together to come and mourn with him, and to comfort him.

If our family does not fulfill Lucifer's intention for us, then he will send our friends. Job still refused to sin, so Lucifer sent Job's three friends to have a little chat with him and straighten him out.

1. Eliphaz the Temanite
   a. Eliphaz, whose name means *"my God is fine gold,"* was a descendant of Esau who sold his birthright for a bowl of pottage because he cared nothing for the inheritance that was rightfully his by blood and position. He thought only of his own immediate needs and pleasures.
   b. He represented the natural pleasures and needs of the world. This is representative of the first test of Jesus in the desert, after He fasted forty days and nights. Lucifer tried to get Jesus to turn stones into bread to satisfy the pressing need of His natural man, but Jesus answered, "Man shall not live by bread alone."
2. Zophar the Naamathite.
   a. Zophar, whose name means *"to leap,"* comes from Naameh, settled by the sons of Ham, the creators of every false religion that has ensnared the world in the grip of untruth.
   b. He represented the religious zealots. This is representative of the second test of Jesus in the desert. Religious zealots will do all sorts of things to themselves or others in the name of God, such as allow themselves to be bitten by poisonous snakes or cutting themselves. Lucifer tried

to get Jesus to leap off the pinnacle of the temple. But Jesus answered him, saying, "You shall not tempt the Lord your God."

3. Bildad from Shuah.
   a. Bildad, whose name means *"Bel has loved,"* was from Shuah, settled by Abraham's son by Keturah, a contender to the righteousness of God. Shuah means "wealth," but wealth from serving another god, not the one true God.
   b. He represented the kingdoms and riches of the world. This is representative of the third test of Jesus in the desert, after He fasted forty days and nights. Lucifer promised to give Jesus all the kingdoms of the world if He would but fall down and worship Lucifer. But Jesus sent Satan away, saying, "You shall worship the Lord your God, and Him only shall you serve."

Matthew 4:3-10 Now when the tempter came to Him, he said, "If You are the Son of God, command that these stones become bread." But He answered and said, "It is written, 'Man shall not live by bread alone, but by every word that proceeds from the mouth of God.'" Then the devil took Him up into the holy city, set Him on the pinnacle of the temple, and said to Him, "If You are the Son of God, throw Yourself down. For it is written: 'He shall give His angels charge over you, and, In their hands they shall bear you up, lest you dash your foot against a stone.'" Jesus said to him, "It is written again, 'You shall not tempt the Lord your God.'" Again, the devil took Him up on an exceedingly high mountain, and showed Him all the kingdoms of the world and their glory. And he said to Him, "All these things I will give You if You will fall down and worship me." Then Jesus said to him, "Away with you, Satan! For it is written, 'You shall worship the Lord your God, and Him only you shall serve.'"

Lucifer will send us *friends* who will buffet us with answers that offer immediate pleasure, easy ways out and untruth to cause us to stray from God's way. If we wait for God to answer our prayers instead of leaping at the easiest way out of our problems, we would not have to go around that same mountain over and over to learn the lesson He would have us learn.

I again asked the Lord how Lucifer, a mere specter of an angel, had power over elements of fire and wind.

"He answered, 'He only has the power I allow Him to have.'"

He can do only what he has permission to do. He must crawl on his belly, in a complete state of subservience, to beg permission to do something...anything at all. He was a created creature. He became a fallen foe. He was banished to the Second Heavens. He will be thrown into the Lake of Fire. He is but a shadow of what he once was. He can do nothing unless he has permission from his Creator...and us in the form of our agreement with his schemes. His judgment in the Lake of Fire is assured. He no longer has the deed to the earth in his possession. He no longer has the keys of death in his possession.

It is written and assured—the only assured thing in all of the universes—that the Word of God will be fulfilled in its entirety.

Our life and our reward on Judgment Day depends solely upon one thing and one thing alone—whose word are we going to believe?

Every word out of the mouth of Lucifer is a lie, a deception cleverly crafted to cause us to accuse God and curse ourselves, bringing death, judgment and loss.

Every word out of the mouth of God is true, bringing life, freedom and gain.

Perhaps it is just me, but I need to understand in my heart what that means. It is one thing to hear the words and know them in one's head, but quite another for it to be made real in one's heart and life.

The power of Lucifer and the satanic kingdom is the power to deceive. We enable their power by allowing the deception to wedge a block between our mind and our heart. Until that block is completely crumbled and destroyed, with absolutely every speck of it blown away, we will remain at the *mercy* of Lucifer and unable to have the abundant life of God, fulfilling the reason of our creation, fulfilling the dreams and aspirations of our hearts, fulfilling the mercies and love He has placed before us.

Our struggle is the eternal struggle of truth and lies.

The truth is that we can do nothing without God. The truth is that nothing exists without God. The truth is that He so loved us, that even after creating us, He gave us free will knowing we would mess up and reject Him. The truth is that even knowing that we would choose the wrong way, He loves us so much that even before He created Lucifer, He set in place the plan of redemption so He could prove His love for us. The truth is, He is God and there is none above Him.

The truth is that Lucifer lost the deed to the planet and his control in this world. The truth is that Lucifer is more than a defeated foe, he is a banished foe who will be sent to the Lake of Fire in due time. The truth is that he knows what he knows because of an incredible network of spies (demons). The truth is that he is only as powerful as we allow him to be in our lives. The truth is that we can get him out of our lives in the name of Jesus because of the sacrificial spilt blood of Jesus.

The truth is that we can be free from his bondage and be free to be who we were created to be—the Bride of Christ.

CHAPTER TWENTY-THREE

The Last Age

I have had several visions of the end times or last age of the seven ages of man before New Jerusalem comes.

Armies of God

I saw the angelic armies of God amassing in great numbers. Horsemen sat waiting upon steeds that pawed the ground in pensive patience. Steed and angel alike wore deep crimson red and silver armor. Great swords of an almost crystal looking steel rested in every hand, their blades so sharp that the very air was sliced as they moved. On their breastplates were insignias of the blood shed upon the cross upon a white crest of purity. The shield seemed to have an invisible but moving wind—if you placed your hand near their breastplate, you could feel the wind blow against your skin. Upon their heads were helmets adorned with living fire, giving the silver the look of rich, shimmering gold.

The horses were magnificent white steeds, their muscles flexing in anticipation. Their manes were raw flame and their hooves were red as if dripping with blood. Their saddles had the appearance of shaped fluid water, glistening with the purity of life and truth.

I heard the voice from the throne call out, "Go! Go to the hills and the valleys. Go to the cities and the country. Go, surround the earth of God and all its people."

The army went forth, galloping at their top speed from the Third Heavens to the First...horsemen and cavalry in numbers impossible to count. I saw them come to the earth and encircle the city and buildings, surrounding every place where there could be found even one person.

They stood, encamped and positioned where the Lord God of all creation had sent them, waiting for the order to come to move out.

These are the soldiers of truth who will sweep across the land.

As I watched them waiting, their horses pawing the ground, the riders kneeling on one knee beside their steeds and holding the reins, I called out to the Lord and asked, "Why do they wait?"

"They wait for man to begin to reclaim the land," a voice answered.

Then I saw man about his business in the earth, doing the daily things that man does, oblivious of the supernatural world around them. But, first there arose one, a woman, the Bride of Christ, and her eyes were opened and she saw the things of heaven. She bowed her knees to the Lord God of heaven and offered her life to the King of Glory. This woman went about, reclaiming the land and the lost souls that had been captured by the enemy. As she moved out to reclaim a section of the earth and the souls within, just before her, wherever her foot stepped out, the angels of truth that were waiting in that land began to move.

The cavalry of truth rode through the dense darkness of fallen spirits, cutting through the enemy, slashing open great areas, co-laboring with the woman. Everywhere the woman went, there was a great awakening of people and truth was placed in their hearts. The darkness was slashed away so the eyes of the people could be opened, and their souls were healed; their lives were eventually reclaimed and the land was made whole.

There is a people who will be called the sons of God. They are a people who have walked into immortality and incorruption and have been translated into their new, eternal bodies. They will be the first fruits of the sons of God that would be raised up after New Jerusalem.

There are three peoples now present in the earth. The sons of God are those who have made their decision totally for God and His way. The sons of Satan are the people who have made their decision totally for Lucifer and his way; those who have given themselves over to the spirits of Antichrist and fight against God and His truth. The great masses of people are those who have not made their decision, and are the harvest unreached.

Everywhere in the world I saw men take up the call and begin to move out against the enemy. As they moved, the army of angels moved, clearing a path, protecting their flanks, and guarding their way. The whole world became mobilized and there was war in the land. The blood of lies covered the land as truth reigned supreme. Truth battled the lies of the devil, and arms were drawn on both sides—the sons of Lucifer drew their swords for blood, and the sons of God armed themselves with mercy and love.

There was a great war that encompassed the entire world…not one corner was spared from the effects of this war. The children of evil shook their sabers at the children of truth, drawing their blood and demanding their lives. They destroyed as much of mankind as they could, their thirst for power, blood and evil insatiable. The devil made one last effort to take as many with him as he could in a last ditch effort to destroy the bride of Christ. Lucifer rose up mighty men of evil to do his bidding, and the world was thrown into darkness and chaos.

Those of God fought those who were not. Muslim fought redeemed Muslim. Hindu fought redeemed Hindu. Brother fought against brother. Every family was touched in every city, town and village in the world. Blood was spilled in every corner, for this was the time when all mankind would stand and make his decision, just as the angels had done so very long ago.

I saw the world from a position far out in space. It was no longer the blue and white jewel nestled against a black tarp. It looked as if it was wrapped in a nest of black vipers that moved and writhed, choking the very life out of the Garden of God and all its inhabitants. The Second Heavens were emptied. The Third Heavens were emptied except for the Godhead. The earth was filled with the life of all three heavens, and it was the last battle of the age. All three heavens drew their weapons and the blood ran.

225

The people of God sent out in His name, the revealed sons of God, were protected by a contingent of angels encircling each one. These people went throughout the world, emboldened by the Spirit. They spoke the truth, delivered people from their bondage, healed bodies and hearts, and comforted the people who were burdened by the raging war. They fed the thousands with manna from heaven for the earth's fruit was eaten up by war. They raised the dead and restored missing limbs and eyes by the power of their word in the name of their King and Savior, Jesus Christ, the Lord.

The Lord's people covered the land as they raised up the hearts of a multitude of peoples. They planted seeds of the Gospel that germinated as quickly as they did in the times of the Apostles. The earth will experience the time of the Apostles once again, but this time in greater power. It will be in a time of great resistance from Lucifer and all his peoples.

There remained during this millennia a people who did not die. They were the people of God who returned to Him before the war; they returned to Him with their whole heart and soul and body. They were one with Him in purpose and heart. They were the sons of God the whole of creation longed to have revealed.

As evil and death touched the earth in a level never before seen, Lucifer manipulated his followers to cause as much havoc as possible. One group of God's people remained untouched. They were a people who had nothing in this world because their provision was from the Lord personally. They did none of their own labors. They did only what the Spirit told them and what they saw the Father doing.

As death, disease and destruction rained down around them, these sons of God went about the earth healing the sick and raising the dead, rescuing from the hands of Lucifer every soul who would be rescued. Wherever they went, they delivered the land and the people from the hand of the evil one, sending the spirits and demons back to the pit until their time of imprisonment was done. They moved throughout the earth until every person was freed from the touch and possession of the fallen angels.

When the land was reclaimed and the spirits cast out to the pit, God's people went among the people healing the wounds left from generations of possession, removing every stain of sin that was in their hearts, on their spirits and in their souls.

The armies of the Lord returned to their homes in the Third Heavens, putting their armor away for a thousand years.

The evil eventually waned, and all that was of the devil crumbled. Those that were of God arose triumphant and took the land sending Lucifer and his fallen host to the pit to be sealed until the end of the age. Angels of Death came and collected the tares that had been scattered throughout the harvest, taking them to be judged and burned. The people of God stayed upon the earth, having reclaimed their inheritance. Like in the days of Noah, the Angel of Death removed the people of Lucifer who had refused to repent of their sins.

The people turned to the precepts of God and in their hearts they longed to learn of Him. They spent their time making Him their priority, and life began to flourish where there had been death. The world prospered with abundant life and every person in the world prospered in every way. The Garden was restored and the people of God were restored to life as in the time of Eden, to live by the principles of God.

The people called for justice and mercy and the courts were established based on the rules of love. Everyone preferred others before themselves and there was no evil in the land.

But it was a learning program, man had to learn about the Lord and His ways. They had to learn who they were and what the Lord intended. It took a very long time for the people to return to the place they had lost in the Garden of Eden, free from the entrapments of Lucifer.

But for many it was a hardship to love one another, even without the influence of the evil one. There had been millennia of changed DNA that had damaged the emotional, mental and physiological aspects of the people. The windows of heaven were opened and the living water from the throne fell upon the earth and the whole land was healed, body, soul and spirit.

These sons of God did not die. The world's population that now lived on the earth still died when their life was finished. Those who died went up to the Throne of Judgment.

At the end of this age, after the world had thrived under the precepts of God, the devil and his fallen comrades were released from the pit for the final battle. Though living under the principles of a righteous God for a thousand years, a lot of the people in the earth ran to Lucifer who had risen from the pit, choosing to follow him instead of their God. The pit was emptied. Hell was emptied. Some of those that were alive joined Lucifer's forces, and they along with all the fallen angels and fallen men encamped against the people of God once again.

The soldiers of heaven were dispatched. They had known for thousands of years that this time was coming and they had waited for their King to give the order. The Lord Himself climbed upon His steed and rode in front of His army. It was the final battle. There would never again be any war in all of creation. This was the last time a sword would ever be drawn.

The battle was over before it began. The army of heaven, led by Jesus Christ, ushered the fallen hordes to the Lake of Fire—Lucifer, the fallen angels, the souls of fallen man and the souls of those who chose now to sin.

The army returned and ushered every person who followed God, alive and dead, to the Third Heavens. Before them was laid one of the biggest parties in the annals of the Kingdom.

While the party went on, the entire dark and light universes were removed and taken to the Lake of Fire for they had been stained with sin. The Lord purged His entire creation of the stain of sin that had marred its perfection. He created a new heavens and a new Garden, while everyone celebrated the peace and unity of creation once again.

All creation was now living in the fullness of the Godhead with one heart and one purpose, fully living by the precepts of God.

Millennium

I was taken to a place where I saw the whole world from an elevated position—my feet did not touch the ground. I stood above the tallest skyscraper.

From my position above the earth, I could see much farther into the horizon. I saw the bustle of life in the villages and towns; people moved back and forth quickly, always in a hurry with never a thought of spiritual matters. Cities were full of busyness and a lack of Godliness—it seemed the larger the city the more devoid of God it was.

A black cloud lay over the land like a mist. The mist hung close to the land smothering it until there was little life left. The contents of the Second Heavens had filled the earth; fallen angels were all given assignments. The time of God was at hand. If their work was completed, the fallen angels returned to their war room where they were given another assignment immediately. As soon as possible, they were once again dispatched to the earth.

Their assignments were in the earth, in the people and even in the animals. They worked over every hemisphere with increased seriousness and intensity. It was make or break, they were all out to play their last card.

There was not one person who was not assaulted by the fallen kingdom of angels. Babies were born with them inside; preachers were surrounded by a group of specific fallen angels to twist their words and break their hearts; religious spirits rose those up to call out the name of god, but not the name of the living God; the mass majority was entrapped in a quagmire of misinformation and brokenness that drained their life and dashed their hopes.

There were multitudes of people who rose up in the name of God but had given their bodies over to the kingdom of Lucifer. They moved in the guise of God's people, saying the words but there was no power within.

I heard a voice cry out, "Oh Lord, how long can this go on? When will the people be free?"

I heard the whole of creation groan and moan, its sound deafening. Creatures, angels, people, rocks, trees…all of creation groaned under the weight of sin that had besieged God's kingdom.

An angel came down and put a sword into my hand and I heard the Lord say, "Clean the earth. Drive the enemy to the pit."

I looked at the angel and said, "But I am a recorder. My call is not evangelism."

The angel looked at me and said, "No one can stand on the sidelines. That time is past. The war is upon the earth. Everyone who is called by God must take part."

I took the sword and began to deliver the earth from one spirit after another, clearing space, and as the small space was cleared, people rose up and taking a sword began to drive back the enemy into the pit. As mile after mile, soul after soul, creation after creation was freed of the enemy, I saw the whole earth become free of the enemy and Satanic influence.

It was the time when people who walked in the name of the Lord had to stand and take their part.

The Angel of Death had come to the earth and separated the tares from the wheat. All those that bowed their knee to God were saved and all those who bowed their knee to Lucifer and violence were removed, taken out by death. All the souls of the dead tares, the people who did not follow God, were confined to their prison in hell.

All the fallen angels were locked beneath a very large circle of the most impregnable metal in the universe—not even a spirit could escape. The metal was not like anything we know as metal; it was created specifically to seal off the entrance from the Second Heaven to this one. It was made a very long time ago waiting to be used, lying in a special room reserved just for this seal.

For a period of this age, men lived free under God. Men called on His name and sang His praises. Angels once again visited the Garden of God and sang in the heavens above the earth, teaching all men about the glory of God. Peace reigned in the earth and the statutes of God were the way of life for every man, woman and child. Life was good.

Children lived with peace, not war—they played. They played in safety—no tears, no threats, no pain. There was no starvation or even hunger. There was no need or poverty. There was no want or lack. Men lived their dreams, working side-by-side with women, fulfilling the call on their lives, bringing up their children in relationship with the Father, Son and Holy Spirit, as well as family. There was, for a very long time, unity once again in the universe—although it was never like the age of innocence before Lucifer sinned.

This was the way it was supposed to be before the fall of Adam and Eve. This was the way the world was to work before the fall, and mankind was sent into the spiral of sin that gripped their hearts and stole their souls.

Then I saw an angel go to the seal and open it, releasing the gates of hell. Every fallen angel poured through the unsealed opening like a black fog vomiting forth. The earth was again filled with their influence. Quite a number of people were pleased as if they had finally been set free from the demanding prison of truth, justice and freedom.

Then I saw the Lord come down with His mighty angels, all riding the cavalry of heavenly steeds; the nostrils of the pure white steeds flared at the scent of war, their manes flowing like live fire in the wind of the Spirit, their eyes ablaze with the fire of the passion of their King. They rode hard and fast. The soldiers sitting upon the steeds wore glistening white armor with swords of fire that emanated far from their hilts. On each head of long, flowing hair was a helmet of radiant gold and silver, the emblem of their King cut from a single ruby.

They rode valiantly behind the King who wore a breastplate of the finest gold and silver that shimmered the deepest hue of blood red in the sunlight. His eyes were pools of love that were so deep and unfathomable that the entire universe could get lost in them. In His hand was the rod of His authority. In His mouth was the sword of His truth. They rode to the earth, as the heaven was emptied of its army.

Around the entrance to the Third Heavens, the Throne and heaven of God, there stood a troop of cherubim that stood nearly eight hundred feet high. These sentries of the King were adorned in blue and gold. A flaming sword was held high before their faces. Each sentry faced towards the First and Second Heavens to prevent any unwelcome visitor from entering the Kingdom of God.

The army rode into the earth, the soldiers of God behind the King. The heavens rumbled under the thundering hooves of the cavalry, and every angel soldier shouted out the cry of the King, "Hallelujah to the Most High God, the King of Heaven and Earth and all that was created."

The fallen angels heard them coming and they trembled for the time of their judgment was upon them. They worked more feverishly to make all fall who would fall. The great army came and surrounded the fallen angels and they drove them into the Lake of

Fire in the farthest corner of the Kingdom of God. All the people who fell were taken up to the judgment seat to be judged for their time on earth. Those who were judged to the Lake of Fire were taken there immediately, to be with the spirits they had followed. Those whose name was written in the book of life were taken to Third Heavens to the celebration of healing.

CHAPTER TWENTY-FOUR

The People Of God

I see a people arise in the land. They rise out of the dust, their mouths and eyes filled with dust...the dust of the ages that have covered their generations.

As they rose, the dust fell away from their arms and bodies. They spit out the dust from their mouths and rubbed the dust from their eyes. A heavy rain fell on the people washing the dust off them. Refreshed, they opened their mouths to let the water flow inside to clean themselves totally.

They were a holy people separated unto their God, cleansed and pure, washed by the Word and filled with the Spirit.

They walked through the land, and everywhere they set their foot, life arose instantly where there had been nothing but death and decay. They walked in twos wherever they went—one man or woman and the Holy Spirit, two walking in complete union of one mind, one heart and one spirit.

This is the generation of freedom. This is the generation of the people of God who will not see death, but like Enoch, they will walk into immortality, leaving the corruptible behind and putting on incorruptibility.

> *1 Corinthians 15:51-58 Behold, I tell you a mystery: We shall not all sleep, but we shall all be changed—in a moment, in the twinkling of an eye, at the last trumpet. For the trumpet will sound, and the dead will be raised incorruptible, and we shall be changed. For this corruptible must put on incorruption, and this mortal must put on immortality. So when this corruptible has put on incorruption, and this mortal has put on immortality, then shall be brought to pass the saying that is written...*

I have seen vision after vision of the man and woman of God, of what we will be, of what we were created to be, and of what Adam and Eve gave away. I have seen hours, days and weeks of the people of God in action; they raise the dead in a moment; they cast out a hiding spirit with a glance; they see into the hearts of people; they see all that is not covered by the redemptive blood of Jesus; disease flees before them; missing limbs are recreated with a kiss; whole lives are saved with a touch; the wind of the Holy Spirit moves before them healing the land as they go. Above their heads, angels constantly sing praises to the God of heaven for His revealing of the sons of God. The body of Christ is a whole, functioning, and complete body in total agreement with the Head, the first fruits of what all redeemed mankind will be in the time to come.

We do not all sleep. There will be those that will walk through the veil between the First and Third Heavens. They will walk through that veil in the natural body as Enoch did, but this time they will walk back out in a new, glorified body. Enoch walked through the veil from the First Heavens to the Third Heavens and stayed there because the time to return was not yet upon the age of man. But there is a people, here in this earth now that will be able to walk back and forth through that veil whenever they please. They will be changed in the twinkling of an eye the first time they walk through the veil. They will return glorified and pure as the body of Christ in the earth, the sons of God revealed.

Mortal will put on immortality. Corruptible will put on incorruption. Death will be swallowed up in victory for man will have returned to their God in the fullness of their life. The sting of death is sin but they are a people who no longer choose to sin. It will be said of them that there is nothing found in them. They have fallen on their faces and repented for all their sins and been forgiven. They have cleansed the stain that has lived in their generations, standing in the gap for the sin their generations have done in the land.

I saw the man of God enwrapped in the righteousness of God, the countenance of his face changed so that it glowed with a pure whiteness mirroring the glory of God he has witnessed. Then I saw myself as I am now and my heart wept. I cried out to the Lord, "Nice words, but how does it happen? How, Lord, do I get from here to there?"

He answered, "Corruptible means to decay and perish. Stop decaying and perishing."

Then He showed me that we were created perfect. We were created without death. We were created to not decay and perish. Adam and Eve lived for perhaps one thousand years in the Garden of Eden before death touched them in two stages. First their spirit man died the very day they sinned and did not repent. Secondly, they died physically some nine hundred and thirty years after their spirit man died.

I saw the sting of death as it attacked Eve. The sting of death was the lie she believed—not the one that Lucifer told causing her to sin, but the one she told herself earlier that prepared her to sin. It is the same lie Lucifer, the fallen angels, the serpent and Adam believed. It was the lie that God had not provided well enough; that they had lack in their lives; that everything God had given them was quite simply not enough.

It is the lie we have told ourselves and believed from others for the entire existence of mankind. It is the lie that has caught us in the trap of corruptibility and has poisoned us until eventually we die after spreading the poison to others, even those we love the most.

But who is our God? What kind of a God is He?

He created the entire Third Heavens out of Himself. He built two universes and filled them with an abundance of star systems so numerous that no man will ever be able to count them. The largest number we have is a googolplex which is 10^{100}; but it is so small it cannot begin to count the number the galaxies the Lord has created, each complete with their suns, planets and moons.

Every planet, moon, star, and galaxy was personally hand crafted by a God so great we cannot even begin to fathom His creativity and imagination. He personally handcrafted and wrote the DNA for everything in creation.

There are planets with purple skies, red grasses and orange waters. There are planets with brilliant yellow skies and blue horizons rising from deep green seas. There are planets where life is smaller than the smallest one-celled life form on earth. There are planets with creatures fearsome to look at due to their immense size.

There are planets where the rain is as gold and thick as honey. There are planets where there is only water wherever you look.

There is one place I have been to where the entire planet is water and the land is only small islands scattered around the globe. These islands lay hundreds of feet above the waves. Its rivers flow across the land before falling off the cliffs into the oceans below, the rushing water of those magnificent waterfalls filling the air with its joyous thunders. In this place, the rainfall comes down only at night. There is such abundant sea life on this planet that their songs fill the air above, the quiet, haunting beauty of it heard even on the land.

The Lord created all the systems, planets, creatures...and all life.

He placed in each planet, habitable or not, precious stones and metals—gold, silver, rubies, diamonds, emeralds, sapphires....

There are metals of every color known to man, and more colors we have not yet seen. There is a metal that is so transparent it is as clear as glass, perfect and unblemished in its beauty and strength. It is harder than steel and more rare than platinum...and yet, it is there for no other purpose than our pleasure.

There are stones that lie so deep near the cores of their planets that they are of the purest color and strength. There are stones the size of basketballs and stones smaller than a single cell. They are all brilliant and sparkling; they are every imaginable shade and depth of color.

There are colored dyes to be discovered that the angels have used for millions of years, but we have yet to see. Everywhere in the universes, there is an abundance of everything we need and would possibly enjoy.

He created every color and texture for the pleasure of our eyes. He created every song and sound for the pleasure of our ears. He created every texture and sensation for the pleasure of our touch. He created every variety of food, beverage and flavor for the pleasure of our taste. He created every scent and fragrance for the pleasure of our smell. He created us with five senses in order to enjoy all that He has created because He is a God of detail and a God of copious abundance.

He created every precious metal and jewel for our adornment and beauty for no other reason than they look good on us.

He created us for His pleasure, but everything else He created for our pleasure.

He did not have to create anything because, after all, each member of the Godhead had each other. He could have just created Lucifer and been done with it because in Lucifer He created Himself a best friend. He could have created the universes and everything in them if He just wanted to see the work of His hands. He could have just filled them with angels who would worship His every move, thought and deed without question. He could have created just Adam and Eve or even a finite number of humans who worshipped His every move, thought and deed without question.

But He is a God of abundance even though it cost Him everything.

He not only created us, the best of His creation, but He gave us everything we could ever possibly desire...most of which we do not even have a clue about right now. He provided for every dream. He provided for everything. Not only did He give us life, and provided everything possible that we could ever want, but He also gave us the unbelievable capability of not wanting Him at all. He gave everything to us, including free will, so that He could not *buy* our affections...He would have to woo us like a lover.

So many Christians have a "Gimme! Gimme! Gimme!" attitude without realizing that it has already been given. We need only reach out and receive it.

What is the veil between this heaven and the Third Heavens? The veil is simply our lack of love for Him and the belief that He does not love us.

Our imaginations of all that He has for us has been atrophied from lack of use and deadened from the disease of lies. The truth about God, the simple, stark, honest truth about God's love and His abundance towards us has been buried under millennia of debris—wars, starvation, rape, murder, abuse, lack, poverty, hardship, evil....

God is a merciful God who gave Lucifer, Eve and Adam, the desires of their heart. He gave Lucifer the people he wanted from the very beginning—the Bride—but only the dust of their empty shells. He gave Eve relationship—children and husband—but she was trapped with always looking to her husband to fulfill her. He gave Adam the very work of his hands he so needed to show his worth—but the earth would no longer co-operate fully with his efforts.

Like the genie in the bottle, we need to be careful what we think our desires are.

II Thessalonians 2:10-12 ...and with all unrighteous deception among those who perish, because they did not receive the love of the truth, that they might be saved. And for this reason God will send them strong delusion, that they should believe the lie, that they all may be condemned who did not believe the truth but had pleasure in unrighteousness.

We do not want to be in the position of having a lie within our minds, emotions, will, thoughts, spirit or body. We must divest ourselves of every lie we have been led to believe...or more accurately, we need to embrace every truth. We each need to let God out of the box we have locked Him in. We need to step outside the limitations of the dark ages that has drowned us in a quagmire of misconceptions and untruths that still have us leg trapped in its teeth. We are just now beginning to break through the revelation of what God is all about and what He has for us, but we are still locked into the traditions of our diverse cultures.

We need to get rid of ALL the dust and cobwebs that are holding us back from ALL that God has for us. We have to get back to the reality of who He is and who we were in Eden before we can even begin to continue on the path. Whenever you find yourself on the wrong path, you need to return to the place where you sinned, repent and continue on the correct path He has for you. We corporately sinned in Eden, and we corporately have to return to that point and regain and reclaim everything we lost there before we can continue on the path to experience something new.

That means we have to be able to see and walk in the spiritual and natural realm to create and co-labor with the Lord. That means we must be one in spirit and union with the Father, Son and Holy Spirit...and each other. That means we must be able to walk through the veil between this heaven and the Third Heavens.

The new thing, the thing that no one has done save one, Jesus, the thing that means we have returned to the purity of Eden before the first lie and sin deadened the spirit, the thing that we will be able to do is...walk out of the Third Heavens again a new creation, immortal and incorruptible.

There is arising a generation who will be able to be a citizen not only of this heavens, but also the Third Heavens, able to go between them at *their* will. In the early hours of the morning they will stand before the Throne of God on the Sea of Glass in person, not vision, and return to a café in New York for lunch. They will touch a withered hand and it shall be restored instantly. They will walk by a legless man and he will walk before their shadow leaves him. They will look at the heart of a man and every spirit of darkness that has held him captive for centuries through his bloodlines will flee to the pit to escape the *dunamous* power of love. They will breathe into the air and the Holy Spirit will fall like fire upon everyone it touches.

They will be in Seattle one moment, and London the next. They will walk across lakes and oceans, across the open space between cliffs, and off platforms into the air. The laws of nature of this dimension will not bind them for they are citizens of both the first and Third Heavens. They will not have to say a word for the whole world will see God by the appearance of their faces, shining with the brilliance of His light. Truth will coat every word and integrity will be found in every cell of their bodies.

They will never see death. They are the body of Christ on earth; Jesus is their head. He will reveal Himself in the earth through them, His body on the earth.

The multitudes will die around them for a thousand years as each generation comes and goes. The multitudes will learn about the goodness of God from the miracle of this non-dying peoples. If they stone a man of God, that man of God will rise up instantly from the burial mound before the first of the men who stoned him turns to walk away.

This people of God will be the second coming of Christ, for they will be the living temple of their God, and He will fill them. They will do nothing they do not see or hear the Father do. There is no striving, work for accomplishment, or struggle. Their only purpose and interest is to be in relationship with the Father, Son and Holy Spirit, and all else pales by comparison. They will never be out of communication with the Godhead, their spirits unable to bear even one millisecond of breach with Them.

Jesus gave up His relation with the Father in His willingness to die on the cross so that we could regain that relationship with the Father. And the body of Christ will have the fullness of the Godhead living within them. The Father, Son and Holy Spirit will be their best friends. The corporate peoples will be one in body, soul and spirit.

They will have the power to create, for they are the body of Christ, the Bride of the Son. They will have the power to heal at will, as true co-laborers and a true helpmate with the Godhead.

They will be as we were supposed to be. Then and only then we will be something new.

CHAPTER TWENTY-FIVE

Heaven

Heaven is a complex myriad of buildings and rooms that are open to everyone. I have not begun to go into all the rooms in the palaces of God, but I know that there are several different palaces. Each room displays the great love the Godhead has for His creation...for us.

I have been to four of the Throne Rooms.

General Court

The Throne Room I spend most of my time in is the General Court. In the General Court is a floor of transparent metal that shows the rest of the universes beneath—a living, changing, transforming blackness that emanates a pale light and evolves in glorious colors as it grows and changes.

What is most interesting about this floor is that anyone can zero in on any part of the universe they would like to see at any given time. Thousands of beings can look into the floor at the same time, everyone seeing a different aspect or view. Through this floor I have seen various homes of the angels, the earth, even into someone's living room or bedroom. I have been able to zero in on a particular face while someone else is looking at something completely different. The Lord has even pointed things out to me through this floor, having it zooming into the very point He wanted to show me as if zeroing into something with a camera lens.

The room is large enough to hold well over ten million angels (rough guestimate). It is the largest congregation of angels I have seen in one place at one time, and I have never seen anyone there except angels. In this Throne Room, the Godhead simply holds court. The angels come there everyday to worship and be in His presence. It is the room spoken of in Job and has been there since the creation of the angels.

The angels congregate, usually in groups, depending how they are praising their Lord. Some dance African style (my favorite) or any other dance; others sing and twirl; others are on their faces. Every small group is doing something different, but the sounds and the sights are tremendously in union.

The ceiling lives and breathes, and is comprised of angels who sing praises to God all day long. They never cease to sing and their song is so transformingly glorious that at the very sound of even a single note, my spirit soars unfettered. I sometimes go there just to hear the music and fall on my face before the Lord, or dance with the angels. Other times I go there to stand in my spot by the Throne and just watch the proceedings and every once in awhile the Father will lean over on one elbow and talk to me.

When there, I am in my transformed body…a beautiful body, fit, healthy, sculptured and lean. It is the same height I am now, unfortunately, which means I will forever be short…but in that short, tiny body, I can dance freely and tirelessly like I have never danced. I can dance, swing, kneel and bow…all the things I cannot do here.

The doors to this Throne Room are solid gold and about eight hundred feet high. They are intricately ornamented and crafted with a design that tells only some of the feats of the Lord and His greatness, a testament to His character.

The walls are horizons—blue skies and clouds, always daylight and bright, always peaceful and beautiful.

The Thrones are on a platform at the top of several steps. Around the thrones is always a mist—the Holy Spirit. Behind the Thrones there is an endless horizon of space that continues on and on.

The Thrones themselves are a shimmering white and gold, almost as if they were alive. The Father and Son shine with a white brilliance that is the purest white I have ever seen.

The congregations of angels that visit the Throne Room every day are from every nation of angels. Each nation is as different from another as the imagination can conceive. There are angels that are thousands of feet high; there are angels who are six feet tall. There are angels with wings; but most of them are without wings. They wear every manner of clothes and colors depending upon their work, duties and tastes. Their clothes shimmer and radiate almost as if they were dressed in vibrant rainbows.

I spend most of my time in this Throne Room facing the crowd. From time to time, the Father will lean over on one elbow and point something out to me or ask me a question, often not related to what is going on. This is the room where I ask Him most of the questions I have relating to the mysteries of the universe and His creation, and this is the room I go to any time I have something to ask. When I am not watching the crowd, I am in the crowd dancing and praising the Lord with the angels.

As I pass the sentries at the door, who themselves are about eight hundred feet tall, welcome me by name, as they do everyone, for my name in heaven is my character—a very long, convoluted name that encompasses all my character. There is simply a knowing, when there, who everyone is because their name is their character and every being there is so transparent that their heart is easily seen.

It was the first Throne Room I visited and remains my favorite.

War Room

I was taken to a very large room in which the only furniture is a very large table. The table is lighted from beneath. On the table is a complete relief of both Dark and Light universes. Any particular area of these universes can be zeroed into at any time by just speaking to the table and requesting what aspect you want to see as instantaneously as the thought occurs.

On the table are placed the strategic positions of every angel, fallen angel and person in the universes, every move made plotted and changed as it happens.

When you look at the table for the overall view, you can see instantly the concentration of activity of the current war that is still raging between God's people and fallen Lucifer's men. There is not one move that can be made in secret as the tokens of each being is intricately tied to them and shifts as they do.

At the head of the table stands Jesus...at least when I was there. Around Him milled several angels, the great and mighty generals of the Lord who dispatch the troops, sometimes going themselves, to fulfill whatever directive and requirement of war.

I stood and watched the activity for what seemed like hours, but was in reality only minutes. Time moves differently in heaven than here on the earth. The tokens moved almost as if they were in an elaborately choreographed ballet. Everything moved so fast I wondered how they could keep up, but every move was noted, measures put in place before an event even happened.

As the tokens moved, the General angels dispatched orders to waiting troops just beyond the city wall. Angels were assigned as extra guardians; angels were dispatched to order circumstances; there was a constant flow of moving tokens and dispatched angels going to and from this War Room.

Just before I left, I was told that I could come back anytime I desired; this room would always be open to me.

Delegation Room

Not all the visions I have had were received when I was in the best of moods. One day, while at church, I was very much wishing I was home in bed instead. I was unhappy while sitting in the chair at church and I was just as unhappy when I was taken into heaven. My mood was so unpleasant I didn't even notice that this was a new room.

I stood in the same spot by the Throne as I always stood, unaware that this room was very much smaller than the more familiar General Court. The walls were a deep scarlet color. The floor was a rich gold.

There were pillars in this room, a row on each side of the Throne near the walls with just enough space for an angel to walk sideways between the wall and column. The walls were outlined with gold relief designs that were simple and strong. The columns were white with a golden hue; they were pillars of golden light.

Angels came into the room in a single line, each waiting their turn to step up to the Throne and receive their orders. The Throne sat upon a single platform that separated it from the general floor. The platform, like the walls, was a deep, rich crimson color outlined in gold relief. The Throne was white, the same color as the columns with the same light emanating a bright golden hue.

The Lord wore a pure white robe and a rich purple cloak with gold trim. On His head was a single golden strand with twelve colored stones. The stones were the deepest hues and richest colors I have ever seen.

I stared off into space, somewhat lost in my misery, as the Father talked to the angels before Him. I was negligent in paying attention to what was actually going on.

The procession of angels continued for about half an hour when the Father stopped everything and spoke to me, "You are missing the point of what is going on. Pay attention."

At the mild but pointed chastisement, my mood broke and I turned to pay attention. The Lord returned to the angel before Him and gave him a set of instructions I couldn't quite hear. The angel then stood, bowed, and flew out of the room quickly.

The Lord turned to me and ordered, "Go follow him."

Outside the room were a number of angels waiting for their friend to come back from the Throne. At his return, the angel gave them their instructions and they left together, heading out of the Third Heaven realm towards the earth. Once there, they went to various points in California, Oregon, Washington and British Columbia. One angel stood in the waters of Juan De Fuca Strait and was so tall that the water came up to only his waist.

They stood where they were stationed, each one waiting for further instructions. Each angel was so large and strong that he could tear the earth apart with his bare hands. Confused about why they were just standing there, I repented for my earlier attitude and asked the Lord why they were just standing waiting as I missed the instructions given them.

He answered by showing me the earth as He and the angels saw it. My eyes were opened and I suddenly saw the earth as if through x-ray eyes. Each angel was standing on a strategic point along a tectonic plate fault line and strategic intersection of cracks. When the order came from the Throne Room, they would disrupt the fault line to cause one of the largest earthquakes this area of the world had ever experienced.

Private Court

There is a Throne Room that is a private room where the Lord meets one-on-one with His people.

This room is a room of comfort and peace. There is a heady aroma of incense and a gentle wisp of smoke filling the room. The walls and ceiling are a deep, rich purple that shimmers with an iridescent appearance that changes the color to a deep scarlet, royal blue and deep gold, depending how you look at it.

The floor is made of wooden boards covered in gold. Through the gold one can see the grain of the wood, and they are all joined together seamlessly. The ceiling glows with a beautiful gentle light infusing the entire room with a warmth that is almost alive.

The Throne is low to the ground, more like a cushioned, comfortable easy chair than a throne. It is not made of gold or silver, but a rich, luxurious fabric that draws the weariness out of one's body. It is big enough for two people to sit cozily and comfortably.

There is no platform separating the Throne from the visitor. The entire room was welcoming and wonderful. Peace pervaded my soul immediately when I entered.

I stood off to one side and watched as the doors opened, allowing only one visitor in at a time. As the person entered, the heavy aroma of the incense changed instantly. Sometimes it was heavier than others...but always with a different perfume. I waited until there was a moment between visitors to ask the Lord why the incense was different for each person.

He smiled, a deep, loving, warm smile and said, "The incense you smell is the prayers of that person that they have prayed all their life. When the incense is heavier, that person has prayed more in their life than another."

Awed, I returned to just watching what happened in that room — seeing several similar rooms at the same time.

Each person entered and sat with the Father on the Throne. Most sat as a little child though they were advanced in years. But there were those who sat with Him as a lover and a friend, and these times touched my spirit with such a tug that I wept for the beauty and love of the sight before me.

When someone sat with the Lord as a friend and lover, their conversation was so personal and joyous that I was continually overcome with emotion. I had never seen anything so beautiful.

This room was open at all hours. Everyone had a room. There were hundreds and thousands of these rooms in the palace of God... and He was in each one, waiting to meet with the Bride that He created with so much love and hope.

We think of God as so one-dimensional. But He is in every room every second of every day. He is so big that He is everywhere at all times. He is in every Throne Room, every other room, and every situation always. He is so big that He is aware at all times what is going on in every corner of His creation. He knows what is happening with the smallest molecule in His creation, aware of every path they take.

He is aware of every word spoken, every thought considered, every dream dreamed, every hope hoped, and every heart broken. He is aware of every prayer and every need. He is aware of every desire hoped for, crushed or realized. He is aware of every tear shed and every laugh.

He is aware of every hand stretched forth to help another in their time of need, whether in comfort or love or just simply to be a friend.

He is aware of every thought, word or deed concerning Him... and every one that does not concern Him. And He longs to hear from us, for each one of us to come and join Him in this special room that is renewed as we enter to come into communion with Him.

The Halls of Judgment

I saw a great room. I have been in this room a few times. It is not my favorite room as it causes me a great deal of discomfort just being there.

There is a very high one step platform with a single, solid white Throne standing upon it. The throne is positioned right in the center of the platform, which is so high, it is totally unreachable by the people standing before it. This room is filled with the shedding of tears and the terrible, deafening sound of shame and wailing.

Beside the Throne is a very large screen that takes up almost half the platform. Before the screen is Jesus who stands the entire time. Upon the Throne is the Father. Both Jesus and the Father are dressed in white. In fact, the entire room is the most brilliant white—ceiling, floor, walls, Throne, screen, platform, doors, angels' garb, etcetera. I looked down at myself and saw that I too was dressed in white, the mandatory uniform of this room. No one except those being judged could be in the room unless they were dressed in white.

Those who were being judged were dressed in the clothes they wore when they died. If they died naked, they appeared in the hall naked.

There was a person standing before the Throne of Judgment, tears streaming down a face that was distorted with agony. Their arms were raised into the air as if they were pleading for their lives, but not one word escaped their lips. On the screen above them played their entire life. Every thought and every motive was revealed over their words and deeds. Everything in their life was revealed from the moment of birth until the moment of death. And they could do nothing except stand before the screen, arms raised in abject horror, as every aspect of their own life condemned them. Every tear they caused to be shed and every drop of blood they caused to flow was called in as witness against them. Every word spoken by them, still held in the air, was called to give testimony in their case.

I found myself weeping as I watched, not so much for the sorrow of a life lost, although that in itself was incredibly grievous, but for the rejection of the very One who created that lost life. There were so many lives that rejected the Lord God who loved them until the moment they died, and even afterwards, that I wept because of the pain it caused the Godhead.

These people died without ever knowing a relationship with the Father, Son and Holy Spirit, but they were not the only ones who lost. The Godhead lost a relationship with them and that pain was felt very much within Their hearts. I found I wept for both of them, the Godhead and the lost soul.

This was the Hall of Judgment for all those who did not have a relationship with the Godhead. There was a countless number of people who thought their works would save them, but were sorely distressed and shamed to find that their works meant little when compared to the rejection of the love of God. When they realized what they had done, and how easy it would have been to accept Their love, they were mortified and speechless.

As each was judged, they immediately were ushered out a great door at the right of the platform that led them instantly into the hell of the Second Heavens.

They were all given the very thing they demanded in life—to be without God. They did not believe in Him during their life so He gave them their freedom in death—freedom to be without Him. He would no longer try to woo them from their path. He would leave them alone, something they had always wanted.

They had not wanted the abundance He offered, choosing instead the works of their own hands, so He gave them the fruit of those works—the penalty of the first death that was hell. They did not want the life He offered, so He gave them the death they chose.

This was a people who put themselves first over God and others because they never learned how to love by His precepts.

Most had a semblance of love and were, in fact, "*good*" people in their time on the earth. But all their goodness had not gained them eternal life. Their own righteousness could not save them or cover their rejection of their Creator. Their own love was found wanting.

Those that were saved, went to another Hall of Judgment. Again, everything in the hall was white, including the uniforms of the angels and myself. There was a large screen that took up half of the platform in this room as well. However, the platform was not as high, allowing the one being judged a closer proximity to the Godhead.

Everyone being judged appeared before the Throne dressed in a white robe. Two angels escorted each person before the Throne, one standing on each side of the person. As the person stood before the Throne, their entire life played on the screen. Before the screen stood Jesus.

On the screen played every scene that had not been covered by the blood of Jesus; every motive and thought played over the words and deeds of the person. Each and every person, in awareness of standing before the Most High, hung their head in their hands and wept.

As their life played, huge sections of their life were missing... these were the vents and portions that had been placed under the blood of Jesus. In place of the events that should have been playing were long periods of red screen, the image of the blood of Jesus applied to their lives, their sins forgotten.

At the end of the movie, four angels came up to the person. One had in his hands the Book of Life. The Father asked if the person's name was written in the book, and the angel looked and said, "Yes, Lord, it is."

The Father looked at Jesus who stepped up and said, "Yes, Abba, I know him."

Sometimes, the Father and Holy Spirit said, "Yes, I know them."

Then one of the angels that came forward placed a crown on the head of the person. Another placed a ring on their finger. Another placed a cloak over their shoulders, a sash around their waist and new shoes on their feet.

The judgment for this person was passed. Their salvation was assured, but their position in heaven needed to be determined. Some were sent to school, the level determined by their judgment. They would learn all that they hadn't learned during their life. Others were taken to gardens, mansions or even other courts where they would meet with other past graduates. Commissions were given to some who had overcome all they were given to overcome on the earth. Some were taken to a banquet.

They were all given their heart's desire—to be with God. They believed in Him during their life, even if it was the last few minutes, so He gave them an eternity with Him. They wanted the abundance He offered, choosing instead His goodness over the works of their own hands, so He gave them an eternity of every good thing He could give them. They wanted the life He offered, so He gave them eternity to share that life with Him.

They became the living temple of the Lord because they wanted to be so close with Him always; He promised them He would never leave or forsake them.

I wept as I saw His heart filled with the joy of acceptance and relationship, and He gladly joined His people in unity and love.

These were the people who had already learned how to love by His precepts.

<u>School</u>

Four years after my mother died, I was sitting in my bedroom watching a movie and working on my computer. I heard a noise and looked over. Beside my bed stood an angel. He raised his hand, wiped his brow, and said, "Whew! Your mother finally learned how to say 'hallelujah.'" As quick as he came he left.

Several years later, I was walking through the gardens of Heaven when I came across a class that was sitting on a lawn of luxurious green grass. An angel was teaching them the things they needed to learn, lessons they had failed to learn while alive. There were hundreds in this outdoor classroom.

There was no man on the face of the earth, save Enoch and Elijah, that had learned the full extent of the lessons they were to learn here on this earth. Every one of them has been sent to school in heaven, staying in whatever class they needed until they *got it*. At the graduation of each class there was a celebration given for their due diligence.

I was also shown a very large complex that was an actual school where they learned the more elementary lessons, from kindergarten upwards. This was the school of those who were saved moments before death with very little real understanding of the Lord's nature or their own place in Him.

In 2005, I was sitting in Bible School myself, learning the spiritual things of the Lord, when an angel came and caught my attention. He pointed to the back of the class, and there I saw my mother in a cap and gown, having graduated. I cannot say from what grade, but I do know that day I was so pleased and proud of her. Long ago I had seen that my mother accepted the Lord while she was in a coma, the Holy Spirit reaching her heart and teaching her the prayer of repentance. I also know that when she was a little girl she gave her heart to the Lord but went another way the rest of her life. She was always a "*good*" person, but her life was less than exemplary. But it was that early commitment that was confirmed while she was in a coma.

When she died, she was sent to school and it took her four years before the first words out of her mouth were "Hallelujah" instead of something more familiar to her. It took her another ten to graduate.

The Unborn

One day, while working on my computer, I was shown another part of heaven. I was taken to the grounds where the general public commune in a great gathering of people. This is a wonderful area where people meet and become friends.

Here I have seen young adults who were the babies once aborted or miscarried. These innocents were brought to heaven, presented with the gospel free from the entrapments of Lucifer, and here they made their choice for their Creator, Lord and King.

Each child was assigned a group of angels who raised the child infant to young adult. Each child spent a lot of time with the Father, Son and Holy Spirit, and they grew strong and healthy in the love that surrounded them. Angels brought these children to family who were already in heaven, regardless of the relationship.

There is not a child in heaven left alone or feeling unwanted. They know no fear, bitterness or abandonment. They are bathed in love. They are fed on love. They know nothing except abundant provision. They are friends with all the angels and know them by name. They sleep with their heads nestled against the breast of their guardian angel who was assigned for their full, eternal life.

These children have seen the homes of angels as well as those of mankind who have died and gone to Paradise. Every child who has died has a special place in heaven where they grow up without the hate and horror this world would have or did inflict on them.

These are the children who starved to death, died from abuse, were tortured and murdered, abandoned and forgotten. These are the children who died despite the valiant efforts made by parents, or medical intervention. These are the children who died before the age of accountability.

I was delighted one day to see someone I knew, the daughter of a friend. She had been aborted several years prior, never able to take a breath of life. But here she was, dressed in a pure white dress with red splashes—her dress was just above her knees and floated in the air as she twirled around in a most vigorous and vibrant dance of love to her Creator. She was happy and content, for although she had never taken a breath on the earth, she breathed in deeply the love of the Godhead every day. She had already gone to school, her young spirit hungry for the relationship with the Godhead, and she excelled quickly through the classes. I had the honor of introducing my mother to her who was delighted to meet the young girl.

This young girl spends all of her time dancing before the Lord and bringing a special joy to the hearts of everyone she meets in heaven. She goes out of her way to bring a very special present of warmth and love to everyone, filling her days with endless giving. She is a complete delight and joy to behold, and my heart, although surprised to meet her in the first place, has come away changed for having met her.

Although these children are in heaven, safe and secure and with the Lord, their blood remains in the earth to testify against the doctor, murderer or abuser in the Hall of Judgment when it is time to give evidence. The face of the one who took their life through commission or omission is embedded in the lifeblood of the unborn or murdered child, and that blood will speak at the court of their abusers. Every mother who has aborted her child and has not been forgiven of this flagrant abuse of God's precious creation will be held accountable in the time of Judgment.

A special angel has lovingly collected every tear shed and preserves them in a special jar. When called, the angel brings the jar to the Seat of Judgment, and each tear is examined, the circumstances of the shedding playing like a movie, the event frozen into the fluid of each tear. These tears will offer up their evidence against whoever had caused them to be shed.

Everyone who thinks that they are not accountable for every word, deed or attitude thrown thoughtlessly at someone else, family or otherwise, will be surprised to find out that it is not only recorded, but every tear shed or drop of blood shed will give testimony at the time of judgment.

While watching a documentary on television about babies born with two heads, I was horrified at the realization that this does happen, and the second head is amputated soon after birth. Though called a parasite, the head blinked its eyes and moved its mouth.

I asked the Lord what happened to the second child who never developed. Were they a living soul? Or were they simply a parasitic growth as was suggested?

He answered me and said, "There are those that are born so deformed that they cannot live. This is due to the interference of Lucifer and the influence of generations of sin in corporate mankind. In cases like this, the soul of the unborn child is taken early while they are still in the womb. What is left is simply the biomass that continues to grow, fed from the mother's body. But the soul of the child is here with Me."

Lake of Fire

My heart was grieved with all that I have seen in heaven because of the Lake of Fire. I saw the judgment of those who had died the first death and were sent either to hell in the Second Heavens or school in Paradise.

I have asked the Lord several times about the teaching that everyone, other than the saved, would burn forever and ever in the Lake of Fire. How could I celebrate and be joyous knowing that someone I had known or loved was in the Lake of Fire forever suffering the torments of fire and brimstone? I asked him how anyone could be happy in heaven knowing their loved ones were suffering for all eternity.

He showed me the Lake of Fire at the end of the ages.

I saw the angels, people, and all that was in the First and Second Heavens that had been thrown into the Lake.

Everyone burned, some fires brighter than others. As I watched, some simply were extinguished into non-existence. Others burned for an incredibly long time. Angels burned forever, and Lucifer even longer.

I asked the Lord how this was so, and He answered me and said, "The fire is fueled by the hate, rejection, fear, all manner of sin in the person's heart. There will come a point when their debt is paid and their hate is extinguished. When that happens, they are simply extinguished into the nothingness of non-existence, the thing they desired all their lives. Their debt was the abuse of the life I gave them."

"Lucifer will never be extinguished for the pit of his hate is bottomless. The angels will never be extinguished for the pit of their hate is bottomless. Their debt is the abuse of the life that I gave them."

"The First and Second Heavens will extinguish when they are completely cleansed of all the sin and hate that stained them. Every man and angel will pay his debt in full and the moment that debt is paid, they are released into nothingness."

"So shall the stain of sin be removed from My creation."

Matthew 18:23-35 Therefore the kingdom of heaven is like a certain king who wanted to settle accounts with his servants…And his master was angry, and delivered him to the torturers until he should pay all that was due to him. So My heavenly Father also will do to you if each of you, from his heart, does not forgive his brother his trespasses.

Revelation 21:8 But the cowardly, unbelieving, abominable, murderers, sexually immoral, sorcerers, idolaters, and all liars shall have their part in the lake which burns with fire and brimstone, which is the second death.

Revelation 20:10-15 The devil, who deceived them, was cast into the lake of fire and brimstone where the beast and the false prophet are. And they will be tormented day and night forever and ever. Then I saw a great white throne and Him who sat on it, from whose face the earth and the heaven fled away. And there was found no place for them. And I saw the dead, small and great, standing before God, and books were opened. And another book was opened, which is the Book of Life. And the dead were judged according to their works, by the things which were written in the books. The sea gave up the dead who were in it, and Death and Hades delivered up the dead who were in them. And they were judged, each one according to his works. Then Death and Hades were cast into the lake of fire. This is the second death. And anyone not found written in the Book of Life was cast into the lake of fire.

CHAPTER TWENTY-SIX

New Jerusalem

New Jerusalem

A new First and Third Heavens were created. The entire universe will forevermore be a place of light, unity, peace and love. The stain of sin has been removed, never again to surface. There is no shadow of darkness. There is no Dark Brane and no hell. The natural and supernatural are joined, and man is citizen of both.

There will never again be a person born who will reject the Lord God Almighty, not because their choice will be taken away, but because they choose not to reject God. Without the effects of sin, brought up in a family of love, a universe of love and knowing the Godhead personally, visually and closely, they will never be drawn to cause a breach.

They will be born with a generational propensity to love. There will never be any mark of sin upon creation. Freedom will reign and peace will be in the hearts of every living thing.

I saw New Jerusalem come down and rest upon a new Garden of God. This is the capital city of Creation, the living temple of the Godhead. The streets are paved with gold. The buildings are the purest white marble with crystal, gold and silver veins, representing the natures of the Father, Son and Holy Spirit. The city of New Jerusalem encompasses the entire Garden of God, the whole planet earth.

Every person has a condo in the city of God, and another residence somewhere else in the universe.

New Jerusalem has been waiting inside the Father for an eternity. It has been the jewel of His eye. It has been a bright spot within Him, something precious and wonderful He has kept within His heart. I watched as the Holy Spirit drew out of the Father the entire new universe. Every detail of this new universe has been thought out and planned before the first creation.

The Father, Son and Holy Spirit knew everything before it happened. They knew everything that would happen before the beginning creation of the Throne Room and of Lucifer. They knew every angel that would be created, every person that would be born, and even every sparrow that would come forth. They had seen it all. They knew every decision that would be made choosing Them; They knew every decision that would be made rejecting Them. They knew it all before one molecule was formed and put in place.

The Father planned New Jerusalem before He planned Lucifer. He placed every marble stone and every gold brick in place. He saw from the very beginning the procession of His people entering the gates of New Jerusalem when the time would come and His heart leapt with joy.

Every tear has been wiped from the face of each person and angel for the loss they suffered. Sin has touched every life in creation, but the smallest to the largest sorrow has been wiped away by the personal, loving touch of the Godhead.

All the redeemed, all those who followed the Lord were called to the great Feast Hall. It was large enough to hold every living person and angel in the universe. Even the cherubim who had remained on duty for millions of years were at the feast. The chairs were solid gold, encrusted with jewels and detailed with a silver platinum metal. The tables in this hall were solid marble. The tablecloths were the finest linen that shimmered with all the shades of a rainbow, depending how you looked at it in the light. The glasses were the thinnest glasses I have ever seen. They looked so amazingly fragile, but each glass was cut from a single diamond and was of such a tensile strength they did not break even when dropped. The plates were also cut from diamonds. Flowers adorned the table in extravagant centerpieces, their aroma filling the air with a rich floral fragrance.

There was no singing or praising because everyone was at the table to dine. No one was on guard. Every person, angel and living creature was at this feast. The foods simply appeared on the table—great platters of every vegetable, fruit and grain imaginable from worlds that would be found in every corner of creation. Spices and aromas mingled with the floral fragrance filling the air with such an incredible orchestra of smells that one's spirit was immediately put at ease and in a state of joy.

The rich crimson wine appeared in the glasses and it tasted of honey. Everyone dug in, eating and drinking their fill. It was the best meal I have ever had, and we sat there for weeks, enjoying each other's company and the magnificent meal before us. It was such a time of communion and pleasantness there was no desire to leave.

While the people of God and the angelic host were at the Feast of Celebration, the Holy Spirit drew the new universe and New Jerusalem out of the Father. As people and angels clinked their glasses and laughed merrily forging eternal friendships, every detail was put in place. Everything was complete and whole before it was drawn from the Father.

When the celebration meal finally drew to a close, everyone arose and slowly moved towards the two gold doors at the end of the hall. The doors opened onto the realm of New Jerusalem, which stood like a glistening jewel in the heavens. Angels and people alike simply stepped through the door to the gates of New Jerusalem, entering the city as a procession of victorious overcomers marching triumphantly through the city streets. They danced and sang praises and worship for their God and King.

They sang a perpetual love song to their King and Maker. The angels danced through the streets and continued onto their homes on every planet. The people danced through the streets to their homes in New Jerusalem.

Every person was pre-assigned their condos and each instinctively knew where their new home was located. The people moved into the city as one, breaking off and dispersing to their new homes as they drew near. Joy filled the air like a visible electrical charge skipping across the atmosphere.

There was no palace here; no government building stood upon a hill or in the center of the city square. The people of God were the living temple of the Godhead. The people themselves were the living city of God. The Lord had given them their hearts desires—they were one with the Lord and they would never be separated forevermore.

The air over New Jerusalem was filled with the odor of delicate, sweet incense. It was like nothing I have ever smelled. It was a new smell in creation that permeated the air with an infusion of peace and beauty. Intrigued, I asked the Lord what it was, and He showed me that it was the entwined incense rising from the hearts of His people. He showed me that the hearts of the people always communed with Him and this was the incense of their prayers. It was the smell of New Jerusalem, the living temple of God, and it would go with His people wherever they went throughout the universe.

Exodus 30:7-8 Aaron shall burn on it sweet incense every morning...And when Aaron lights the lamps at twilight, he shall burn incense on it, a perpetual incense before the LORD throughout your generations.

The people danced and twirled to their new homes. When they opened the doors to their new home in the city, the rooms were empty and bare. I saw each person stand in the space of their new home, their imaginations on fire. As they stared at the space, the look of *endless possibility* moved upon their faces. I saw hundreds of these people in their new condos at the same time—each and every one drew out of the Third Heavens the furnishing and décor, down to the last detail of kitchen and bath. Each and every one drew out of the Third Heavens the wardrobe that filled their closets and dresser drawers.

Every window looked out upon hills over the single river that wound throughout the earth touching every corner. The earth is not like we know it today. There is no mark of a curse. No meteorite strike, earthquake or volcano mars its beauty—and never would again. Everywhere the endless bounty of the earth is anxious to offer up its fruit. If I could say that the earth was pleased and proud to be able to give freely of all its gifts to the sons of God, it would not truly express what I see.

The bounty of the earth is so abundant that a single grape can feed several people. The bounty of every planet in the universe is so abundant that there is absolutely no end of the things that are created by God.

The entire size of the expanse will never be filled with everything that God will create...it is so inexpressively large. I saw eternity pass in fast forward—the expanding universe He creates ongoingly moves out to the horizon of the expanse in every direction, only to have another horizon appear beyond.

And every planet, moon and system created is anxious to give up the endless abundance of its fruits with all its tastes, smells, touch, sight and sound that have not yet been explored or discovered.

I saw that the Lord takes such immeasurable delight in creating something new. He is so pleased with being able to supply things He knows we will enjoy, He is almost childlike in His excitement. He smiled as He created a new treasure, new sensation, new taste, new sound, new scent, all for His children to discover. His smile is so big and beautiful the joy of His pleasure is remarkable. He just cannot give enough.

When He creates, He takes into account each person in His kingdom. Every millisecond He creates something new for each person all at once. And then He comes and tells each of them, "Come and look. Come and see this new thing I have made just for you."

Then they go together, the created and the Creator to see this new thing made just for them...and together they share the delight and joy, the pleasure and thrill, the love and blessing, the love and gratitude.

Everywhere in New Jerusalem, which is the name of the age that will never end, there is unity and peace. It pervades every cell.

Once again, I found myself in the center of the expanse. I floated as the expanse was refilled with the voices of everything singing the praises of God. Unity joined everything together and washed over my spirit, overwhelming me with a peace that was so great I didn't think I could bear it. The innocence of creation had returned, only this time it was different. There was a determination of choice in this innocence, because everything here was here because they wanted to be…not because they knew nothing else. It gave the praise a headiness to it like a deep aroma of musk. In fact, remembering the first time I was taken to this place, before Lucifer sinned, there had been no odor. This fragrance was a new thing.

The beauty of this praise so overwhelmed me, the deep infusion of aroma so overcame me, I wept with a joy I had never known and I could not control. It exploded within me like a geyser of emotion. Every cell in my body, soul and spirit joined the praise and sang forth the love…I cannot begin to describe the incredible love that so filled me. It was like an agony of pleasure. I became lost in the love.

James, The Clockmaker

The Lord brought me to the second home of James, a resident of New Jerusalem.

James lived in a very large mansion with rooms that are gargantuan in size. He has one room that can hold the tallest angel with ease because angels and people from all over creation come to his home on a regular basis. They love to watch James work, and some even have the work of James' hands in their homes.

James is a clock maker. He makes the most incredible clocks I have ever seen. My grandfather taught me to love clocks, and I have placed my order to have one of James' clocks when the time comes.

James fashions his clocks out of the living water from the Garden of God. He commands the water into shape by the words of his mouth and the touch of his hands, and the water maintains the form he so orders forever. The water, because it is living water, flows around the shape in a never ending mini-river, the gentle sound of its babbling crooning praises of love for the God of creation.

Time does not pass in eternity as it does here. There are no years or days. It is a perpetual Sabbath. Time passes by events and memories. The water marks time not by moving hands and numbers, but by the event it witnesses being impressed upon a single water molecule, all the memories flowing in one river of peace forever.

The face of the clock looks like a living image of New Jerusalem—its rolling hills, rivers and lakes. The intriguing image was designed by the water itself. The hues of the water, which looked very much like the colors of a rainbow as it appears on minute water molecules, fused together to form the picture. This gave the picture a very liquid, living appearance. When you put your hand on top of the clock, the face changes, bringing up one event after another impressed on each water molecule, almost like a living photo album.

Michael, the archangel, has one of these clocks in his home. James gives his wonderful clocks as gifts to all he desires.

Economy

There is no commerce in the eternity of New Jerusalem. There is no need to struggle for income to purchase clothes, housing, food or the necessities of life.

The Lord provides for every need and everyone in creation. All He provides is drawn out of the endless supply of the Third Heavens which is drawn out of Him.

There are no taxes, sales or trades because they were part of the invention of Lucifer's sin that stained the universe. People give of the works of their hands to share the bounty of their provision and the creation of their own hands with others to bless them, as the Lord selflessly blessed them.

There are no squabbles. There are no disagreements, fights, wars, arguing…or anything disagreeable. There is only peace in the heart of everyone. Each and every person prefers everyone else in all things. They think of how they can make someone else's life happier, how to bless each other. New Jerusalem, which means the "*new teaching of peace*," is overflowing with the precepts of God, which are love, peace, joy, patience, kindness, goodness, faithfulness, gentleness and self-control.

It is a creation of loving and giving, and no one is more pleased and happy than the Lord, for everyone is manifesting His nature of love.

The government and economy of God is love and generosity, and it is the basis of all of creation for all of eternity.

One Day In The Life

One of my biggest fears had always been that life in eternity would be boring. I had heard stories from well-meaning Christians that we will all be gardeners and would spend eternity in the Garden of Eden tending the plants. I am not a gardener even in the broadest sense of the term.

I asked the Lord in a sort of quiet desperation, "What will it be like?"

Since then, I have seen day after day of things I, and others, will be doing in the eternity of New Jerusalem.

I have been to the Throne Room where everyone was gathered. Angels and people alike were dancing, singing, praising, talking, milling, lying on their faces, or lying on their backs....

The four living creatures were above and before the Throne of God, crying "Holy! Holy! Holy!" Before the Throne was a row of low, red clothed golden chairs, each one with a man sitting on it. The ceiling was filled with angels singing the glories of the Godhead. Over in one corner was a group of people dressed in plain, white clothes. They danced and sang continuously without stop, as if they were in a world all their own. They were a special group of people who never left the Throne Room because they could not bear to leave the presence of the Father, Son and Holy Spirit.

I watched them, and I asked the Lord, "Please, I am not one of those people, am I?"

The Lord smiled at me. I felt terrible that I did not want to be one of those people who never left the Throne Room as that meant that I didn't want to be in the presence of the Lord all the time, but it came out of my mouth without thinking. The Lord smiled again, knowing what I was feeling, and said, "I made you to be like you are. You are an explorer and an adventurer. I created you with a need to know and see everything because it is your calling to be a reporter. No, you are not one of them. You will travel to the very corners of creation and explore every part of My creation."

Each one of us has been created with an inherent nature placed there specially by God. There are as many different natures as one can imagine, each one created to enjoy His creation and Him individually. Every one of us is created to commune with a different side of the Godhead and to enjoy a different viewpoint of His creation. In this way, the fullness of the Godhead can be appreciated and enjoyed. He is so incredibly diverse that we can only enjoy one aspect of Him. We can share that aspect with each other, and therefore there will be no end of sharing with everyone else, all the parts making up the whole. And because we can only see one aspect of God's nature, we need everyone else to help us see the whole.

There will be those who stay in New Jerusalem, never wanting to leave. There are those who will never leave their neighborhood, while others will be content to explore the city itself for the rest of eternity. In New Jerusalem are all aspects of culture without the entrapments of the perversities, prejudices and sin of the current world. We will celebrate the unity of our diversity, appreciating the differences in food, clothing, manners, and living styles with anticipation rather than criticism and fear.

As for myself, I will travel and visit every planet and system in creation. I will visit every home and mansion, and talk with every person and angel. I will see every animal, bird, sea creature and insect. I will sail on every sea, walk across every ocean, stand in every desert, climb every mountain, and taste every delicacy....

I will go to every concert and live theatre. These concerts will hold audiences in the millions. The acoustics are so stupendously engaging that even the lowest whisper courses through the body, feeling every note and word. There will be plays and concerts that will inspire our souls to soar to the highest reaches of heaven where it will join in praise of God until we feel like our hearts will burst with love.

I cannot describe how overwhelmed that much love makes one feel. I have been to several of these concerts, and each one goes on, not for hours, but for days and weeks without end. The chairs are comfortable, not like the miserable chairs we have here in our concert halls. No matter how nice we try to make them, it is always a marathon of endurance for me to see the end of a musical or theatrical festivity. But there, the very atmosphere will be our chairs as we float in space, oblivious of anything except the absolutely glorious music and singing that envelopes us.

There will be speakers in every corner of the universe speaking on an endless variety of topics. They will discuss how the animals on their world behave. They will show living documentaries of sunsets, sunrises, oceans, lands...every part of God's magnificent creation will be shared and taught and shared again.

And when we think we have it all, He will create a whole new something for us to explore.

As I stood looking at everyone attending a musical concert, the Lord said to me, "Why people like action and horror movies is because they cry out for the rush of adrenaline. But, when they experience the spiritual and emotional high from one of these concerts, they will never again remember the cheap movies they used to watch." He answered one of my biggest concerns because I am an action movie addict.

We will share every taste, texture, sound, smell and sight as we go from place to place celebrating the absolutely incredible diversity of the Lord God Almighty, always finding new aspects to His nature.

On the planets we live, we will know the names of each animal, bird, fish and insect; not their genus name, but their real name for we will all be friends. Nothing dies. No longer will one eat another in the struggle to survive. Blood will never again be shed in all of creation. Life will procreate at a much slower rate than now. There is no rush. There is no timetable that must be met; no ticking clock. All life is prized and precious not only to God, but to mankind as well.

No longer will we treat God's creation with the utter contempt that has been the hallmark of mankind. We will stop throwing away the life He has created as if it is garbage, but we will honor Him and His precepts. We will no longer be children of destruction but children of life and love.

There are no signs and wonders in New Jerusalem. There will be no need. What we consider as miracles now will be common occurrences in eternity. There is no sickness or disease. There may be the occasional injury or accident to an animal, but a broken leg is healed quicker than the words can be spoken...and animals will speak the words and we will hear and understand them. There will never again be confusion of communication between any creature of creation.

There will never again be any confusion in an effort to express or understand our thoughts, for our minds will be clear and uncluttered, working at full capacity.

Every dream will be realized. Every hope will become real.

I will spend time with my mother and my grandfather in heaven. I will spend time with my children. In fact, my grandfather has not seen the clocks James makes, because James is a citizen of New Jerusalem. I would be thrilled to give him my clock because of his passion for clocks, the passion he shared with me.

My grandfather will work with his hands and he will craft beautiful things. My mother will sometimes travel with me for adventure is her heart.

I have seen the home of my dearest friend. Her world is a water world where the whales sing day and night. She will swim in the oceans with the dolphins as if she were one of them. She will walk on the most beautiful white beach that has only the finest sand with no pebbles that might hurt her foot. Her house is one of clear crystal walls, floor and ceiling so that not one aspect of the sea she loves is obscured from view.

I have had breakfast there, a plate of the most tantalizing and delicious fruits of vibrant reds, blues and purples, while listening to the sounds of the waves, peace saturating everything around. Then she went for a swim with her water friends while I walked along beside them, atop of the water.

Sometimes, I have gone to the art galleries were I saw hanging the most beautiful art. Paintings are made in the most incredible colors. At this particular gallery they were 3-D. There are some paintings that you can actually walk into. They capture the essence of a complete moment in time that can be shared over and over again.

I was told by the Lord that I will write a series of books dealing with stories of actual people in New Jerusalem and their lives there, very much like James the clock maker.

CHAPTER TWENTY-SEVEN

Getting Back To Eden

I have obeyed and the vision is written. Now I find myself on the last chapter and I feel like the most unqualified person in the world to write it. I cannot think of this chapter without tears welling up in my spirit.

I have seen the end of the matter, what we were created to be. I have danced in my new, translated body while in vision, and yet, here in the natural, I suffer physically. "How…just how do I get from here to there?"

In my spirit, I find myself on my face before the Throne of God, weeping from the very depths of my heart, unable to stop. "Oh wretched woman am I!"

I have seen visions all my life and there has been an underlying understanding in my spirit of the world they reveal. Most times that understanding did not get through to my natural man, and it was that very duality that has caused me so much trouble. I wish I had parents who were so steeped in Godly things that they could have guided me in the total reality of what I was witnessing in my spirit, which would have made things so much easier. But that wasn't where I was placed.

The mere thought of the separation of what I have observed and what I am actually walking in causes tears to well up in my eyes and the Spirit of Repentance to overcome me. I would like the Spirit of Repentance to stay on me until I am completely emptied of whatever stands between me and God, but the agony of my sin is so grievous I cannot bear the pain very long.

Some people think that they must repent of the Ten Commandments—don't covet, don't murder, don't steal, etcetera. But the agony of repentance is every second I have chosen to be separate from God, my Creator, my King, my Lord and my Love. The agony of how much I have hurt Him is so great I don't think I will ever be able to rise again.

But what is it that stands between me and my God? I can see it. I can feel it. I can even touch and taste it, but how can I explain it?

I have been bowed beneath the burdening grief of the Holy Spirit that was so immense I thought I could not bear it one moment longer.

I have seen tears stream down the Father's face because of the grief that has pierced His heart. He has cried for the loss of life Lucifer and mankind has inflicted on his fellow man, the loss of each one felt deeply. He had lovingly thought of each one, every angel, and creature with the hopes of enjoying eternity with them. But His hopes were dashed when the angels and mankind chose to reject Him and go their own way. It hurt Him deeply, so deeply that Jesus offered to give up His life so that each one would be able to regain a relationship with the Father, the same relationship He had. Jesus offered to give up the very thing He held dearest to His heart, the communion with the Father and Holy Spirit, the two people He loved most in all of life so that we might possibly know the joy that filled His heart.

That was His test...to give everything up so that we might know what He knew—a relationship with His Father and Holy Spirit.

Lucifer fashioned himself as a god that exacts life and demands penalty and blood. He knew nothing of love or sacrifice. He knew nothing of giving. His is the kingdom of taking...taking everything from his followers including their very lives. His is a kingdom built on the death and bones of every angel and person who listened to his suave lies. He demands more and more bones to be heaped beneath him so his vantage point is ever higher—never achieving enough.

That is the simple, stark truth of Lucifer—everything for him and nothing for us.

Oh, Lucifer promises wealth and power. I bent under that promise for awhile. He promised me a very high office in his kingdom. He promised me that I could live with them forever in one of those face-less, cold cubicles. What was I thinking? There is nothing Lucifer has that is his...he hasn't created anything. He has simply deformed everything he has ever touched.

I have spent my life following two lies at the same time with great earnestness. The first was that I was in control of my life; the second was that Lucifer was in control of my life.

When I was four years old, I remember sitting on the Father's lap, Him holding me tight. He looked down at me, tears in His eyes, and said, "You have to go away for awhile now."

When I got down from His lap, being sent away was the only part of the vision I remembered. All I understood was that He was sending me away and I hated Him for that. I hated Him for forty-eight years. I didn't know I hated Him. I just didn't pay attention to anything regarding Him. And yet, I have considered myself a Christian my entire life, even when I was on the wrong side.

It was not until two years ago, sitting in church, when I was in a vision in the General Court, that I was overcome with emotion. I began to weep inside, tears escaping from my pridefully dry natural eyes. I found myself oblivious to the entire congregation of angels that were doing whatever they were doing. I found myself moving towards the foot of the stairs, my spirit overcome with grief. When I got to the foot of the stairs, the Father and Jesus looked down at my prostrate body lying on the steps. I couldn't see Them with my face buried in my arms, but Their love washed over me. Jesus sat down on His Throne, something I don't see Him do very often.

He smiled and said to me, "Arise."

I pushed myself up from the stairs, my eyes filled with tears. I felt as if I had just come home. I was overcome with emotions I couldn't recognize. Oh, I have been to the Throne Room thousands of times and talked with the Godhead face to face in the spirit even more times. I have treated these visits as commonplace, because for me, they were. I had been here before, but for some reason, this was the first time I actually felt like I had returned home. Suddenly, I was four years old again, sitting on the lap of my Father. The reality of that moment suddenly overtook me, and I remembered every feeling of sadness, loss and despair that I had felt at four. I began to weep uncontrollably, unable to deal with the feeling coursing through me...an emotion I have yet to comprehend.

I looked up into Their eyes, my voice choked with joy and sorrow—joy because I was back and sorrow for having been gone so long. I looked into the eyes of Jesus and my Father, felt the warmth of the Holy Spirit wrap around me, and I said, "I have come home."

The Lord Jesus held out His scepter to me like Esther and said, "You can have anything you want, up to half of My kingdom."

Without hesitation or a moment's thought, I blurted out what must have been in my heart, "I want to free your people."

The Father and Son smiled a broad, grin. Jesus said, "So be it. Go, and free My people."

I kicked myself for days afterward. I could have asked for anything—riches beyond belief. I could have become anything I wanted with His blessing. But, instead, I asked to free His people without a thought of what that would mean. I am still learning what that might entail.

So, now I find myself being told to write the visions I have had over the past several years. And now I am at the final chapter and every time I think about it I just want to cry. I would prefer to write some profound theology that would turn the hearts of the people back to God, but that just escapes me.

Instead, I want to tell you about my friend.

He is someone who cared so much for me that He sent me home from the hospital into His care to take me out of danger and save my life.

He is someone who cared so much for me that He brought me to His home for four years so I wouldn't suffer from the emotional deprivation living isolated from human touch and bonding.

He is someone who cared for me so much that He had to send me back to the earth so that I could learn how to live in the natural world with other people.

He is someone who cared for me so much that He has stayed with me for forty-eight years while I was less than caring about Him.

He is someone who loves me and has loved me despite the tears I have caused Him...and I have caused Him a great many tears.

I know that one day I will walk into the Third Heavens just as Enoch did. And I will be able to walk out again. I have been shown this in vision. But I have no theological idea how to get there, just this ever present realization that it is a very simple process. And as my heart goes through the process, the Spirit of Repentance overtakes me, welling up in my spirit with such an urgency that I just want to throw myself on the floor before the Lord.

For some reason, I had never thought that I caused Him grief. And yet, I have actually said the words to the Lord, "Not today, I don't feel like it." That grief was very much caused by me. I need to take this personally just as we all need to take it personally. We need to stop spiritualizing the Lord into a comfortable theology that will fit our lifestyle without too much adjustment. We need to take Him to heart. Each one of us has caused many tears to flow down His cheeks, whatever our personal reasons. We have all rejected His love and desires.

The burning question then is, "What is sin?"

Sin is the Hebrew word, "chatta'ah" meaning "*an offence.*" It comes from the root word, "chatta" which means "*to miss.*"

Could it be said that sin in our lives is actually the offence of *missing* the relationship with Him and forcing Him to *miss* a relationship with us?

Sin should not be made into anything difficult or complicated. Sin isn't anything mystifying or distant, unable to touch us. It is as simple as the act of rejecting the one person in the whole of Creation that so completely accepts us and loves us as no other ever will.

I come from a long line of sinners who rejected Him, beginning with Adam and Eve in the Garden of God.

Not only have I rejected God, but I have also rejected everyone else He died for, judging them to be unworthy of my affections or my time. Not only have I rejected God and others, but I have rejected myself, calling Him a liar for thinking that I was not worth loving.

Sin is very simple. It is telling the God who created everything that my way is better, based on my fifty-three years of experience, and His way just isn't good enough, and, He simply does not do things fast enough.

How do I get back to Eden? It is very simple in theory, but difficult to do.

We must follow the Ancient Paths set out by the Ancient of Days. It is the path of love.

Jeremiah 6:16 Thus says the LORD: "Stand in the ways and see, and ask for the old paths, where the good way is, and walk in it; then you will find rest for your souls."

Jeremiah 18:15 Because My people have forgotten Me, they have burned incense to worthless idols. And they have caused themselves to stumble in their ways, from the ancient paths, to walk in pathways and not on a highway

Isaiah 58:5-14 Is it a fast that I have chosen, a day for a man to afflict his soul? Is it to bow down his head like a bulrush, and to spread out sackcloth and ashes? Would you call this a fast, and an acceptable day to the LORD? Is this not the fast that I have chosen: to loose the bonds of wickedness, to undo the heavy burdens, to let the oppressed go free, and that you break every yoke? Is it not to share your bread with the hungry, and that you bring to your house the poor who are cast out; when you see the naked, that you cover him, and not hide yourself from your own flesh? Then your light shall break forth like the morning, your healing shall spring forth speedily, and your righteousness shall go before you; the glory of the LORD shall be your rear guard. Then you shall call, and the LORD will answer; you shall cry, and He will say, 'Here I am.' If you take away the yoke from your midst, the pointing of the finger, and speaking wickedness, If you extend your soul to the hungry and satisfy the afflicted soul, then your light shall dawn in the darkness, and your darkness shall be as the noonday. The LORD will guide you continually, and satisfy your soul in drought, and strengthen your bones; you shall be like a watered garden, and like a spring of water, whose waters do not fail. Those from among you shall build the old waste places; you shall raise up the foundations of many generations; and you shall be called the Repairer of the Breach, the Restorer of Streets to Dwell In. If you turn away your foot from the Sabbath, from doing your pleasure on My holy day, and call the Sabbath a delight, the holy day of the LORD honorable, and shall honor Him, not doing your own ways, nor finding your own pleasure, nor speaking your own words, Then you shall delight yourself in the LORD; and I will cause you to ride on the high hills of the earth, and feed you with the heritage of Jacob your father. The mouth of the LORD has spoken.

I need to repent of pretending that I am walking in the way of Christ when it is still far from me. He was in communion with His Father and the Holy Spirit continually every day. That is what it means to be a Christian.

For a long time now, I have seen vision after vision that the people of God will be on their faces, their hearts rent under the weight of their sin. They will be slain completely under a Spirit of Repentance. We must repent as a corporate people and as an individual. We must repent because of our lack of relationship with Them.

The Hebrew word for *repent* is from the primitive root "nacham," literally meaning, *"to sigh."* It goes on to say that it is to breathe strongly, by implication, to be sorry. I can't help but feel that it literally means to sigh. God gave us our breath, breathing life into Adam in the Garden. He gave us His breath. To repent is to expel our breath, every breath we have taken separate of God in rebellion and rejection. To repent is to give up our breath. In other words, it is to give up our life in the matter, placing us in the position of needing His breath to live.

The Greek word for *repent* is "metanoeo," meaning, *"to change one's mind (heart) for the better, to amend heartily with abhorrence of one's past sins."* It is not enough to give up just our breath, but also to amend our way heartily with abhorrence of our past rejection of God.

I can think of nothing more humbling than having someone give me mouth-to-mouth resuscitation. By my giving up my breath and allowing God to give me mouth-to-mouth resuscitation, I am completely vulnerable.

Several years ago I had two wisdom teeth removed. Bad dentistry years ago resulted in chronic TMJ, which, at times, causes severe headaches. During one such session, which lasted for four weeks, I went to hospital four times for drug-induced relief. No matter what they did, the spasms did not stop and the pain did not leave. Finally, in sheer desperation, I agreed to use Morphine to relax me so totally the spasms would stop. I was given an overdose.

I remember the complete and utter vulnerability of those several hours, as I lay on my bed, alone in my room, unable and unwilling to move. My breath kept stopping. At the time I did not realize that Morphine was a respiratory suppressant, nor did I realize that I had a reaction to the drug.

I felt my breath slip away as my lungs simply slowed until there was no automatic response. At that moment, I realized that no matter how hard I tried I could not will my body to breathe. Even my own breath was out of my control. It was a terrifying awareness that has caused a profound change in my thinking.

As I lay there, feeling the life ebb out of me, I saw an angel sit on the side of my bed. He was the same one that had lifted me out from behind the bed when I was a toddler. He reached out his hand and prodded my lungs causing them to work again. He sat there with me for two days, never once leaving my side. Every time my lungs succumbed to respiratory suppression, he would reach out his hand and prod my lungs once more into action. Slowly I began to realize just how much of my life I actually control—absolutely none. I began to realize just how much of my life Lucifer controlled—absolutely none. He can only do what he has permission to do. He may try to take my life with the overdose of Morphine I allowed him to give me through the hands of my doctor, but he couldn't do it. The Lord intervened and sent an angel to once again protect me and save my life.

Slowly I began to realize just how much of my life God actually controls—absolutely all.

I wish I could write some phenomenal theological premise that would get the recognition and accolades of those around me, saying, "Well, done." But this is not a theological matter. I wish I was a clever Bible scholar that could awe everyone. But I'm not. I can only report the visions I have seen. And as I am wishing I was a theologian or scholar, I can hear the Lord saying to me, "I don't want theology. Tell them My heart."

What is God's heart? He misses you. He misses me.

As much as your heart aches because you are alone, His heart aches more for you. As you lie in your bed, weeping into your pillow because your heart cries out to be loved, He has shed more tears because He is always there, right beside you saying, "Here I am! I love you!"

But you see, we *miss it*. We turn to others, anybody else, saying, "...please, somebody, anybody come and love me." And then in our desperation, our lack of knowledge, our ignorance, or our simple self-absorption, we reject Him and send Him back to heaven empty handed and rejected.

Oh my God, I repent of rejecting you.

But how have I rejected Him? In short I have rejected Him twelve different ways. I have followed the path of Lucifer, breaking the Ten Commandments of the Old Testament as well as the two given by Jesus.

1. I didn't trust that He could give me enough to fulfill my needs and desires. I regarded what He gave me as lack. (Exodus 20:17)
2. I have called Him a liar when He said He loved me, knowing I was unlovely and not worth love. (Exodus 20:16)
3. He created me for His pleasure, and I have stolen my life from Him, keeping it for myself. (Exodus 20:15)
4. I have chased after anyone I could for my validation and love. (Exodus 20:14)
5. I have murdered Him in my heart each time I sent Him away empty handed. I have murdered His friends in my heart each time I sent them away. (Exodus 20:13)
6. I have dishonored my Father, who fashioned me before I was born. (Exodus 20:12)
7. I have relied on my own works, choosing to labor and struggle in my own pitiful ability. I rejected the provision

of God who keeps me in the palm of His hand and calls me the apple of His eye, giving His life for me. (Exodus 20:8)

8. I have blasphemed His name—Fortress, Deliverer, The Lord Will Provide, The Lord Who Heals.... I have blasphemed His name every time I have not run to Him for my protection, or gone to Him for my provision or healing. (Exodus 20:7)

9. I have refused His company every time I have let something take up my time other than Him. (Exodus 20:4)

10. I have forgotten what He has saved me from. It is so long ago that it is but a vague memory. (Exodus 20:3) Because I have forgotten what I was before, I have not loved Him with all my heart, my soul and my mind. (Matthew 22:37)

11. I have rejected all His friends, the rest of the people He created. (Matthew 22:39)

12. I have rejected myself, calling Him a liar because I am not worth loving. (Matthew 22:39)

To get back to Eden is very simple. I need to love Him so much—the Father, Son and Holy Spirit—that they are My greatest love. Like a love-struck lover, I need to spend time with Him—all of Them together and individually. I need to stop putting them far away into the stratosphere of some far off star system and be more intimately aware that all three of Them are right here with me. I need to make this relationship personal. I need to remove, or allow Him to remove all the dust of my generations, which are the lies, half-truths and misunderstandings we have picked up along the way.

There are only three things I need to do to get to Eden.

1. I need to love the Father, Son and Holy Spirit with all my heart, letting it flutter and miss a beat in excitement at the very thought of Him looking my way; letting Their love touch me personally and intimately. I need to love the Father, Son and Holy Spirit with all my soul—the seat of my feelings, desires, and affections. I have to be excited to be with Him, longing every moment to be with Him, desiring to know how He feels, what He thinks, what is

He doing, how has His day gone? My affections should be towards Him, the lover of my soul. I need to love the Father, Son and Holy Spirit with all my mind—deep thought and understanding, looking to know and understand everything about Him.

2. I need to love His friends. Back before creation was created, He not only thought of me, but He thought of everyone else. He made them all for my good. Each one of them was given the opportunity to see a different side of Him, and I need absolutely every one of them to see Him fully. I need to love who He loves, and His love for them does not depend on my personal response to them.

3. I need to love myself and stop saying He made a mistake with me. He did not make other people any better. It does not matter what the enemy has interfered with or stolen. It is time to stop blaming Him for what the enemy has done or what I have allowed the enemy to do.

Enoch walked the Ancient Path with God.

Jesus walked the Ancient Path with God.

I saw Jesus on the cross. His body hung broken and bruised beyond recognition. The Lord said to me, "The seven last words that Jesus spoke upon the cross correspond with the seven sins that led to Lucifer's downfall. It follows exactly the ten commandments as I have shown them to you."

I asked the Lord, "But why only seven commandments? Why not all ten?"

And He said to me, "Because Lucifer had only seven curses against him. The other three curses were against mankind for their sin."

And then I was shown the angels watching the crucifixion. They all understood how Lucifer fell. They all understood the ramification of His last words as He refused to take one step onto the path Lucifer had followed. I understood His last words were more for them than us as He embraced both supernatural and natural realms in His sacrifice upon the cross.

Let our example be Jesus. He chose to follow the Ancient Path even unto death so that we could live and find the way back to relationship with the Father, Son and Holy Spirit. He gave up all the glory and comfort of His godhood to become human. He gave up all the companionship and comfort of His humanity to become the ultimate sacrifice as they stripped away the very vestige of his mortal body. And yet, even in the face of death, at the most bleak and painful moment of life, He did not sin. His last seven words upon the cross reveal the strength of His resolve, knowing the Godhead and knowing the significance of His obedience. He chose, to His dying breath, to keep His eyes on the Father and not on the path that Lucifer chose into his downward fall into sin.

1. "Father, forgive them, for they do not know what they do." (Luke 23:34-37)
    a. Pain raged through His broken body which hardly resembled a human being by this point. At no time, even for the briefest second, did He regret His decision and the path He had chosen. He still would not say, "I wish I was any one of those people standing watching, whole and healthy before Me."
    b. He chose not to break the tenth commandment, "Thou shall not covet…" (Exodus 20:17)
2. "Assuredly, I say to you, today you will be with Me in Paradise." (Luke 23:43)
    a. He stayed firm in His words, not swaying once from beginning to end. He told the whole truth, about everyone He encountered including Himself from the beginning to the end.
    b. He chose not to break the ninth commandment, "You shall not bear false witness against your neighbor." (Exodus 20:16)
3. "Behold, your mother!" (John 19:27)
    a. He ensured the security of Mary to the end. As oldest son, it fell to Jesus to look after His mother in her old age. In the face of death, when the thoughts of most people are on themselves and their own miserable situation, He chose to not steal what little time He had left from his mother. He continued to look after her affairs and safety.

He did not steal from her by shirking His obligations and responsibilities.

b. He chose not to break the eighth commandment, "You shall not steal." (Exodus 20:15)

4. "My God, My God, why have you forsaken Me?" (Matthew 27:46)

a. Even to the moment of death, Jesus stood faithful to His God, His Father. Never wavering in His affection and obedience. He had not turned aside to another for even a moment, nor had He ever thought of forsaking His God, His Father.

b. He chose not to break the seventh commandment, "You shall not commit adultery." (Exodus 20:14)

5. "I thirst." (John 19:28)

a. His mouth full of congealed, dried blood. His tongue and cheeks swollen from the beatings. His teeth probably loosened. In the heat of the day, He had been dragged from the Garden to Pilate to Herod to Pilate where He was beaten and whipped. He was forced to carry a heavy cross through the dusty streets and the crowds up the hill to the place of His execution. And yet, though His body must have been screaming for some cool water, He chose not to rail or curse the very people who crucified Him, as He watched them gamble over His clothes, and laugh drunkenly beneath His feet.

b. He chose not to break the sixth commandment, "You shall not murder." (Exodus 20:13) He chose not to murder even His executioners in thought or word.

6. "It is finished." (John 19:30)

a. He honored His Father by doing the will of His Father until the very end, not wavering for one moment to accomplish all the Father would have Him do.

b. He chose not to break the fifth commandment, "Honor your father and mother..." (Exodus 20:12)

7. "Father, into Your hands I commit My spirit." (Luke 23:46)

a. Even unto the very end, He did not get off the cross, which He could have, to save Himself by His own works. He trusted in His Father, doing only those things He saw His Father do. Even in the face of the most horrible death, He chose to do nothing of Himself, but rested in the will of His Father, believing He knew best. He trusted completely in the provision of His Father and His God.

b. He chose not to break the fourth commandment, "Remember the Sabbath day, to keep it holy." (Exodus 20:8)

To get back to Eden, we need to walk with God, His way, not ours. That is the Ancient Path that Jesus walked.

We need to follow the ancient paths to get back to God and Eden:

1. be content with everything God provides, taking the whole of it, not just picking the stuff we like and saying "no thanks" to the stuff less cool or comfortable;
2. be filled with the truth about who He is and who we are in Him, to stop putting GOD in a box;
3. stop compromising to keep the peace, but follow His way to make peace;
4. stop allowing our conscience to be seared, let it heal and be the protection it was meant to be;
5. walk in ALL the ways of the Lord, rather than just the ones we like best;
6. listen to the watchmen (prophets) He has set in our midst, speaking His words.

Our answer is found in the Song of Solomon and the words of the Shulamite who was wooed by the King. Her words show her need and her changing attitude.

God is not ours, there to do our will. We are His, here to do His will. We need to drop the "Gimme!" attitude. We need to stop the frantic search for every anointing, ministry, mantle, gift, etcetera, while forgetting the One who gives the gifts. It is not "He who loves me is mine...and, oh yeah, I am his."

Song of Solomon 2:16 My beloved is mine, and I am his.

It is not even, "I am his, *but* He who loves me is mine." This smacks of blackmail. It is saying to God that I am yours only as long as you do the things I like.

Song of Solomon 6:3 I am my beloved's, and my beloved is mine.

Oh Spirit of Repentance, come upon your people now. Oh Spirit of Repentance, come upon me now. Slay us with the revelation of our sin and the Lord's mercy and greatness.

We need to be completely His, knowing, without a shadow of a doubt, that his desire is towards us all the time because He loves us and He knows what is in us. We need to understand a new concept of life. Life in His kingdom, even today, He does provide all things. He wants to look after us in all things because we are His Bride. We need to stop doing things our way and begin doing things completely His way. We need to see Him how He really is and not how we would like to perceive Him.

We need to follow in the footsteps of Jesus, our Beloved, binding the lies and hate of Lucifer, and releasing the truth and love of God.

We need to let God be God.

Song of Solomon 7:10 I am my beloved's, and his desire is toward me.

APPENDIX A

Reference Materials

Fingerprints of the Gods, Graham Hancock, 1996 A Mandarine
  Paperback, Reed International Books Ltd., Michelle House,
  81 Fulham Road, London SW3 6RB

Heaven's Mirror, Quest for the Lost Civilization, Graham
  Hancock, Santha Faiia, 1998, Crown Publishers, Inc., 201
  East 50th Street, New York, New York 10022

Walking With Dinosaurs, A Natural History, Tim Haines, 1999,
  BBC Worldwide Ltd., 80 Wood Lane, London W12 OTT

The Twilight Labyrinth, Why Does Spiritual Darkness Linger
  Where It Does, George Otis Jr., 1997, Chosen Books, A
  Division of Baker House Co., Grand Rapids, MI 49516

Dictionary of World Myths, General Consultant: Roy Willis, 2000,
  Duncan Baird Publishers Ltd., Sixth Floor, Castle House,
  75-76 Wells Street, London W1P 3RE

Secrets of the Lost Races, Rene Noorbergen, 1977, The Bobbs-
  Merrill Company, Inc., New York, New York

The Mars Mystery, Graham Hancock, 1998, Crown Publishers,
  Inc., 201 East 50th Street, New York, New York 10022

The Living Earth Plate Tectonics, Unraveling the Mysteries of the
  Earth, Jon Erickson, 2001, Checkmark Books, An Imprint
  of Facts on File Inc., 11 Penn Plaza, New York, New York
  10001

Egyptian Gods and Goddesses, The British Museum,
   http://www.ancientegypt.co.uk/gods/explore/main.html
Social Science Data Lab, University of Colorado at Boulder,
   http://socsci.colorado.edu/LAB/GODS/
Egyptian Mythology, Tour Egypt, http://www.touregypt.net/gods1.
   htm
The Spirits of Nature, Religions of the Egyptians by Ottar Vendel,
   http://www.nemo.nu/ibisportal/0egyptintro/1egypt/
Ancient Egypt, Gods and Goddesses, http://www.rom.on.ca/egypt/
   case/about/gods.html
Directory of Ancient Egyptian Gods, http://www.osirisweb.com/
   egypt/director.htm
Aldokan Ancient Egyptian Gods, http://www.aldokkan.com/
   religion/gods.htm
Wikipedia, The Free Encyclopedia, http://en.wikipedia.
   org/wiki/Main_Page
T. Multamaki & Ø. Elgarøy: "The integrated Sachs-Wolfe
   effect as a probe of non-standard cosmological evolution", Astronomy & Astrophysics 423 (2004) 811
   astro-ph/0312534
I. Brevik, S. Jojiri, S. D. Odintsov & L. Vanzo: "Entropy and
   universality of Cardy-Verlinde formula in dark energy
   universe", Phys. Rev. D 70 (2004) 043520, hep-th/0401073
I. Brevik, K. Ghoroku & M. Yahiro: "Radius stabilization and
   brane running in RS1 model", Phys. Rev. D 70 (2004)
   064012, hep-th/0402176
P. Callin & F. Ravndal: "Higher order corrections to the Newtonian
   potential in the Randall-Sundrum model", Phys. Rev. D 70
   (2004) 104009, hep-ph/0403302
Ø. Elgarøy & T. Multamaki: "Cosmic acceleration and extra
   dimensions: constraints on modifications of the Friedmann
   equation", MNRAS 356 (2005) 475, astro-ph/0404402
I. Brevik: "Viscous Cosmology, Entropy, and the Cardy-Verlinde
   Formula" gr-qc/0404095
F. Ravndal: "Scalar Gravitation and Extra Dimensions"
   gr-qc/0405030

A. K. D. Evans, I. K. Wehus, Ø. Grøn & Ø. Elgarøy: "Geometrical Constraints on Dark Energy", Astronomy & Astrophysics 430 (2005) 399, astro-ph/0406407

P. Callin: "Corrections to the Newtonian potential in the two-brane Randall-Sundrum model" hep-ph/0407054

M. Amarzguioui & Ø. Grøn: "Gravitational entropy of perturbed FRW models" gr-qc/0408065, Phys. Rev. D71, 083011 (2005)

K. Tywoniuk & F. Ravndal: "Scalar field fluctuations between parallel plates" quant-ph/0408163

T. Koivisto, H. Kurki-Suonio & F. Ravndal: "The CMB spectrum in Cardassian models" astro-ph/0409163, Phys.Rev. D71 (2005) 064027

M. Amarzguioui, Ø. Elgarøy and T. Multamaki: "Combined constraints on Cardassian models from supernovae, CMB and large-scale structure observations", JCAP 01 (2005) 008, astro-ph/0410408

O. Lahav and Ø. Elgarøy: "Weighing Neutrinos with Large-Scale Structure" astro-ph/0411092

Ø. Elgarøy and O. Lahav: "Neutrino Masses from Cosmological Probes" hep-ph/0412075, New J. Phys. 7 (2005) 61

Ø. Elgarøy, D. F. Mota and T. Multamaki: "Loitering universe models in light of the CMB", Phys.Rev. D71 (2005) 067301

C. P. Burgess, R. Easther, A. Mazumdar, D. F. Mota and T. Multamaki: "Multiple Inflation, Cosmic String Networks and the String Landscape", JHEP 0505 (2005) 067

A. W. Brookfield, C. van de Bruck, D. F. Mota, and D. Tocchini-Valentini: "Cosmology with massive neutrinos coupled to dark energy", astro-ph/0503349

M. Manera and D. F. Mota: "Cluster number counts dependence on dark energy inhomogeneities and coupling to dark matter", astro-ph/0504519

C. Skordis, D. F. Mota, P. G. Ferreira, and C. Boehm: "Large scale structure in Bekenstein's theory of relativistic MOND", astro-ph/0505519

P. Callin and F. Ravndal: "Lagrangian formalism of gravity in the Randall-Sundrum model", hep-ph/0412109

H. Alnes, F. Ravndal, and I. K. Wehus: "Black-body radiation in extra dimensions", quant-ph/0506131

H. Alnes, M. Amarzguioui, and Ø. Grøn: "Can a dust dominated universe have accelerated expansion?", astro-ph/0506449

I. Brevik, M. Wold Lund, and G. Ruø: "Expanding AdS5 Branes: Time Dependent Eigenvalue Problem and Production of Particles", hep-th/0406156

I. Brevik and O. Gorbunova: "Dark Energy and Viscous Cosmology", gr-qc/0504001

I. Brevik, K. Ghoroku, and A. Nakamura: "Meson mass and confinement force driven by dilaton", hep-th/0505057

M. Amarzguioui, Ø. Elgarøy, D. F. Mota and T. Multamaki: "Cosmological constraints on f(R) gravity theories within the Palatini approach", astro-ph/0510519

Science Watch, http://www.sciencewatch.com/jan-feb2004/sw_jan-feb2004_page1.htm

Space.com, http://www.sciencewatch.com/jan-feb2004/sw_jan-feb2004_page1.htm

Physicsnetbase.com, http://www.physicsnetbase.com/

Eurekaalert.com, http://www.eurekalert.org/pub_releases/2004-06/uocs-ndt061004.php

A Brief Introduction to the Ekpyrotic Universe by Paul J. Steinhardt, Princeton University, http://wwwphy.princeton.edu/~steinh/npr/

Ekpyrotic Universe, http://en.wikipedia.org/wiki/Ekpyrotic

WMAP, http://map.gsfc.nasa.gov/m_uni.html

Cosmology Tutorial by Ned Wright, http://www.astro.ucla.edu/~wright/cosmolog.htm

Official String Theory, http://www.superstringtheory.com/cosmo/

Cambridge Cosmology, http://www.damtp.cam.ac.uk/user/gr/public/cos_home.html

High Redshift Supernova Search, Berkeley Lab, http://panisse.lbl.gov/

Theoretical Cosmology, http://cfa-www.harvard.edu/~jcohn/tcosmo.html

Age of the Universe, http://www.astro.ucla.edu/~wright/age.html
Age of the Universe Revised,
http://www.space.com/scienceastronomy/age_universe_030103.
html
WMAP Age of the Universe, http://map.gsfc.nasa.gov/m_uni/uni_
101age.html
AISH.com, Society Today, http://aish.com/societywork/sciencena-
ture/Age_of_the_Universe.asp
Age of the Universe, by Jon Covey, B.A., MT (ASCP), CLS, Anita
K. Millen, M.D., MPH, editor, http://www.ldolphin.org/
univ-age.html
An Ancient Universe, http://www.astrosociety.
org/education/publications/tnl/56/
Has the Garden of Eden been Located at Last, Dora Jane Hamblin,
http://www.ldolphin.org/eden/
Garden of Eden, Wikipedia.com, http://en.wikipedia.
org/wiki/Garden_of_Eden
The Extinction Files, http://www.bbc.co.uk/education/darwin/
exfiles/massintro.htm
Mass Extinctions of the Phanerozoic Menu, http://hannover.park.
org/Canada/Museum/extinction/extincmenu.html
Space.com, The Five Worst Extinctions in Earth's History, http://
hannover.park.org/Canada/Museum/extinction/extincmenu.
html
Phanerozoic Mass Extinctions, http://member.biodiversity.org.
uk/teddy/projecta/
The Late Pleistocene Extinctions, http://www.museum.state.il.us/
exhibits/larson/lp_extinction.html
Catastrophic and Mass Extinctions, http://www.pibburns.com/
catastro/extinct.htm
The Sixth Extinction by Dr. Niles Elderidge, http://www.actionbio-
science.org/newfrontiers/eldredge2.html
Changing Paleoclimates and Mass Extinctions, http://webspinners.
com/dlblanc/climate/index.php
Asteroid and Comet Impact Craters and Mass Extinctions, http://
webspinners.com/dlblanc/climate/index.php
Dinosaur Extinctions, http://www.dinoruss.org/de_4/5c524c9.htm

Prehistoric Man, http://www.dinoruss.org/de_4/5c524c9.htm
The Antiquity of Man and Prehistoric Archaeology, http://www.
    infidels.org/library/historical/andrew_white/Chapter7.html
Hominid Species Timeline, http://www.wsu.edu:8001/vwsu/gened/
    learn-modules/top_longfor/timeline/timeline.html
Prehistoric Man Timeline, http://www.cartage.org.lb/en/
    themes/Sciences/LifeScience/PhysicalAnthropology/
    PrehistoricMan/ManTimeline/ManTimeline.htm
The Story of Mankind, http://www.authorama.
    com/story-of-mankind-5.html
Bonobos Monkeys, http://williamcalvin.com/teaching/bonobo.htm
Tree of Origin, www.cord.edu/faculty/landa/presentations/
    TreeOfLife.ppt
World Population Since Creation, http://www.ldolphin.org/popul.
    html
The Global Flood of Noah's Day, http://www.biblicalarcheology.
    net/Bible&History/Flood1.htm
The Great World Wide Flood, http://www.bible-truth.org/GEN6.
    HTM
Genealogies of Genesis, http://en.wikipedia.
    org/wiki/Genealogies_of_Genesis
Genealogy of Shem, http://en.wikipedia.org/wiki/Shem, http://
    en.wikipedia.org/wiki/Semitic
Genealogy of Ham, http://en.wikipedia.org/wiki/Ham%2C_son_
    of_Noah, http://en.wikipedia.org/wiki/Hamitic
Genealogy of Japheth, http://en.wikipedia.org/wiki/Japheth, http://
    en.wikipedia.org/wiki/Japhetic
Table of Nations, http://www.biblebelievers.org.au/natindx.htm
Table of Nations, http://www.osterholm.info/man/
Table of Nations, http://www.freemaninstitute.com/RTGham.htm
Table of Nations, http://www.mazzaroth.com/TableOfNations/
    IntroTableOfNations.htm
Hittites, http://www.crystalinks.com/hittites.html
Mesopotamia, http://www.wsu.edu:8080/~dee/MESO/HITTITES.
    HTM
Hittites, All About Turkey, http://www.allaboutturkey.com/hitit.htm
Hittites, http://www.asor.org/HITTITE/HittiteHP.html

Hittites in the Bible, http://www.absoluteastronomy.
  com/reference/hittites_in_the_bible
History of the Ancient Hittites, http://history-world.org/hittites.htm
Who Were the Hittites, http://history-world.org/hittites.htm
Hittites, http://en.wikipedia.org/wiki/Hittites
Girgashites, http://philologos.org/bpr/files/t005.htm
Girgashites, http://www.bible-history.com/map-israel-joshua/map-
  israel-joshua_the_girgashites_encyclopedia.html
Canaanites, http://www.mazzaroth.com/ChapterFour/
  TenCanaaniteTribes.htm
Amorites, http://www.mazzaroth.com/ChapterFour/
  TenCanaaniteTribes.htm
Amorites, http://en.wikipedia.org/wiki/Amorites
Jebusites, http://en.wikipedia.org/wiki/Jebusites
Perizzites, http://www.bible-history.com/map-israel-joshua/map-
  israel-joshua_the_perizzites_encyclopedia.html
Perizzites, http://en.wikipedia.org/wiki/Perizzites
Perizzites, http://bible.tmtm.com/wiki/Perizzites
Hivites, http://en.wikipedia.org/wiki/Hivites
Seven Nations of Canaan, http://www.crystalinks.com/canaan.html
Viracocha and the Coming of the Incas, http://www.sacred-texts.
  com/nam/inca/inca01.htm
Pre-Inca Civilization, http://www.crystalinks.com/preinca.html
The Legend of Viracocha, http://www.cantaremusic.com/stories/
  viracocha.htm
Incan Mythology, http://www.godchecker.com/pantheon/incan-
  mythology.php?deity=VIRACOCHA
The Fisher Kings, http://www.labyrinthina.com/fisherkings.htm
Viracocha's Voyage, http://www.philipcoppens.com/viracocha_
  voyage.html
Peruvian Myths of the World, http://www.sacred-texts.com/etc/
  omw/omw78.htm
Lake Titicaca, http://en.wikipedia.org/wiki/Lake_Titicaca
Viracocha, http://en.wikipedia.org/wiki/Viracocha
Lake Titicaca, http://www.crystalinks.com/laketiticaca.html
Tiahuanaco, http://www.crystalinks.com/tiahuanaco.html

Tiahuanaco and the Deluge, http://www.crystalinks.com/preinca2.html

Tiahuanaco and the Deluge, http://www.thule.org/tiahuanaco.html

Tiahuanaco, http://www.mnsu.edu/emuseum/prehistory/latinamerica/south/sites/tiahuanaco.html

Tiahuanaco, http://www.astrofilitrentini.it/mat/puerta/

Tiahuanaco and Pumapunka, http://www.world-mysteries.com/mpl_6.htm

Tiahuanaco and the Gateway of the Sun, http://www.athenapub.com/tiahuan1.htm

Civilizations in the Americas, http://www.wsu.edu:8080/~dee/CIVAMRCA/TIA.HTM

Tiwanaku, http://en.wikipedia.org/wiki/Tiahuanaco

Tiahuanaco, http://www.encyclopedia.com/html/T/Tiahuana.asp

Tiwanaku, a Photo Gallery, http://www.jqjacobs.net/andes/tiwanaku.html

The Pre-Inca Ruins at Tiahuanaco, http://bolivia.freeservers.com/photo4.html

Elle Fraile, http://www.alovelyworld.com/webbolivie/htmfr/bol117.htm

Mystery Babylon the Great, http://www.biblenews1.com/babylon/babylon1.html

APPENDIX B

Referenced Scriptures

Jeremiah 6:16
Luke 16:22-31
Luke 11:24
Jude 1:10-13
Psalm 9:17
Isaiah 5:14
Revelation 20:14
Ezekiel 28:12-14
Ezekiel 28:14-16
Exodus 20:17
2 Timothy 3:2-5
Exodus 5:2
Exodus 7:17
Genesis 4:7
Exodus 20:16
Exodus 8:2-4
Exodus 20:15
Genesis 15:16
Daniel 4:30
Exodus 20
Exodus 20:14
Exodus 8:20-21

Exodus 9:27-28
Exodus 20:13
Exodus 9:1-3
1 Peter 5:8
Ezekiel 28:12
Revelation 3:17-19
Ezekiel 28:16
Ezekiel 27:32-36
Ezekiel 28:12-20
Ezekiel 31:1-18
Exodus 10:8-11
Exodus 20:12
1 Corinthians 2:10
Revelation 2:23
Ezekiel 28:2-10
Ezekiel 28:12-19
Exodus 9:8-9
Revelation 13:18
Exodus 10:16-17
Jeremiah 4:22-30
Ezekiel 31:16-18
Job 38:22-24

Exodus 20:8
Genesis 2:1-3
Exodus 9:22
John 8:44
Ephesians 2:2
Numbers 22:28-34
Romans 8:22-25
Revelation 4:11
Psalms 36:6
Revelation 22:17
Joshua 10:24-26
Job 1:6-12
I John 3:8-10
Exodus 20:7
Genesis 2:16
Exodus 10:4
Isaiah 5:20
Genesis 5:29
Luke 21:34
Revelation 22:17
Genesis 3:17-19
Exodus 10:21-23
Genesis 6:3
II Thessalonians 2:11-12
Matthew 25:24
Revelation 2:7
Revelation 22:14
Genesis 5:24
Matthew 13:44-46
Romans 7:15-25
Joshua 24:15
John 10:10
Daniel 10:12-14
Jeremiah 1:5
Isaiah 49:1
Lamentations 2:17
John 15:25

Ecclesiastes 1:9-10
Romans 8:19-23
1 Timothy 4:1-2
Exodus 34:7
Genesis 6:4
Jeremiah 17:9
Genesis 6:5-7
Ezekiel 31:8
Luke 8:26-39
Numbers 31:16
Genesis 6:9
Matthew 7:21-23
John 15:13-14
Romans 8:19-23
Job 1:7-19
Job 1:22
Job 2:3-7
Job 2:9-10
Job 2:11
Matthew 4:3-10
1 Corinthians 15:51-58
II Thessalonians 2:10-12
Matthew 18:23-35
Revelation 21:8
Revelation 20:10-15
Exodus 30:7-8
Jeremiah 6:16
Jeremiah 18:15
Isaiah 58:5-14
Exodus 20:17
Exodus 20:16
Exodus 20:15
Exodus 20:14
Exodus 20:13
Exodus 20:12
Exodus 20:8
Exodus 20:7

Exodus 20:4
Exodus 20:3
Matthew 22:37
Matthew 22:39
Matthew 22:39
Song of Solomon 2:16
Song of Solomon 6:3
Song of Solomon 7:10
Book of Job
Book of Genesis
Book of 1 Kings
Book of II Kings
Book of Revelation
Jeremiah 6:11-20
Luke 21:26
John 1:1-3
Ephesians 1:22-23
II Thessalonians 2:1-17
Matthew 12:43-45

Printed in the United States
92363LV00003B/100-132/A

9 781600 341816